Potluck
on the Pedernales
SECOND HELPING

Also by the
Community Garden Club
of Johnson City

POTLUCK ON THE PEDERNALES
The First Volume

Regional Winner of the
Tabasco Community
COOKBOOK Award

Potluck

on the Pedernales

SECOND HELPING

Compiled by

Community Garden Club of Johnson City

Johnson City, Texas

EAKIN PRESS ★ Austin, Texas

Proceeds

The proceeds from the sale of *Second Helping* will be used for civic and community projects sponsored by the Community Garden Club of Johnson City.

A portion of the royalties from the sale of this cookbook is pledged to Friends of the Blanco County Historical Commission. Preserving, protecting, educating, and promoting Blanco County's rich historical heritage is it's purpose. Funds will go toward the restoration of the beautiful historic Blanco County Courthouse in Johnson City. Due to the many years of neglect, this 1916 classical revival limestone structure is in dire need of restoration. Thank you for supporting this project.

Remember . . . **"Kissin don't last, cooking do!"** There is one other old adage worth repeating . . . **"The way to a man's heart is through his stomach,"** or turned another way, **"A man who can cook is worth a lot to a working woman,"** and lastly, **"To be able to cook for yourself is to survive!"**

What's for Supper

Clean Your Plate Now . . .

"Much Obliged"

Cookbook Chairman . . . Holly Lawson
Business Manager . . . Cynthia Smith
Recipe Coordinator . . . Joycelyn Carter
Cover Art . . . Geneva Eubanks
Design and Divider Page Art . . . Geneva Eubanks
Legal Advisor . . . Dean Myane
Recipe Testers . . . Community Garden Club of Johnson City

COOKBOOK BOARD MEMBERS

Joycelyn Carter	Kittie Clyde Leonard
Thelma Elm	Ola Matus
Geneva Eubanks	Jane Mills
Robyn Henderson	Cynthia Smith
Holly Lawson	Janey Wiemers

Thanks to everyone who bought our first cookbook, *Potluck on the Pedernales*. We could not have published our second cookbook, *Second Helping*, without the recipes from the people of Johnson City and the surrounding Hill Country areas. Thanks also to those who shared old photos and history. ***Much obliged!***

"The well-prepared dish is a source of pleasure, as well as a builder of health, strength and family ties. The housewife realizes that good appetites go with good humor. She is in little danger of losing the affection of her loved ones if she sets a good table." — by Helen Mayfield

Still Cooking ... Second Helping

Our first cookbook, *Potluck on the Pedernales* is a great cookbook. The best in the whole Southwest as a matter of fact! In 1991 we entered McIlhenny Company's Tabasco Community Cookbook contest and won first place in the Southwest Region. We are very proud and excited to have won such an honor, and said, while we were waiting for the news of the winners ... "if we win, we'll do another." We are pleased to offer our second effort ... *Second Helping – Potluck on the Pedernales*.

The potluck supper or covered dish supper is a tradition carried on in most parts of the country. It is a wonderful way to share home cooked foods with neighbors, friends or family. We do it a lot in the Hill Country of Texas. It is both an inexpensive and charming way to entertain.

The dictionary says:

POTLUCK (pot'luk') "whatever food might have been prepared for the family ... ordinary, nothing special" but this cookbook, and its recipes, are anything but ordinary, so get ready for something special.

The Pedernales River is one of the last free flowing rivers in Texas with no major dams. The river bisects the LBJ Heartland, rising in southeast Kimble County flowing eastward for 106 miles through southern Gillespie County, central Blanco County and onward to northern Hays County, finally joining the Colorado River in western Travis County. The river cuts a rugged path that was home to prehistoric hunters, and determined pioneers who finally tamed the Hill Country.

PEDERNALES RIVER (Purd'nalis) local pronunciation, Spanish definition means; "River of flint."

One of the most difficult jobs in putting together a cookbook is choosing the recipes. With so many excellent recipes so generously shared, it was quite a task choosing and testing. We gained a few pounds, had a few laughs, and enjoyed the food, "but someone had to do it!"

We know what you said you like in a cookbook; good down-home recipes that one could cook without having access to a gourmet grocery. Recipes anyone could follow, and a good index, done. You liked the stories and personal comments about the recipes and we have done that again. People like to know how a recipe got its name and how and when it was used, so we'll tell that if we can.

There are several new sections in *Second Helping;* Look Who's Cooking (men's recipes), the Good Old Days (recipes over fifty years old) and Melting Pot (a blending of ethnic recipes).

The Cookbook Committee is very proud to publish this book containing local recipes and folklore. This is a true LBJ Country Cookbook, the *Second Helping – Potluck on the Pedernales,* from the people who made the history of this area unique and the food so great. So read on . . . get in the kitchen, cook up something wonderful, CLEAN YOUR PLATE NOW!

☆　☆　☆　☆　☆　☆　☆　☆　☆　☆

Good friend who would these pages test,
A whisper in your ear;
These dishes are the very best
Your husband's heart to cheer!

Let none escape, but try them all
To boil or fry or bake;
We'll warrant they are just as good
As Mother used to make.

SELF-GUIDED TOUR MAP

The drawings in this cookbook were done by local artist, Geneva Eubanks. They are set in "yesteryear" when life was simple and folks gathered in town to shop, transact business, worship, and visit friends.

This map is a guide if you wish to tour these sites.

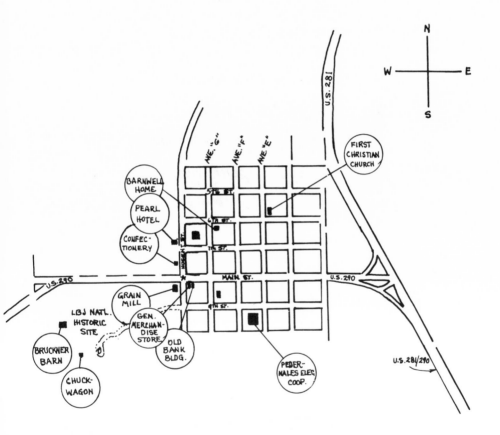

The recipe that is not shared with others

will soon be forgotten,

but when it is shared it will be enjoyed

by future generations.

First Things First, Beginnings
Appetizers, Dips, Beverages

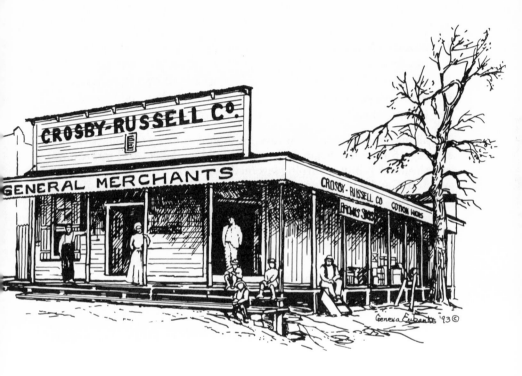

GENERAL MERCHANDISE STORE — Early 1900s

One of the earliest buildings of Johnson City was constructed in 1893 by Ed Wallace for his dry goods business. Through many changes of owners, a wide variety of goods passed through its double doors. Later enlarged and used as a wool warehouse, this historical building was acquired by the late President Lyndon Johnson, who deeded it to the American people. It presently serves as maintenance office of the LBJ National Historic Site. The exterior has been restored in appearance, circa 1915–1920.

1

MARINATED MUSHROOMS
Margaret Dannecker

One of my young daughters annoyed me by picking the mushrooms out of any dish in which she found the offending ingredient. I made these marinated mushrooms ahead for a dinner party and refrigerated them. By the time I was ready to serve them, there were not enough left to serve. I was even more surprised to discover the identity of the culprit; but then, she never picked the mushrooms out of anything again!

⅔ cup olive oil	½ cup water
Juice of two lemons	1 pound small whole, fresh
1 bay leaf	mushrooms, washed and
2 cloves garlic, crushed	trimmed <u>or</u> 3 (2½-ounce)
6 whole peppercorns	jars whole mushrooms,
½ teaspoon salt	drained

Put all ingredients except mushrooms in skillet. Bring to boil, cover and simmer 15 minutes, strain and return liquid to skillet. Add mushrooms and simmer 5 minutes, turning several times. Cool in the liquid, then chill, covered. Can be prepared several days ahead. To serve, lift out of liquid with slotted spoon. Yield: about 2 cups.

PARTY PUFFS
Bernice K. Weinheimer

1 cup water	½ teaspoon salt
½ cup butter or margarine	1 cup flour
1 teaspoon sugar	4 eggs

Bring water to boil in sauce pan with butter, sugar and salt. Remove from heat and quickly stir in flour. Stir vigorously with wooden spoon over low heat until mixture forms a ball. Remove from heat, beat in eggs, one at a time, until batter is smooth and shiny. Drop by rounded ½ teaspoon on ungreased baking sheet. Bake at 400 degrees for 20 to 25 minutes. Puffs should be light and airy, slightly brown and dry. May freeze. If frozen, place in 425 degree oven 3 to 4 minutes to thaw and crisp. Yield: 70–80 puffs.

Fill with one of the following:

Tuna or Chicken Filling

1 (6½-ounce) can tuna <u>or</u> chicken	3 tablespoons mayonnaise
3 ounces cream cheese	Celery or onion, chopped,
Salt and pepper to taste	optional

Mix filling together, split puffs, fill and serve hot or cold. If served hot, place in 350 degree oven for 8 minutes.

Ham Filling

3	(4½-ounce) cans deviled ham	1	tablespoon prepared horseradish
1	teaspoon onion salt	½	cup sour cream

Blend all ingredients together, split puffs and fill. Serve cold.

BARBECUE CUPS
Robyn Henderson

Best served hot right out of the oven.

2	cups buttermilk biscuit mix	½	cup onion, chopped
½	cup cold milk	½	cup barbecue sauce
1	pound ground beef	½	cup Cheddar cheese, shredded
1	clove garlic, crushed		

Mix biscuit mix with cold milk to form soft dough. Beat vigorously with a spoon for 20 strokes. Drop by spoonfuls into 12 medium ungreased muffin cups. Press dough on bottom and up sides of each cup with floured hands. Stirring frequently, cook ground beef, garlic and onion in a skillet until beef is brown; drain. Stir in barbecue sauce; heat through. Spoon beef mixture into cups; sprinkle with cheese. Bake at 400 degrees for about 15 minutes or until crust is golden brown. Yield: 12

CHAFING DISH MEATBALLS
Janey Wiemers

When I first heard about this recipe, I thought it was strange, but the flavors blend and it tastes great!

1	pound ground beef <u>or</u> ground turkey	1	teaspoon salt
½	cup bread crumbs	⅛	teaspoon pepper
⅓	cup onion, minced	½	teaspoon Worcestershire sauce
¼	cup milk	¼	cup shortening
1	tablespoon parsley, snipped		12-ounce bottle chili sauce
1	egg		10-ounce jar grape jelly

Mix all ingredients except shortening, chili sauce and jelly. Shape into 1-inch balls and brown in melted shortening in a large skillet, drain. (May be cooked in the oven in a shallow pan at 375 degree oven, turning the meat-

balls once in order to brown). Heat chili sauce and jelly together, add meatballs and simmer for 30 minutes. Serve hot in a chafing dish. Yield: 5 dozen.

HONEY BACON HULAS
Holly Lawson

I like to serve these at family get-togethers. Don't leave off the dipping sauce, the sweet sauce with the salty bacon is excellent.

2 pounds bacon	½ cup barbecue sauce
1 (20-ounce) can pineapple chunks, drained	½ cup honey

Preheat oven to 350 degrees. Cut bacon in half. Wrap ½ slice of bacon around each pineapple chunk. Secure with toothpick. Continue until all chunks are used. Bake in shallow pan for about 30 minutes. Drain grease before serving. Mix barbecue sauce and honey together for a dipping sauce. Yield: Approximately 50.

HAM CRESCENT SNACKS
Gwen Pickett

1 (8-ounce) can Pillsbury Crescent Dinner Rolls	1 cup Swiss <u>or</u> Cheddar cheese, shredded
4 thin slices ham, 4 x 7 inches	2 tablespoons sesame seed
4 teaspoons prepared mustard	

Unroll dough into 4 long rectangles. Press perforations to seal. Place one slice ham on each rectangle. Spread ham slices with mustard; sprinkle with cheese. Start with shortest side, roll up each rectangle and press edges to seal. Coat rolls with sesame seed. Cut each of the 4 rolls into 5 slices. Place each side down on ungreased cookie sheet. Bake at 375 degrees for 15 to 20 minutes or until golden brown. Remove from cookie sheet immediately. Serve warm. Yield: 20.

HAM ROLL-UPS
Jane Mills

1 (8-ounce) package cream cheese, softened	2 teaspoons prepared horseradish
8 stuffed green olives, chopped fine	Dash of garlic salt
	½ pound very thin sliced ham

Soften cream cheese to room temperature. Add rest of ingredients except

4

ham and mix very well. Spread mixture on ham slices, then roll in jelly-roll style. Chill. When ready to serve, cut into about 3/4-inch slices. Freezes well. Yield: 40-50 slices.

SAUSAGE MEATBALLS
Suzanne Law

2	pounds mild sausage	1	(16-ounce) can sauerkraut
1	pound hot sausage	½	cup onion, chopped
2	(15-ounce) cans Italian bread crumbs	½	cup cheese, shredded
2	eggs		Salt and pepper to taste

Mix all ingredients together. Mix into small balls and place in a shallow baking pan. Bake 20-25 minutes at 325 degrees. Freezes well. Yield: about 10 dozen.

SAUSAGE STUFFED BISCUITS
Janey Wiemers

1	pound plain pork sausage	1	cup soft bread crumbs
2	(4-ounce) cans stems and pieces mushrooms, drained	½	cup parsley, chopped
4	tablespoons onion, chopped	1	teaspoon pepper
2	tablespoons water	1	(10-ounce) can Hungry Jack Flaky Biscuits

Sauté sausage, stirring until cooked but not browned. Drain off fat. Add mushrooms and onions; cook a few minutes until tender. Add water and remaining ingredients. Cool, if necessary, and mix well with fingers to combine. Separate biscuits into very thin slices; each biscuit should separate into 3 or 4 sections. Press dough into miniature cup-cake tins. Fill with sausage mixture and bake 15 minutes at 375 degrees. May be frozen and reheated. Makes 30.

SAUSAGE ON RYE
Jewell Sultemeier

Every time I serve these they are enjoyed.

1	pound hot pork sausage	½	teaspoon garlic salt
1	pound ground meat	1	pound Velveeta cheese, cubed
1	tablespoon flaked oregano		
½	teaspoon Worcestershire sauce	2	loaves party rye bread

Fry and drain sausage and ground meat. Add seasonings and cheese, mix well. Heat until melted. Spread meat mixture on bread. Freeze on cookie sheets then put in freezer bags. At party time, bake directly from freezer at 400 degrees for 10 minutes. Yield: 50.

HOT RYES
Flora Cox

These delicious appetizers were served by my friend, Leona Lynch, at her daughters wedding. Leona was always bringing the most tasty dishes to school luncheons.

1 cup grated Swiss cheese	¼ cup celery, finely chopped
¼ cup crumbled crisp cooked bacon	¼ cup mayonnaise
1 (4½-ounce) can chopped ripe olives, drained	1 teaspoon Worcestershire sauce
⅓ cup green onions, finely chopped	¼ teaspoon salt
	1 loaf party rye <u>or</u> pumpernickel bread

Mix all together and spread cheese mixture on slices of bread. Bake at 350 degrees for 10-15 minutes or until cheese melts. To freeze: Place rounds, uncooked, on cookie sheet and freeze. When frozen, place in bag or an air tight container. Bake frozen 15-20 minutes. Yield: 30 rounds.

SHRIMP MOUSSE
Jan Christensen

1 envelope Knox gelatin	1 (4-ounce) can small shrimp, drained
¼ cup cold water	
1 can tomato soup	½ cup onion, chopped fine
1 (8-ounce) package cream cheese, softened	½ cup celery, chopped fine
1 cup mayonnaise	½ cup green pepper, chopped fine

Dissolve gelatin in cold water. Set aside. Heat soup, add cheese, blend well. Remove from heat and add remaining ingredients. Pour into a 10 to 12-ounce mold sprayed with Pam. Refrigerate overnight. Serve with assorted crackers. Yield: 1 large mold.

HINT:
1 teaspoon dried herbs is equal to 1 tablespoon chopped fresh herbs.

ꔖ ꔖ ꔖ ꔖ ꔖ ꔖ ꔖ

SPINACH BALLS

Gail Rucker

Some people may turn up their noses at spinach, but these do not taste like spinach and they are colorful and delicious.

½	cup margarine, melted	¾	cup Parmesan cheese
2	(10-ounce) packages chopped spinach, cooked and well-drained	1	large onion, chopped fine
		1½	teaspoons garlic salt
			Black pepper to taste
4	eggs, beaten		Accent to taste
2	cups Pepperidge Farm Stuffing Mix		Cheddar cheese

Mix above ingredients except Cheddar cheese together. Cool overnight in refrigerator or at least 3 hours. Shape into small balls, about 1½-inch diameter, and place on cookie sheet. Place a small square of Cheddar cheese on top of each ball and press down slightly. Bake at 325 degrees for 20 minutes.

CREAM CHEESE BALL

Pat Althaus & Maxine Parrott

2	(8-ounce) packages cream cheese	2	tablespoons onion, finely chopped
1	(8-ounce) can crushed pineapple, drained	2	tablespoons green pepper, chopped
2	cups pecans, finely chopped, divided		Garnish: pineapple chunks, maraschino cherries, parsley
1	tablespoon Lawry's Seasoned Salt		

Soften cheese, gradually stir in pineapple, 1 cup pecans, salt, onion, and green pepper. Mix well. Chill. Make into a ball and roll in remaining pecans. Best made a day or so before needed to blend flavors. Leftovers can be rolled again in nuts after reshaping and served another time. Serve with Ritz crackers. Yield: 20 servings.

☆ ☆ ☆ ☆ ☆

HINT:
To stuff eggs or celery or to put cream cheese on crackers use a pastry tube for a decorative look.

☆ ☆ ☆ ☆ ☆

DIANE'S CREAM CHEESE BALL

Geneva Eubanks

This came from my cousin Diane Friesen who is a very good cook.

3 (8-ounce) packages cream cheese, softened
1 (4-ounce) can mushrooms, stems and pieces
1 (4-ounce) jar black olives, chopped
3 to 4 green onions with tops, chopped

1 (2-ounce) jar pimiento, chopped
1 (2¼-ounce) jar dried beef, chopped
Garlic powder to taste, optional

Mix all ingredients together and form into two balls. Chill. Yield: 2 balls.

HAM CHEESE BALL

Moline Lorenz

This recipe was given to me by Diane Watson of Madera, California. It is very delicious and makes a pretty holiday dish served on red plate with sprigs of parsley around it.

2 (8-ounce) cream cheese, softened
4 (6-ounce) packages thin wafer ham, chopped
1 tablespoon Accent

1 tablespoon garlic salt
½ (3-ounce) bottle chives, chopped
1 (2-ounce) jar chopped pimientos, optional

Mix cream cheese and 2 packages of ham, Accent, garlic salt, and chives. Make into 2 balls. Roll in remaining ham. Yield: 2 balls.

SALMON BALL

Jewell Scott

Substitute non-fat sour cream for cream cheese to make this a low-fat healthy treat.

1 (15½-ounce) can salmon, drained and flaked
1 (8-ounce) package cream cheese, softened
½ cup pecans, chopped
2 tablespoons onion, grated

1 tablespoon lemon juice
1 tablespoon prepared horseradish
¼ teaspoon salt
¼ cup fresh parsley, chopped
Lemon slices, optional

Combine first 7 ingredients; stir well. Chill. Shape into a ball and roll in parsley. Serve with assorted crackers and garnish with lemon slices, if desired. Yield: 1 ball.

STUFFED CHEESE TORTILLAS   *Robin Taylor*

1   (8-ounce) package cream cheese, softened
1   (8-ounce) carton sour cream
1½ cups sharp Cheddar cheese, grated
1   cup ripe olives, chopped
1   (4-ounce) can green chilies, chopped and drained
1   tablespoon pimientos, chopped
1   teaspoon garlic salt
1   tablespoon onion, minced
12 flour tortillas

Mix all ingredients together except tortillas. Spread mixture on flour tortillas; roll up in jelly roll style. Chill several hours. Slice in half-inch slice. Serve. Yield: 72 slices.

ZESTY PARMESAN CRISPS   *Margaret Dannecker*

Nice because they can be made ahead of time and kept on hand in the freezer for use on short notice.

8   slices white bread
1½ cups Parmesan cheese, grated
1¼ teaspoons chili powder
1   cup butter or margarine, melted

Remove crust from bread. Cut each slice into 8 sticks. (Easier to do when slightly frozen). Place on baking sheet and toast at 400 degrees for 5 minutes. Meanwhile in shallow dish, combine cheese and chili powder. Into another dish pour butter. Roll each stick in butter, then in cheese mixture. Then freeze. To serve, place as many as you need on baking sheet and bake at 400 degrees for 5 minutes. Good as cocktail snacks or with soup. Yield: 64 sticks.

HINT:
Butter a flour tortilla and sprinkle a little cinnamon and sugar on it, fold over and place on paper plate. Heat for 20 seconds in a microwave on HIGH. This is a great after-school snack.

HILL COUNTRY TRASH   *Vanessa Luce*

1	cup bacon drippings <u>or</u> margarine	3	teaspoons red pepper
1	tablespoon liquid smoke	3	teaspoons Accent (optional)
5	teaspoons Worcestershire sauce	1	(16-ounce) box Wheat Chex
		1	(12-ounce) box Rice Chex
2	teaspoons Tabasco sauce	1	(12-ounce) box Corn Chex
1	teaspoon seasoned salt	1	(10-ounce) box Cheerios
4	teaspoons garlic powder	2	(12-ounce) boxes thin pretzels sticks
2	teaspoons chili powder	3	cups salted nuts with sesame sticks
2 to 3	teaspoons curry powder		

Melt bacon drippings or margarine and mix with sauces and seasonings. Mix dry ingredients in very large container and pour liquid over dry ingredients. Use egg turner to stir. Bake in large roaster 1½ to 2 hours in a 250 degree oven. Stir several times while cooking. Yield: 15 to 20 quarts.

FRUIT FOR DIPPING   *Cathy Woods*

This recipe was given to me by a very dear friend, Martha Ashley of Nixon, Texas. The dip is very rich, a little goes a long way. Try different fruits.

1	(14-ounce) can sweetened condensed milk	3	green apples
		3	bananas
1	(7-ounce) jar marshmallow cream	4	kiwi
		1	bunch red seedless grapes
1	(8-ounce) package cream cheese, softened	1	bunch Thompson grapes
		1	pint fresh strawberries
3	red apples	2	large lemons

With mixer blend the first 3 ingredients until smooth and refrigerate until serving time. Core apples and cut into wedges; peel bananas and cut into 1 inch pieces; peel kiwi and cut into quarters, remove grapes from stems; cut strawberries into halves. Cut lemons in half and squeeze juice over apples and bananas to keep them from becoming discolored. Place the "Dip" into a serving bowl and place in the center of a serving platter, arrange fruit around the bowl of dip on platter. Serve at once or keep refrigerated until serving time. Yield: 12 to 15 servings.

BACON-CHEESE SPREAD
Holly Lawson

This is very similar to the olive spread that comes in the cute little glass jars.

1 (8-ounce) package cream cheese, softened	½ cup green olives, finely chopped
½ cup Cheddar cheese, shredded	8 slices bacon, fried and crumbled

Combine cheeses, olives and ½ of bacon, mix well. Chill until firm. Mixture can be shaped into a design or log or served in a dish. Sprinkle reserved bacon on top. Serve with crackers. Yields: about 1½ cups.

CHILI-CHEESE DIP
Mary Ruebsahm

This will be on the thin side as you start to simmer slowly.

1 pound Velveeta	1 large onion, diced
1 can Cheddar cheese soup	Dash or two of garlic salt
1 (15-ounce) can chili, medium hot	1 tablespoon Worcestershire sauce
Few drops hot sauce	

Heat cheese and soup until cheese melts, add chili and mix well. Add remaining ingredients. Simmer slowly about 2 hours, or until thickened to desired consistency. Stir frequently. Serve hot. Yield: 5-6 cups.

CREAM CHEESE DIP
Mary A. Moursund

1 (5-ounce) jar dried beef, chopped	1½ cups sour cream, more or less
2 (8-ounce) packages cream cheese, softened	Garlic salt and pepper to taste
½ green pepper, diced	½ to 1 cup pecans or walnuts, chopped
2 tablespoons onion, diced	

In a bowl, mix together beef and cheese. Add green pepper, onion, sour cream, garlic salt, and pepper to taste, about a teaspoon of each. Place in 8½-inch Corning skillet about 1½ inches deep. Sprinkle heavily with nuts. Bake 350 degrees for 30 minutes. Serve warm on crackers. Yield: about 2½ cups.

❖ ❖ ❖ ❖ ❖ ❖ ❖

HOT BEEF DIP

Flora Cox

This is good for any fun get-together or party. You will get compliments.

¼ cup onion, chopped
1 tablespoon margarine
1 cup milk
1 (8-ounce) package cream
    cheese, cubed
1 cup dried beef, chopped
1 (3-ounce) can sliced
    mushrooms, drained

¼ cup Parmesan cheese,
    shredded
2 tablespoons parsley,
    chopped
Toasted party rye
    bread rounds
Toasted bread sticks

Cook onion in margarine until tender. Stir in milk and cream cheese, mixing until well blended. Add remaining ingredients except bread. Serve hot in chafing dish with toasted bread rounds and bread sticks. Yield: 2 cups.

CLAM DIP

Jane Mills

1 (6½-ounce) can minced
    clams
1 (3-ounce) package cream
    cheese, softened
1 tablespoon mayonnaise
1 tablespoon chives, chopped

1 tablespoon parsley, chopped
½ teaspoon Worcestershire
    sauce
½ teaspoon prepared mustard,
    regular or hot

Drain clams very, very well. Place in container with a lid. Add the rest of the ingredients. Mix well and chill several hours. Serve with Fritos or some type of cracker. Yield: about 1½ cups.

SALMON PATE

Holly Lawson

I can my own carp, yes, the fish most of you throw back! It tastes just like salmon and can be interchanged in recipes with salmon. I have used it in this recipe several times and no one can tell the difference. The salmon is excellent, also.

1 (7¾-ounce) can salmon, drained
1 (1.05-ounce) Good Seasons
    Italian Salad Dressing Mix

1 (8-ounce) package cream
    cheese, softened
⅓ cup cucumber, chopped

Line a 2 cup bowl or loaf pan with plastic wrap. Blend the salmon with the dressing mix, cream cheese, and cucumber. Press into bowl and chill at least 1 hour. Unmold and serve with cucumber slices or crackers. Yield: 2 cups.

SHRIMP DIP
Susan Thomas

1½ (8-ounce) packages cream cheese
1 teaspoon Worcestershire sauce
2 teaspoons fresh lemon juice
1 teaspoon onion, grated
½ pound fresh shrimp, steamed, cut into very small pieces

1 cup ketchup
3 tablespoons lemon juice
1 tablespoon horseradish
3 drops Tabasco or to taste
½ teaspoon celery salt
½ teaspoon salt
Parsley for garnish

Mix cream cheese, Worcestershire sauce, 2 teaspoons lemon juice, and onion together. Spread into flat serving dish. Top with shrimp pieces. In another bowl, mix ketchup, 3 tablespoons lemon juice, horseradish, Tabasco, celery salt, and salt. Cover shrimp with the red sauce. Garnish with parsley. Let sit overnight in refrigerator. Serve with crackers. Yield: A party.

VEGETABLE DIP
Flora Cox

This dip is very good with all vegetables. It is also tasty with sliced apples and pineapple chunks. Bill and I first had this dip while visiting Leland and Thelma Stevenson in Austin. I liked it so much that when I was preparing for a party in Borger, I called Thelma for the recipe, and I use it often.

1 (8-ounce) carton of small curd creamed cottage cheese
1 cup Hellmann's mayonnaise
Minced onion or onion powder to taste

¼ teaspoon Accent
¼ to ½ jar of Imitation Bacon Bits
Garlic salt to taste

Place all ingredients in a blender or food processor until well mixed. Yield: 2 cups.

⭐ ⭐ ⭐ ⭐ ⭐

HINT:
A quick and easy dip is 8-ounces cream cheese, softened and ½ cup jalapeño jelly mixed well. Picante or hot sauce may be substituted for the jelly.

MEXICAN RELISH

Gail Rucker

Goes fast at our family reunions!

1 (4-ounce) can chopped ripe olives	2 large tomatoes, finely chopped
1 (4-ounce) can chopped green chilies	3 tablespoons vegetable oil
1 bunch small green onions, finely chopped	1½ teaspoons garlic salt

Mix all ingredients together. Serve with Fritos or Tostado chips. Yield: 2½ to 3 cups.

SALSA FRESCA

Robin Taylor

3 large tomatoes, chopped	1 (4-ounce) can chopped green chilies
1 bunch green onions with tops, chopped	1 to 2 fresh jalapeño peppers, chopped
3 to 4 cloves fresh garlic, chopped or 1 teaspoon garlic powder	1 teaspoon or more salt
1 (2½-ounce) can sliced black olives, drained	¼ teaspoon black pepper
	1 tablespoon vinegar
	3 tablespoons olive oil

Mix all the ingredients well and serve with tortilla chips, garnishment for fajitas or add to pinto beans. Yield: 3 to 4 cups.

CITRIC ACID PUNCH

Suzanne Law

This is a great and inexpensive punch for a crowd. I received this recipe from Daisy Cox.

5 pounds sugar	12 ounces lemon juice
4 cups hot water	2 ounces almond extract
1 cup cold water	2 ounces vanilla extract
2 tablespoons (1 ounce) citric acid (canning section)	14 (1-liter) bottles ginger ale

Mix sugar and hot water; mix citric acid in cold water. When hot water mixture has cooled, combine all ingredients together except ginger ale. When ready to serve, mix 1 cup syrup with 1 liter bottle ginger ale. Yield: 100 servings.

14

EASY HOT FRUIT PUNCH
Mary Pat Carter

2 (48-ounce) jars apple juice
1 (48-ounce) can pineapple juice

2 cups orange juice
1 (9-ounce) package red hots

Heat juices together, add red hots and stir until melted. Serve hot. Keeps well in refrigerator. Yield: about 24, 6-ounce servings.

LET'S HAVE A PARTY PUNCH
Cynthia Smith

I made this punch for our Chamber of Commerce Citizen of the Year dinner. Before asking your husband to help when you triple this recipe, make sure your marriage is strong.

2 quarts boiling water
5 cups sugar
¼ cup citric acid (canning section)
1 (10-ounce) can frozen strawberry daiquiri mix, thawed

1 (12-ounce) can frozen pink lemonade, thawed
1 (46-ounce) can unsweetened pineapple juice
4 quarts water
8 (10-ounce) bottles ginger ale

Combine boiling water, sugar and citric acid in a ceramic, heatproof container stirring until citric acid dissolves. In a large stainless steel or ceramic container for mixing combine daiquiri mix, lemonade, pineapple juice, and 4 quarts of water. Add citric acid mixture and stir well. Divide mixture evenly into 4 one gallon size freezer zip lock plastic bags. FREEZE. When ready to serve remove from freezer 30 minutes before serving. Place in punch bowl and break into chunks. Add 2 bottles of ginger-ale to each bag of mixture. Stir until slushy. This recipe may be doubled or tripled. Yield: 50 6-ounce servings.

LIME FROSTED PARTY PUNCH
Aline Slack

4 cups pineapple-grapefruit drink, chilled
⅔ cup lemon juice
2 quarts cold water
3 (0.5-ounce) packages unsweetened lemon-lime soft drink mix

2 cups sugar
2 pints lime sherbert
4 (7-ounce) bottles lemon-lime carbonated beverage, chilled

In punch bowl, combine first five ingredients stirring until soft drink mix and sugar are completely dissolved. Top punch with large spoonfuls of sherbert. Resting bottle on rim of punch bowl, carefully pour in carbonated beverage. Serve some sherbert with each cup of punch. Yield: 30-35 servings.

PASTEL PUNCH
Joycelyn Carter

1 (3-ounce) package strawberry gelatin
1 cup boiling water
1 (6-ounce) can frozen orange juice
1 (6-ounce) can frozen pineapple juice

1½ cups sugar
1 (28-ounce) bottle ginger-ale, chilled
Ice

Dissolve gelatin in boiling water, stir in fruit juice and stir well until thawed. Stir in sugar. Chill. When ready to serve add ginger-ale and ice. Yield: 10, 4-ounce servings.

QUICK AND EASY PUNCH
Lucia Carbary

This recipe comes from Dorothy Lackey of Johnson City. It is not very sweeet but kids like it for school parties.

1 (6-ounce) can frozen orange juice
1 (6-ounce) can frozen lemonade

1 (6-ounce) can frozen Hawaiian punch
3 quarts 7-Up

Dilute juices with the 7-Up. Add ice or ice ring. Garnish with slices of oranges and lemons to float on top. Quick and easy. Yield: 30 servings.

SOFT DRINK PUNCH
Joycelyn Carter

1 (46-ounce) can Hawaiian Punch
3 packages lemon-aid sweetened soft drink mix
1 package cherry sweetened soft drink mix
1 package orange sweetened soft drink mix
1 (46-ounce) can pineapple juice

¼ cup maraschino cherry juice
¼ teaspoon almond extract
½ teaspoon vanilla
Water to make two gallons
Red food coloring, optional
2 to 3 (12-ounce) cans 7-Up, Sprite, or Gingerale

16

Mix all ingredients together except 7-Up and add water to make 2 gallons. Chill or freeze. Just before serving add 7-Up. If using unsweetened soft drink mix use a cup of sugar for each package used. Yield: 50, 5-ounce servings.

SPECIAL PUNCH
Inez Steolyn Evavold

- 2 (10-ounce) package frozen strawberries, thawed
- 1 (6-ounce) can frozen lemonade
- 2 quarts Mountain Dew

Blend strawberries and lemonade in blender. Add 1 quart of Mountain Dew and freeze. Thaw slowly and add more Mountain Dew. Yield: 20, 4-ounce servings.

SUE'S EASY PUNCH
Sue Sultemeier

- 1 (46-ounce) can pineapple juice
- 2 liters Lemon-Lime Slice
- Almond extract to taste, about 1 tablespoon
- Vanilla extract to taste, about 1 tablespoon
- Red food coloring, optional

Mix all together. Serve over ice. Try freezing some of the punch to use as ice. Yield: 25, 4-ounce servings.

TEA CONCENTRATE
Ray Sultemeier

- 6 cups water
- 1 cup tea leaves
- 1 teaspoon baking soda
- 6 cups sugar

Bring water, tea, and soda to a boil. Turn off heat and allow to steep for 10 minutes. Strain over sugar. Stir well. Will keep 2 to 3 weeks in refrigerator. At mealtime or as needed simply add water and ice. Yield: about 1 quart.

HOT CHOCOLATE MIX
Jewell Sultemeier

- 1 (8-quart) package powdered milk
- 2½ cups powdered sugar
- 2 (6-ounce) jars Coffee Mate
- 1 (14.5-ounce) box Hershey's Chocolate Mix

Mix well and store in covered containers. To serve use ⅓ cup mix in cup and fill with hot water. Stir. Add one marshmallow per cup.

Gettin' Started

Soups, Sandwiches, Sauces, Salads

PEDERNALES ELECTRIC COOPERATIVE, INC.
E. BABE SMITH HEADQUARTERS BLDG.

Through the efforts of then-Congressman Lyndon B. Johnson, Pedernales Electric Cooperative, Inc. was allotted federal funds to assist in the construction of a head-quarters building in Johnson City. Construction began in 1939 by seventy-five members of the National Youth Administration (NYA) from San Antonio. NYA workers cleared the land, quarried the native limestone rock used in construction, laid the water lines and built the structure. Construction was completed in 1940. The building has been remodeled, renovated, and added to several times over the years. The most recent addition was completed in 1985. In 1986, the headquarters building was officially renamed and dedicated as the E. Babe Smith Headquarters Building to honor the Oakalla rancher who co-founded the Cooperative with Lyndon Johnson.

GARBANZO BEAN SOUP   *Robyn Henderson*

When I get into a vegetarian cooking mood, I start the meal with this dish. Garbanzo beans are high in protein and low in fat.

2   cups dried garbanzo beans
Water to cover
½   teaspoon dried rosemary
3   tablespoons olive oil
3   cloves garlic, chopped fine
3   tablespoons onion, chopped fine
2   tablespoons diced green chilies

1   tablespoon Worcestershire sauce
3 to 4 tablespoons tomato paste
1   cup shell macaroni
Salt and pepper to taste

Soak the beans overnight in enough water to keep them covered. The next day, add salt and rosemary and more water if needed. Simmer for 2 to 3 hours, until the beans are tender. Heat olive oil in a small saucepan, add garlic and onion and cook until onion is transparent. Stir in green chilies, Worcestershire sauce and tomato paste and add to beans and their liquid. Season with plenty of pepper and salt. Add more water to make room for the macaroni. When liquid simmers add macaroni and continue cooking until it is tender, another 20 minutes. Serve steaming hot with French bread. Yield: 8 to 10 servings.

CHEESE VEGETABLE CHOWDER   *Jeanne Hudson*

10   slices bacon
1   cup onion, chopped
1   cup carrots, chopped
1   cup water
2½   cups potatoes, diced
2   chicken bouillon cubes
3   cups milk

1   (16-ounce) can whole kernel corn, drained
3   cups (12-ounces) Cheddar cheese, shredded
3   tablespoons flour
Pepper to taste

Cook bacon in 4 quart Dutch oven until brown. Remove and crumble, set aside. Sauté onions in drippings until tender. Add bacon, carrots, water, potatoes, and bouillon cubes. Bring to a boil, reduce heat, cover and simmer 20-25 minutes until vegetables are tender. Stir in milk and corn. Combine cheese and flour and add to soup stirring until cheese melts. Yield: 2½ to 3 quarts.

SPLIT PEA SOUP
Mae Hernlund

Family favorite for thirty years.

1	cup dry split peas, green or yellow	2 or 3	stalks of celery, chopped
2	quarts water	¼	teaspoon powdered ginger
1	bay leaf, remove after cooking	¼	teaspoon black pepper
1	large carrot, sliced		Salt to taste
1	large onion, chopped		Ham bone or leftover ham

Rinse peas. Place in a 3 to 4 quart pot with other ingredients. Simmer 2 to 2½ hours. Recipe can be doubled. Ways to serve: 1. After cooking, sieve through a strainer. Reheat and serve with a dollop of sour cream with horseradish. This may be first course of a company dinner. 2. Unstrained with bits of meat. 3. Add sliced frankfurters last 15 minutes of cooking. 4. Cool, chill, remove bones, cut meat into bite-size pieces, simmer uncovered to further thicken soup. Serve with crusty bread or crackers. Yield: serves 8 to 16.

PENNSYLVANIA DUTCH POTATO SOUP
Mae Hernlund

A family and guest favorite since 1974.

4	cups potatoes peeled, thinly sliced		Several peppercorns
		1½	cups milk
3	cups onion, thinly sliced	2	tablespoons butter or margarine
3	cups water		
2	small bay leaves		Black pepper
2	teaspoons salt		Nutmeg, optional

Place the first 5 ingredients in a 3 quart saucepan. Cover and bring to boiling. Reduce heat and simmer until tender, about 15-20 minutes. Stir in milk and butter. Heat. Add few twists of black pepper to taste. Sprinkle nutmeg on top of each bowl if desired. Serve with crackers. Yield: 6 servings.

HINTS:

The one who gets the bay leaf in their bowl of soup is the lucky one.

For flavor, rub soup pot with pod of garlic.

20

SUPER SLIMMING SOUP
Opal Weirich

2 large onions, chopped
1 red bell pepper, chopped
1 stalk celery, chopped
3 cloves garlic, chopped
1 tablespoon oil
5 cups chicken broth
2 cups zucchini, chopped

1 cup carrots, chopped
2 tomatoes <u>or</u> 1 (16-ounce)
  can tomatoes, chopped
2 cups cabbage, chopped
1 tablespoon parsley, chopped
¼ teaspoon pepper
Salt to taste

Slowly brown onions, pepper, celery and garlic in oil in a 3-4 quart pot. Add remaining ingredients, bring to boil and simmer about 30 minutes. 50 calories per cup. Yield: 10 servings.

COLD TOMATO SOUP
Frana Keith

2 ripe tomatoes, peeled
1 cucumber, peeled, diced
¼ cup green pepper, diced
¼ cup onion, diced
1 cup canned tomato juice

2 tablespoons olive oil
1½ tablespoons vinegar
Dash Tabasco sauce
Salt, pepper, garlic salt <u>or</u>
  minced garlic to taste

Blend all ingredients in a blender and chill. Leave the cucumber chunky as it gives the soup a good crunchy consistency. Yield: 4 servings.

MINETA'S FREEZER SOUP
Cynthia Smith

This is my step-mother's recipe and a favorite of mine and my husband. She is a very frugal person, never throws anything out, into the 'soup jar' in the freezer it goes. She does buy the shank meat, it is so tender. I have tried other stew meat but it is tough and not as tasty. A pan of cornbread with this is a great winter meal. When the soup jar is full, it is time to make soup!

4 quarts water
1 medium onion, quartered
1 whole rib of celery
1 package soup meat, shank cut
1 clove garlic, chopped

1 (8-ounce) can tomato sauce
Pasta, optional
Potatoes, optional
Quart jar of frozen left over
  vegetables, pasta, meat etc.
½ head raw cabbage, chopped

Bring water, celery and onion to boil with soup meat. Reduce heat and add garlic and tomato sauce. Let simmer for a few hours, adding water as needed. Remove cooked celery and meat, remove meat from bone, cut-

ting into smaller pieces. Put meat and bone back into liquid and add uncooked pasta and uncooked potatoes if you like. Cook this for 15 minutes and then add contents of soup jar with the cabbage. Cook just 10 minutes and serve. Yield: 6 to 8 servings.

BUSY DAY VEGETABLE BEEF SOUP   *Joycelyn Carter*

1 pound ground meat, browned	1 (46-ounce) can V-8 juice
1 onion, chopped	1 tablespoon sugar
1 bell pepper, chopped	Salt and pepper to taste
1 (20-ounce) package frozen mixed vegetables	

Put all ingredients into crock-pot and mix well. Cook on low 10–12 hours. Yield: 8 servings.

CRAB BURGER   *Vanessa H. Luce*

This was a favorite of my children, Deborah, Karen, Gary and Laurie, when they were young.

1 (6-ounce) can crab meat	3 tablespoons mayonnaise
¼ cup celery, diced	Salt and pepper to taste
1 tablespoon prepared mustard	Swiss or Cheddar cheese slices
	Hamburger buns

Mix crab meat, celery, mustard, mayonnaise, salt and pepper well. Put mixture on bun. Place slice of cheese over mixture. Broil until brown. Yield: 2-4 open-face sandwiches.

CUCUMBER-CREAM CHEESE SANDWICHES/DIP   *Sadie Sharp*

I often serve these sandwiches/dip at club parties or family gatherings and have requests for the recipe.

1 (8-ounce) package cream cheese, softened	1 cup pecans, ground
½ medium cucumber, peeled, seeded and grated	1 tablespoon sweet pickle relish or grated sweet, dill or sour pickle, drained
1 (8-ounce) carton sour cream	1 teaspoon lemon juice
¼ cup salad dressing, more if needed	1 large loaf thin sandwich bread

22

Mix all ingredients except bread. If cucumber seems too watery, reserve some of juice. Spread mixture on one slice and cover with another slice. Cut into wedges or fingers. Crust of bread may be removed. 8-ounce can crushed pineapple, drained, may be substituted for cucumber.

Dip: To make mixture a dip add more liquid; lemon, cucumber or pineapple juice. Yield: 20 to 30 sandwiches or 2 pints dip.

ROAST BEEF SANDWICHES   *Joycelyn Carter*

4   cups roast beef, ground
½   cup celery, chopped fine
½   cup sweet pickle relish <u>or</u>
     sweet pickle, chopped

1   tablespoon prepared
     mustard
1   cup mayonnaise
½   teaspoon salt

Mix all ingredients well except bread. Chill. Serve on very thin white bread with crust removed. Spread may be frozen. Good as small party sandwiches. Yield: 4 cups of spread.

TUNA-PUFF SANDWICHES   *Margaret Dannecker*

If you're one of those who thinks you would never serve tuna-anything to guests, try this on the next football-watching crowd at your house. Attractive and delicious!

1   (7-ounce) can tuna, drained
      and flaked
1½ teaspoons prepared
      mustard
¼   teaspoon Worcestershire
      sauce
¼   cup mayonnaise
1½ teaspoons onion, grated

2   tablespoons green pepper,
      chopped
3   hamburger buns, split
6   tomato slices
½   cup mayonnaise
¼   cup American cheese,
      shredded

Blend first 6 ingredients and spread onto bun halves. Top each with tomato slice. Blend mayonnaise with cheese. Spread on tomato slices. Broil 4 inches from heat until topping puffs and browns. When hot, mayonnaise topping tends to slide, so be careful removing from broiler and eating. Yield: 6 servings.

WATERCRESS SANDWICHES   *Jewell Sultemeier*

1   (3-ounce) package cream
    cheese, softened
⅓   cup sour cream
1   tablespoon homemade
    mayonnaise (rec. p. 254)
1   tablespoon chives, chopped
    or 1 teaspoon onion, finely
    chopped

18 slices thin sliced white or
    wheat bread
1   bunch watercress
    Watercress sprigs, garnish

Combine cream cheese, sour cream, homemade mayonnaise until blended. Stir in chives or onions. Remove crust from bread and cut each slice into 2 rectangles. Spread each rectangle with 1 teaspoon of cream cheese mixture. Arrange watercress on half of rectangles, top with remaining rectangles. Garnish, if desired. Yield: 18 sandwiches.

GARLIC BREAD SPREAD   *Suzanne Law*

½   pound butter, softened
1   tablespoon garlic powder
1   teaspoon basil
1   teaspoon oregano

1   teaspoon red pepper flakes
½   cup Parmesan cheese,
    grated

Mix all ingredients together. Spread generously on thick Italian bread. Broil until bubbly and golden. Spread keeps for months in refrigerator. Yield: about 1 cup.

"YOU CAN DO IT, HOLLANDAISE SAUCE"   *Peggy Green*

Always successful.

½   pound butter or margarine
4   egg yolks
2   tablespoons lemon juice

¼   teaspoon salt
    Pinch cayenne pepper

In a small saucepan, heat butter just to bubbling. In container of electric blender put yolks, lemon juice, salt and cayenne pepper. Cover container, turn on high speed. Immediately remove cover and add hot butter in a steady stream. Yield: about 2 cups.

RAISIN SAUCE

Geneva Eubanks

My sister-in-law, Gail Eubanks, gave this recipe to me in 1958.

1	cup sugar	¼	cup lemon juice
¼	teaspoon salt	½	cup water
2	tablespoons cornstarch	½	cup seedless raisins
1	tablespoon flour	1	tablespoon margarine
1¼	cups orange juice		

Cook all ingredients, except margarine over low heat until boiling. Cook 3 minutes. Remove from heat and add margarine. Keeps well. Serve hot with baked ham. Yield: 2⅓ cups.

TARTAR SAUCE WITH A DIFFERENCE

Margie Sultemeier

½	cup mayonnaise	1	tablespoon black <u>or</u> green
¼	teaspoon Worcestershire		olives <u>or</u> both, diced
	sauce	1	tablespoon lemon juice
½	teaspoon onion, grated		
1	tablespoon dill pickle relish		

Mix together, use for seafood. Yield: ⅔ cup.

APRICOT CHEESE SALAD

Janey Wiemers

It is great with fried chicken or baked ham. This was entered in an annual recipe contest in Anchorage, Alaska, by Monica Kennedy, a dear friend, who won honorable mention.

1	egg	2	cups mild Cheddar cheese,
½	cup sugar		grated
3	tablespoons flour	1	cup nuts, chopped
2	(16-ounce) cans of apricots,		
	drained, save juice		

Beat together egg, sugar and flour in a small saucepan. Add juice from apricots and cook until thick, stirring constantly. In serving bowl put one layer of apricots, sprinkle with layer of cheese, a layer of nuts and then a layer of sauce. Continue to layer the ingredients until they are all used. Chill before serving. Can be made a day ahead and refrigerated. Yield: 6 servings.

CRANBERRY SALAD   *Dorothy Lackey*

1 (14-ounce) can sweetened condensed milk
¼ cup lemon juice
1 (16-ounce) can whole cranberry sauce
1 (20-ounce) can crushed pineapple, drained

½ to ¾ cup walnuts or pecans, chopped
1 (9-ounce) carton whipped topping, thawed
4 to 5 drops red food coloring (optional)

In a large bowl combine milk and lemon juice. Stir in cranberry sauce, pineapple and nuts. Fold in whipped topping and red food coloring if desired. Spread in a 13 x 9 x 2-inch dish or place in paper muffin cups or muffin pan. Freeze until firm. Serve on lettuce leaves with whipped topping on top. Yield: 15 servings.

VAL'S CRANBERRY WALDORF SALAD   *Pauline Edwards*

This tasty, festive salad is a good addition to a holiday meal and is low in calories and fat. It is a traditional holiday favorite of the Edwards family.

1 cup apple, chopped
1 to 2 tablespoons lemon juice, optional
1 cup celery, chopped
1½ cups cranberries, chopped
⅓ cup walnuts or pecans, chopped

1 cup green grapes, halved
⅓ cup raisins, soak 30 minutes
2 tablespoons brown sugar
¼ teaspoon cinnamon
8 ounces vanilla lowfat yogurt

Mix apples with lemon juice to reduce browning, if desired. Mix all ingredients except yogurt together and stir well. Fold in yogurt. Refrigerate 2 to 3 hours before serving. Yield: 8 servings.

FOO-FOO SALAD   *Holly Lawson*

I fix this at Easter with cherry gelatin. It is so good and simple.

1 (8-ounce) carton cottage cheese, drain thoroughly
1 (3-ounce) package gelatin, any flavor
1 (15-ounce) can crushed pineapple, drained well
2 cups whipped topping
1½ cups miniature marshmallows

Mix cheese, pineapple and dry gelatin together. Fold in whipped topping and marshmallows. Chill 30 minutes before serving. Yield: 12 servings.

FROG EYE SALAD

Lee Caruthers

The pasta in the salad look like eyes, the reason for the name.

¾ cup sugar
1 tablespoon flour
½ teaspoon salt
⅔ cup pineapple juice
1 egg, beaten
1 teaspoon lemon juice
1 cup Acini Di Pepe (rice-like pasta)
2 (11-ounce) cans Mandarin oranges, drained

1 (20-ounce) can chunk pineapple, drained and saved
1 (20-ounce) can crushed pineapple, drained and saved
1 (8-ounce) carton dairy whipped topping
1 cup miniature marshmallows

In a small sauce pan, mix sugar, flour and salt. Stir in pineapple juice and egg. Cook over medium heat, stirring constantly until thickened. Add lemon juice and set aside to cool. Cook pasta as directed on box. Combine cooked mixture and pasta. Cover and place in refrigerator to chill. Combine remaining ingredients, stir lightly. Chill at least 1 hour before serving. Good frozen. Yield: 10-15 servings.

FROZEN FRUIT SALAD

Barbara Taylor

1 (21-ounce) can peach <u>or</u> apricot pie filling
1 (20-ounce) can crushed pineapple, undrained

3 to 4 bananas sliced
1 (10-ounce) package frozen sweet strawberries <u>or</u> raspberries

Mix all together using all juices. Pour into a bundt pan sprayed with vegetable spray. Freeze. When ready to serve, unmold on large plate covered with lettuce leaves. Cut serving like cake. Yield: 12-16 servings.

HINTS:

To peel oranges and grapefruit without the membranes sticking to sections, soak the fruit in hot water for 5 minutes before peeling.

Melted jelly makes a quick glaze for fruits.

To keep fresh cranberries as fresh as the day you bought them, put them in the freezer . . . will keep for months.

LEMON FRUIT SALAD

Annie Dee Ebeling

1   (16-ounce) can fruit cocktail, undrained
1   (4-ounce) package miniature marshmallows
1   (3¼-ounce) package lemon instant pudding, dry
1   teaspoon lemon extract
1   (16-ounce) can sliced peaches, drained

1   (16-ounce) can pears, drained and diced
1   (16-ounce) can pineapple chunks, drained
1   (16-ounce) can apricots, drained and chopped

Mix fruit cocktail, marshmallows, pudding mix and lemon extract. Add drained fruit and mix well. Refrigerate overnight or a day or two before using. Keeps well. May freeze leftovers and serve as frozen salad. Other fruits may be added or some deleted. Yield: 16-20 servings.

FRUIT MEDLEY

Lee Caruthers

1   (13-ounce) can pineapple tidbits, drained
2   (11-ounce) cans mandarin oranges, drained
1   cup seedless grapes, red <u>or</u> green, halved
2   large ripe bananas, sliced
1   pint fresh strawberries, halved

3   tablespoons fresh lemon juice
¼   teaspoon almond extract
1   (21-ounce) can peach pie filling
Fresh mint leaves

Combine all the fruit. Mix lemon juice and almond extract with peach pie filling. Stir in fruit. Chill. Garnish with mint leaves. Freeze any leftovers and serve as frozen salad. Yield: 10-12 servings.

MILLION DOLLAR SALAD

Elisca Parsons

This can be used as a salad or a dessert. Try other fruits along with pineapple or by themselves.

4   cups cooked rice, chilled
2   envelopes Dream Whip topping mix
½   cup milk
1   teaspoon vanilla

2   cups sugar
2   (16-ounce) cans crushed pineapple, drained
2   cups pecans, chopped

28

Chill rice. Place topping mix in bowl with milk and vanilla. Beat on high speed of electric mixer until soft peaks form. Add sugar and whip until sugar dissolves. Mix pineapple, pecans, and rice, fold in whipped topping. Refrigerate. Serve chilled. Recipe can be halved. Yield: 28 servings.

SPRINGTIME FRUIT SALAD
Mary A. Thurlkill

3	cups, red, black, <u>or</u> green seedless grapes, whole
2	cups fresh strawberries, whole
3	bananas, sliced
3	apples, cut in bite-size pieces
1	(15¼-ounce) can pineapple chunks, drained

1	(8-ounce) jar red maraschino cherries, drained
1½	cups buttermilk
1	(3.4-ounce) box pistachio instant pudding mix
1	(8-ounce) container Cool Whip Lite
½	cup angel-flake coconut

Combine all fruit in large bowl. Set aside. Mix buttermilk with pudding. Fold in Cool Whip. Add pudding mixture to fruit. Place in serving bowl and garnish with coconut. Chill and serve. Yield: 12 servings.

TANGY FRUIT SALAD
Lucia Carbary

Originally came from Leola Mills.

1	(16-ounce) can chunk pineapple, drained, reserve juice
1	(11-ounce) can mandarin oranges, drained
1	(15½-ounce) can fruit for salad, drained

3	bananas, sliced
10	Maraschino cherries, optional
1	(3½-ounce) package vanilla instant pudding mix
3	tablespoons Tang, orange drink mix

Mix fruit together in a large bowl. In another bowl mix pudding mix, Tang and reserved pineapple juice, blend well. Pour over fruit and stir gently. Chill and serve same day. Yield: 6 servings.

HINTS:
Marshmallows can stay fresh for an indefinite length of time when frozen.

To remove congealed salad from mold, coat mold with vegetable cooking spray before filling.

☆ ☆ ☆ ☆ ☆

SUPER DUPER FRUIT SALAD

Ruth Teague

2 eggs
4 tablespoons sugar
1 tablespoon butter
4 tablespoons vinegar or
   lemon juice
1 (3-ounce) package lemon
   gelatin
1 envelope of Dream Whip
   topping mix

1 cup milk, divided
½ teaspoon vanilla
1 (16-ounce) can crushed
   pineapple, drained
1 (16-ounce) can fruit
   cocktail, drained
2 cups miniature
   marshmallows

Beat together the eggs, sugar, butter, vinegar or lemon juice. Cook until thick. Remove from heat and stir in dry gelatin. Cool 10 minutes. Prepare Dream Whip with ½ cup milk and vanilla. Fold into cooled mixture. Blend in other ½ cup milk, drained fruit and marshmallows. Chill. Colored marshmallows make a prettier salad. Yield: 12 servings.

APPLE CINNAMON MOLDED SALAD

Janey Wiemers

This was given to me by a friend, Verona, many years ago. She has always been a wonderful hostess. This is a beautiful salad for Christmas and Valentines. The salad could be put directly into a glass serving dish and served from it at the table.

1 cup water
¼ cup red cinnamon candies
1 (6-ounce) package lemon
   gelatin
1 tablespoon Knox gelatin,
   optional

1 (16-ounce) can applesauce
1 (8-ounce) package cream
   cheese, softened
½ cup salad dressing
½ cup nuts, chopped
½ cup celery, finely chopped

Combine water and candies; bring to a boil, reduce heat and simmer until candies are melted, stirring frequently. Add gelatin and Knox gelatin, if desired, stirring until dissolved. Add applesauce; mix thoroughly. Pour half of mixture into 4 cup mold; chill until firm. Beat cream cheese and salad dressing together with a fork. (Milk may be added if it is quite thick). Stir in nuts and celery. Spoon cream cheese mixture evenly over firmed gelatin. Pour remaining gelatin on top and chill until firm. To serve, unmold and turn out on plate lined with lettuce leaves. Yield: 8-10 servings.

ROSIE'S APRICOT SALAD

Rosie Hunter

1   (6-ounce) package apricot
    gelatin
½   cup sugar
1   (15-ounce) can of crushed
    pineapple
1   cup Cheddar cheese, grated

1   cup pecans, chopped
1   (6-ounce) jar junior size
    baby apricots
1   (8-ounce) carton Cool Whip

Bring to boil the gelatin, sugar and pineapple. Cool long enough that the cheese will not melt when added. Add cheese, pecans and apricots and mix well. Add Cool Whip. Pour into 8 x 8-inch dish and chill until set. Yield: 6 to 8 servings.

CHERRY SHERRY MOLD

Peggy Hudspith

1   (16½-ounce) can pitted
    dark sweet cherries, drained,
    reserve juice
1   (6-ounce) box cherry gelatin
1   (6-ounce) box raspberry
    gelatin

Toasted almonds
½   cup sherry
Dash lemon juice
Whipped cream
Mayonnaise

Heat cherry juice. Measure one cup of this juice and add enough boiling water to make 3½ cups liquid. Stir in gelatin. When gelatin is cool but not set, add ½ cup sherry. Stuff each cherry with an almond; fold into gelatin mixture. Add a dash of lemon juice. Gently pour into a 2-quart ring mold. Serve with whipped cream to which a small amount of mayonnaise has been added. Yield: 10 servings.

CHRISTMAS JELLO (COKE SALAD)

Susan Thomas

1   (6-ounce) box cherry Jello
4   cups Coca-Cola
½   cup pecans, chopped
1   (8-ounce) can crushed
    pineapple, drained

1   (3-ounce) package
    Philadelphia cream cheese,
    cut into small chunks

Substitute boiling coke for boiling liquid required on Jello directions. Stir to dissolve completely. Add cold coke in amount required for cold water on Jello package. Chill until partially set. While Jello is setting, mix pecans, pineapple, and cream cheese. Stir all together and place in refrigerator until firm. Yield: 8 servings.

CRANBERRY PINEAPPLE SALAD   *Genevia Bushnell*

I like to serve this when we have turkey and dressing and it covers the need of having a dessert.

1   (6-ounce) box cherry or
    strawberry gelatin
1   (15¼-ounce) can of
    crushed pineapple

1   (16-ounce) can whole
    cranberry sauce
¼   cup pecans, walnuts or
    almonds, chopped

Prepare gelatin as directed on package leaving out ½ cup cold water. Mash the cranberry sauce into bottom of a 13 x 9 x 2 pyrex dish. Add pineapple. Pour gelatin mixture over cranberry sauce and pineapple and stir. Sprinkle nuts on top and chill for 2 to 3 hours or until firm. Yield: 15 servings.

MANGO SALAD   *Linda Slack Hugghins*

3   (3-ounce) package lemon
    gelatin
3   cups boiling water
1   (8-ounce) package cream
    cheese

1   (16-ounce) can mangoes
    with juice or apricots
Garnish: lettuce, sour cream
    and brown sugar

Dissolve gelatin in water. Blend cream cheese and mangoes in blender. Combine gelatin and cheese mixture well. Pour into a 1½ to 2 quart pyrex dish or individual molds. Serve on lettuce with dab of sour cream and sprinkle of brown sugar. May be frozen. Yield: 12 servings.

ORANGE JELLO SALAD   *Suzanne Law*

1   (16-ounce) can crushed
    pineapple, undrained
1   (6-ounce) package orange
    Jello
1   (11-ounce) can Mandarin
    oranges, drained

1   (9-ounce) carton Cool Whip
2   cups buttermilk
½   cup pecans, chopped
Garnish: mayonnaise, cherries,
    orange sections

Heat pineapple and dissolve Jello in it. Let cool completely. Place in large bowl and add oranges, Cool Whip and buttermilk. Fold in nuts. Pour into a 13 x 9 x 2-inch pyrex dish. Refrigerate until firm, about 2 hours. When serving top with a dollop of mayonnaise and cherries or orange sections, if desired. Yield: 15 servings.

CHAIN LETTER ORANGE SALAD   *Cynthia Smith*

This came to me in a recipe chain letter. It is very good. I use it as dessert or salad.

1 (6-ounce) package orange gelatin	½ cup pecans, chopped
1 cup boiling water	½ cup Maraschino cherries, chopped
1 cup orange juice	
1 (11-ounce) can Mandarin oranges, drained	1 pint vanilla ice cream (I use Blue Bell), softened
1 (8-ounce) can crushed pineapple, drained	Lettuce leaves

Mix gelatin with boiling water until dissolved. Stir in orange juice, oranges, pineapple, pecans and cherries. Freeze until at the syrupy stage. Mix in the softened ice cream, pour into a 2 quart mold or 13 x 9 x 2-inch pyrex dish and put back in the freezer until firm. Slice and serve on lettuce leaf. Top with whipped cream and a cherry, if desired. Yield: 12 to 15 servings.

ARTICHOKE & AVOCADO SALAD   *Aline Slack*

If you have never tasted artichokes . . . Try this recipe. You may discover, like I did, that they are good.

1 (14-ounce) can artichoke hearts, drained and quartered	½ teaspoon salt
1 medium avocado, peeled and cut in chunks	¼ cup lemon juice
½ teaspoon crushed fresh garlic	¼ teaspoon dried dillweed
	¼ cup vegetable oil

Place avocado and artichoke in small salad bowl. Combine garlic, salt, lemon juice and dillweed, slowly beat in oil. Pour over vegetable mix. Serve as appetizer or salad. Yield: 4 servings.

BROCCOLI SALAD

Susan Thomas

1   bunch fresh broccoli
2   (1.05-ounce) packages Italian dressing mix, divided
1   (2¼-ounce) can ripe olives, drained and sliced
1   (5-ounce) can water chestnuts, drained
1½   cups small fresh mushrooms

Cut broccoli into bite-size pieces. Mix one package of dressing mix according to the directions on the package. Mix broccoli, olives, water chestnuts and mushrooms in large bowl. Sprinkle with other package of dry Italian dressing mix. Pour the mixed dressing over all; toss and chill. Yield: 6-8 servings.

BROCCOLI SUPREME SALAD

Margaret Withers

For broccoli lovers (ignoring former President Bush) this is a winner.

1   large bunch broccoli
2   green onions, white part only
½   teaspoon salt
½   teaspoon pepper
2   hard boiled eggs, diced
¾   cup mayonnaise

Remove the tough ends of lower stalks, and wash broccoli thoroughly; cut the flowerets and a few stems. Steam broccoli until crisp tender, about 5 to 10 minutes, then blanch in ice water. Slice onions into 1/8th-inch pieces and separate into tiny rings. Add salt, pepper, eggs and mayonnaise; toss very gently. May garnish with onion rings. Yield: 6 servings.

KIDNEY BEAN SALAD

Geneva Eubanks

This salad is so good and filling that it can serve as a whole meal with crackers and fruit.

1   (16-ounce) can kidney beans, drained
2   medium tomatoes, diced and drained
2   hard boiled eggs, diced
4   slices cooked crisp bacon, crumbled
2   ribs celery, diced
3   green onions and tops, diced
1   cup sharp Cheddar cheese, diced

Mix all ingredients together and toss lightly with dressing.

Dressing

⅓ cup mayonnaise
1 teaspoon ketchup
Juice of one orange, ⅓ cup

Juice of one lemon, 3 tablespoons
Dash of salt
1 tablespoon sugar

Mix well and chill. Yield: 6-8 servings as salad or 4 servings as main meal.

RED BEAN SALAD
Cynthia Smith

A Cajun delight!

1 cup cooked red beans, rinsed and drained
1 small sweet pickle, chopped fine
1 tablespoon onion, minced
2 teaspoons capers
¼ teaspoon prepared mustard

2 tablespoons salad dressing or mayonnaise
Salt and pepper to taste
1 egg, hard boiled and minced
Lemon wedges

Combine beans, pickle, onion, capers, mustard and salad dressing. Mix well. Season with salt and pepper. Chill. Serve on lettuce leaves, garnish with egg and lemon wedge. Yield: 2 servings.

COTTAGE CHEESE SURPRISE
Vanessa H. Luce

On one of our morning walks, my sister and I came up with this recipe. I experimented and came up with this delicious light and tasty salad. Makes a pretty Christmas salad.

1 (16-ounce) carton lite cottage cheese
2 medium cucumbers, peeled, cut in bite size pieces
½ green bell pepper, cut in ¼-inch pieces

½ red bell pepper, cut in ¼-inch pieces
1 (6-ounce) jar marinated artichokes, cut in bite size pieces, reserve juice
Pepper to taste

Pour cottage cheese in bowl, add cucumbers, peppers and artichokes. Pepper to taste. Add ½ jar of artichoke juice and mix. Save the rest of juice for salads later on. Yield: 6 servings.

REFRIGERATOR CUCUMBERS   *Aline Slack*

7 cups cucumbers, thinly sliced	1 tablespoon salt
1 cup onion, sliced	1 tablespoon celery seed
1 medium green pepper, chopped	2 cups sugar
	1 cup vinegar

Combine cucumbers, onion and green pepper. Mix remaining ingredients, pour over vegetables. Refrigerate at least 3 hours, stir several times. Yield: 12 servings.

LIMP SALAD   *Cynthia Smith*

A Smith family favorite. The Smith kids, when younger, would fight for the bit of liquid, if there was any, in the bottom of the bowl and eat it with a spoon. Hmmmnn tastes so good. This is also good the next day, a little more limp. My husband's grandmother's cook used to make this in Bremond, Texas.

Half a head of Iceberg lettuce torn into small pieces	Whop of mayonnaise (¼ cup)
1 large tomato, chopped	1 tablespoon dill pickle juice
2 hard boiled eggs, chopped	½ teaspoon celery salt
3 ribs celery, chopped fine	Garlic powder to taste
½ medium onion, grated or chopped fine	Pepper to taste

Toss lettuce with tomatoes, eggs, celery and onion. Thin mayonnaise with pickle juice, add celery salt, garlic powder, and pepper. Pour over vegetables and toss well. Refrigerate for at least 30 minutes. Stir again and serve. (Do not use salad dressing or fat free mayonnaise.) Yield: 6 servings.

SESAME SEED SALAD   *Aline Slack*

1 large head lettuce	1 cup Swiss cheese, grated
5 green onions and tops, thinly sliced	⅓ cup toasted sesame seeds
	Vinegar and oil dressing

Tear lettuce into bite-size pieces. Add onions, cheese, and sesame seeds and toss. Add dressing and toss again. Yield: 6 servings.

❦ ❦ ❦ ❦ ❦ ❦ ❦

FRESH VEGETABLE MARINATE

Mary A. Thurlkill

Excellent. A favorite of mine for years.

1	pound fresh broccoli	1	small onion, chopped
1	small head cauliflower	1½	cups vegetable oil
8	large fresh mushrooms, sliced	½	cup sugar
		½	cup vinegar
3	ribs celery, chopped	2	tablespoons poppy seeds
2	carrots, peeled and sliced	2	teaspoons dry mustard
1	small bell pepper, chopped	1	teaspoon salt

Trim off large leaves of broccoli. Remove tough ends of lower stalks and wash broccoli thoroughly. Cut into bite size pieces. Wash cauliflower thoroughly and separate into flowerets, slicing large flowerets into bite size pieces. Combine all vegetables in a large bowl. Combine remaining ingredients; stir well. Add to vegetables, tossing to coat. Cover and refrigerate at least three hours or overnight. Keeps well in refrigerator for several days. Yield: 10 servings.

BRENDA'S CHICKEN SALAD

Geneva Eubanks

This recipe was given to me by my daughter, Brenda Chambers, and it is delicious.

1	(6.8-ounce) box chicken flavor Rice-A-Roni	2	green onions with tops, chopped
2	(14-ounce) cans or jars artichoke hearts, diced, drained, and reserve juice	1	(2½-ounce) can black olives, diced
		½	bell pepper, chopped
4	chicken breasts, cooked and diced <u>or</u> 1 pound cooked, boned chicken	⅓	cup mayonnaise <u>or</u> salad dressing

Cook Rice-A-Roni according to package directions except use ¼ cup less water. Mix artichoke, chicken, onions, olives, and bell pepper in bowl. Add cooked rice. Mix the mayonnaise with the reserved artichoke liquid and stir into chicken mixture. Chill about 6 hours and serve on toasted English muffins or avocado halves. May be used as filling for stuffed tomatoes. Yield: 6-8 servings.

⬧ ⬧ ⬧ ⬧ ⬧ ⬧ ⬧

CHICKEN FRUIT SALAD

Opal Weirich

2	cups chicken, cooked and cut in bite size pieces	3	tablespoons mayonnaise
2	apples, diced	¾	teaspoon curry powder
1	cup pineapple chunks, drained	¼	cup pecans or almonds, chopped
		1	cup seedless grapes

Toss all ingredients together. Spoon portions onto salad greens. 220 calories per serving. Yield: 6 servings.

WALDORF LUNCHEON SALAD

Norma Honeycutt

A grand old favorite and low fat too!

3 or 4	apples, unpeeled	Salt to taste
1	cup cooked chicken or turkey, chopped	Lowfat mayonnaise
1½	cups celery, thinly sliced	Walnut or pecan halves
½	cup walnuts or pecans, chopped	

Cut thin slices of apple for garnish, allow three slices per serving. Cube remaining apples; mix with chicken, celery, and nuts. Salt to taste and mix with enough mayonnaise to moisten. Spoon mixture into lettuce cups, garnish with apple slices. Top with mayonnaise and nut halves. Yield: Serves 6.

HOT CHICKEN SALAD

Susan Thomas

2	cups chicken, cooked and diced	1	cup mayonnaise
2	cups celery, diced	½	pound American cheese, grated
½	cup toasted almond slices	1	(5-ounce) can Chow Mein noodles
2	teaspoons onion, grated		
2	tablespoons lemon juice		

Combine all ingredients except cheese and noodles. Put in buttered 1-quart casserole and heat at 350 degrees for 20 minutes. Sprinkle cheese on top. Heat 10 minutes or until cheese is melted. Serve on Chow Mein noodles. Yield: 6 servings.

SHRIMP SALAD
Leah Mauck

My mother originated this salad and we have all adjusted it to our own taste. I like more Tabasco sauce in mine.

2 cups cooked shrimp	*Sauce*
1 cup celery, chopped	2 cups ketchup
1 cup green onions, chopped	2 tablespoons lemon juice
1 cup stuffed green olives, sliced	2 tablespoons Worcestershire sauce
Garlic salt to taste, add at serving time	1 tablespoon Tabasco sauce

Mix first four ingredients in bowl. In another bowl mix sauce ingredients and pour over shrimp and stir. Cover with paper towel to absorb excess liquid, then over with plastic wrap. Refrigerate overnight. Add garlic salt to taste before serving. Yield: 4 servings.

LORETTA'S COLE SLAW DRESSING
Sallye Baker

1 cup cider vinegar	1 teaspoon whole mustard seed
1 cup sugar	1 teaspoon celery seed
¾ cup salad oil	1 tablespoon salt

Put all ingredients in blender and mix well. Pour over shredded cabbage, chopped onion and celery. Keeps well in the refrigerator or freezer. Yield: 1¾ cups.

LETTUCE WEDGE ITALIAN
Cynthia Smith

¾ cup sour cream	⅛ teaspoon salt
⅓ cup mayonnaise	1 (2½-ounce) jar B&B
½ to 1 (1.05-ounce) package Italian salad dressing mix	Brand mushrooms with liquid, chopped
1 teaspoon sugar	Lettuce wedges

Combine first 5 ingredients, add liquid from mushrooms. Mix well. Pour over lettuce wedges, topping with chopped mushrooms. Yield: 1½ cups dressing or 8 lettuce wedges.

POPPY SEED DRESSING
Adelia Felps

This is one of the best fruit salad dressings I have come across and have used it for years. It is also very good on green salads.

¾   cup sugar
1   cup vegetable oil
1   teaspoon dry mustard
1   teaspoon salt

⅓   cup vinegar
1½   tablespoons onion, finely chopped
2   tablespoons poppy seeds

Combine all ingredients in blender and mix. Lasts indefinitely in covered jar in refrigerator. Use on fruit salads or green salads. Yield: 2 cups.

AUNT MINNIE'S WATERCRESS DRESSING
Margie Sultemeier

In the spring and fall when watercress is plentiful, gather and clean using only the leaves not stems.

½   cup evaporated milk
2   tablespoons sugar
Pinch salt
1   tablespoon vinegar

1   egg, hard boiled, chopped and crumbled
Watercress

Mix first four ingredients well. Wash watercress, drain and blot dry. Pour dressing over watercress. Add crumbled egg, toss. Yield: ½ cup dressing.

SHRIMP SPICE MIX
Margie Sultemeier

Messy but good.

1   tablespoon cayenne pepper
1   tablespoon black pepper
1   tablespoon salt
2   tablespoons Italian seasoning

2   tablespoons lemon pepper
1 to 2 tablespoons garlic powder

Mix all the above ingredients together. Sprinkle desired amount over steamed or boiled shrimp with or without their shells. Chill for about one hour. Peel and eat. Don't rub your eyes until you wash your hands, burn you good. Yield: ½ cup mix or enough for several 2-3 pound batches of shrimp.

Some Serious Eating

Main Dishes: Beef, Pork, Poultry, Seafood, Game

Geneva Eubanks '93©

FIRST CHRISTIAN CHURCH OF JOHNSON CITY

This congregation was organized in 1903 by the Rev. Tom Smith, an evangelist with the Texas Christian Missionary Society, and twenty-six charter members. Land for a church building was given by Judge N. T. Stubbs and a sanctuary was completed in 1905–06. In its early years the congregation was served by traveling ministers. Lyndon B. Johnson joined the congregation in 1923, following his baptism in the PEDERNALES RIVER. Few structural changes were made over the years.

41

BRISKET OF BEEF

Dorothy C. Lackey

5 to 8 pound brisket	6 beef bouillon cubes
1½ teaspoons pepper	3 cups water
5 onions, sliced	1 cup beer
4 ribs celery, chopped	
2 (12-ounce) bottles chili sauce, divided	

Place brisket in roast pan, fat side up. Season with pepper. Place onions, celery, and 1 bottle of chili sauce on top. Dissolve bouillon cubes in water and add to pan. Cover with heavy duty foil and bake for 3½ hours at 325 degrees, basting at times. Pour beer and second bottle of chili sauce and bake ½ hour longer, covered. Slice thinly. Yield: Enough for a gang.

LOW-SLOW ROAST BEEF

Jeannette Stanton

This also turns out well served at a party, sliced thin, and placed in a biscuit.

1 tablespoon vinegar	1 teaspoon salt
¼ teaspoon allspice	1 tablespoon brown sugar
¼ teaspoon pepper	5 to 8 pound rolled or
½ teaspoon dry mustard	standing rib roast
1 teaspoon paprika	

Mix first seven ingredients together and spread over entire surface of the meat. Place uncovered in a 200 degree oven for 3½ hours. Turn oven down to 175 degrees and cook for 3 more hours. The roast will be a rare pink throughout. There is no shrinkage; all the juices are retained. Cook longer if you want a medium roast. Yield: 12 servings.

DEVILED STEAK

Sallye Baker

Beef arm steak, 1-inch thick	⅛ teaspoon paprika
¼ cup flour	1 teaspoon salt
2 tablespoons shortening	⅛ teaspoon pepper
1 large onion, sliced	3 tablespoons vinegar
1 teaspoon dry mustard	1 cup hot water

Dredge steak with flour and brown both sides in shortening. Place onion over meat. Add seasonings, vinegar, and water. Cover tightly and cook in a slow oven, 300 degrees for about 1 hour or until tender. Thicken the remaining liquid for gravy. Yield: 4-6 servings.

BEEF BIRDS IN RED GRAVY   *Cynthia Smith*

My mother-in-law used to serve these, only she called them veal birds. Forty years ago, veal was a cheaper cut of meat than beef. Some people do about the same, but add a dill pickle or Bleu cheese and call it roulades, making a brown gravy. Either way it is delicious.

1 pound or more round steak, tenderized	2 (8-ounce) cans tomato sauce
Meat tenderizer	Salt and pepper to taste
1 onion, cut in cubes	Water as needed
Bacon strips	1 tablespoon flour, optional
	½ cup water, optional

Trim fat from steak, sprinkle with tenderizer. Cut meat into strips about 4 or 5 inches long. Place a piece of cubed onion in each strip, roll up and then wrap a piece of bacon around the meat securing with a toothpick. Brown the 'birds' (I guess they call them 'birds' because they look like a dove breast) in a skillet sprayed with vegetable spray. It will make a lot of grease as the bacon cooks. When brown, pour off some of the grease and add the tomato sauce. Bring to a boil, reduce heat, cover and simmer for about 45 minutes, adding water as needed. If more gravy is needed, make a paste of flour and ½ cup water and add to red gravy. Serve over white or wild rice. Good enough for company. Yield: 4 servings.

CHICKEN FRIED STEAK   *Joan Winters*

A Texas cookbook could not be complete without a recipe for chicken fried steak.

2 pounds lean tenderized round steak	1 teaspoon pepper
1 cup flour	1 egg, beaten
2 teaspoons salt	1 cup milk
	1½ cups Canola <u>or</u> vegetable oil

Cut steak into serving-size pieces. Mix flour, salt and pepper, and place on plate or wax paper. Mix egg and milk in small flat bowl. Dredge meat in flour mixture, dip in egg mixture and into flour mixture again. Heat oil in a large skillet (cast-iron is the best) until very hot, but not smoking. Add steaks to hot oil and cook for about 5 minutes on each side or until golden brown. Drain on paper towels; serve warm with cream gravy. Buttermilk may be substituted for egg-milk mixture.

Cream Gravy

4 tablespoons pan drippings	1 teaspoon salt
3 tablespoons flour	¼ teaspoon pepper
2 cups milk	

Pour off drippings, leaving 4 tablespoons. Blend in flour, stirring constantly, until bubbly. Stir in milk while stirring. Add salt and pepper. Continue stirring until gravy thickens. If too thick add a little more milk. Yield: 8 servings.

LONGHORN LEAN RANCHERO

*The "Stonewall" Jacksons,
Velna, Don, Donna, and Donny*

This recipe was developed by Velna Jackson to use the beef her family raises at Stonewall Valley Ranch. It is served to the many guests who come to see the Longhorns. It was selected "Best of Beef" dish in 1988 by the Beef Industry Council in Austin, Texas.

2 pounds lean round steak	2 (8-ounce) cans tomato sauce
Flour	1 tablespoon chili powder
Salt, pepper, paprika	1 teaspoon cumin
2 tablespoons vegetable oil	1 cup water
1 cup onion, chopped	Cilantro, to taste, chopped
½ cup bell pepper, chopped	Garnish: Longhorn Cheddar
2 (14½-ounce) cans Mexican style stewed tomatoes	cheese, shredded

Cut round steak into strips or cubes. Roll meat in flour seasoned with salt, pepper, paprika. Brown meat in hot oil in heavy skillet. Add onion, pepper, stewed tomatoes, tomato sauce, chili powder, cumin, cilantro, and water. Cover tightly and simmer slowly for about 1 hour. To serve, arrange steak on hot serving platter. Cover with cheese to melt. Serve with rice, buttered noodles or mashed potatoes. Yield: 6 to 8 servings.

HINTS:

Sprinkle salt in frying pan to prevent fat from spattering.

After removing a roast from the oven, let it set 15 minutes for easier carving.

For a juicier burger, rub both sides with cold water before grilling.

SKILLET BEEF AND GREEN BEANS   *Sallye Baker*

½	pound lean, tender beef	1	tablespoon soy sauce
2	tablespoons oil	1	(3-ounce) can sliced mush-
1	onion, chopped		rooms, drained, reserve
2	cups fresh green beans	¾	cup liquid, juice from
1	cup celery, sliced		mushrooms plus water
1	tablespoon cornstarch		Garnish: pimientos

Cut beef in strips, brown in oil. Add onion, beans, and celery. Cook 4-6 minutes. Stir. Combine cornstarch and soy sauce with liquid. Add to skillet with mushrooms. Stir, cooking until liquid is shiny. Cover, cook until beans are tender. Garnish with pimiento. Serve with rice. Yield: 4 servings.

SHERRIED BEEF   *Dolores Fasel Bozeman*

This is great for large groups and easy to fix.

3 pounds beef, cut into small chunks	2 cans golden mushroom soup
1 or 2 (5-ounce) cans sliced water chestnuts, drained	1 envelope dry onion soup mix
1 or 2 (3-ounce) cans mushrooms	1 cup cooking sherry

Put all ingredients into a crock-pot and mix it all together. Cook for 6 or more hours or until meat is tender. May be cooked in a Dutch oven with lid at 300-325 degrees for 3 to 4 hours or until tender. Serve over rice. Freezes well. Yield: 12-15 servings.

ALL DAY STEW   *Bernice K. Weinheimer*

Wine makes it better. A healthy, hearty stew.

1 can tomato soup, undiluted	4 medium potatoes, cut in 1½-inch chunks
1 cup water <u>or</u> red wine	½ cup celery, cut in 1-inch slices
¼ cup flour	12 whole large fresh mushrooms
2 pounds beef chuck, fat trimmed, cut in 1-inch to 2-inch cubes	2 beef bouillon cubes
3 medium carrots, cut in 1-inch slices	1 tablespoon Italian herb seasoning mix
6 white boiling onions or yellow onions, quartered	1 bay leaf
	3 grinds fresh pepper

Mix together soup, water/wine and flour until smooth; combine with remaining ingredients in covered roasting pan. Bake at 275 degrees for 4-5 hours. Yield: 8 servings.

HONEYCUTT GOULASH   *Norma Honeycutt*

This recipe was passed on to me as a new bride by my mother-in-law. It was easy, inexpensive and a husband pleaser and after thirty-eight years it still is!

1	pound ground beef	2	tablespoons chili powder
1	large sweet green pepper, chopped	1	(8-ounce) can tomato sauce
¾	cup onion, chopped	5	ounces elbow or shell pasta
			Salt and pepper to taste

Brown ground beef in heavy skillet. Add green pepper, onion and chili powder and enough water to sauté vegetables about 5 minutes. Add tomato sauce and mix well. Turn heat to low, cover and simmer about 20 minutes. Cook pasta and add to meat mixture; stir to mix. Continue to cook on low about 30 minutes, stir occasionally. Serve with a salad and hot bread. Yield: 4 servings.

STUFFED MEAT PATTIES   *Holly Lawson*

This is great served with English peas and a salad.

2¼	pounds ground meat	5 slices American cheese
10	teaspoons onion, chopped	Salt and pepper to taste
10	teaspoons bell pepper, chopped	Garlic powder to taste
5	teaspoons picante sauce <u>or</u> jalapeño peppers, chopped, optional	Seasoning salt to taste

Divide hamburger into 10 equal portions. Put plastic wrap or foil on counter. Take 1 portion at a time and flatten as a hamburger patty on plastic wrap. Repeat with second patty. On one patty sprinkle 2 teaspoons onion, 2 teaspoons bell pepper, 1 teaspoon Picante sauce and 1 slice cheese. Place second patty on top and press edges together to seal well (cheese will ooze out if patties are not sealed well). Place on large pan. Sprinkle with seasonings to taste. Repeat to make 4 more patties. Preheat oven at 350 degrees. Bake for 25 to 30 minutes for well done patties. Yield: 5 servings.

HUNGARIAN STUFFED PEPPERS
Thelma Elm

1	small onion, diced	6	medium green peppers
1	tablespoon butter or margarine	¼	cup butter or margarine
		2	tablespoons flour
4	tablespoons regular rice	2	teaspoons sugar
1½	cups water, divided	1½	cups tomato puree
1	pound ground beef	2	tomatoes, peeled and quartered
1	teaspoon salt, divided		
¼	teaspoon pepper, divided		

Sauté onion in the butter until soft in a large skillet. Add rice; cook over low heat, stirring constantly 1 minute. Stir in ½ cup water; cook until rice is almost tender, about 10 minutes. Remove skillet from heat; add ground beef, ½ teaspoon salt and ⅛ teaspoon pepper, mixing thoroughly. Wash peppers; cut off tops; scoop out seeds and heavy ribs. Stuff loosely with rice-meat mixture. Melt ¼ cup butter in a small heavy kettle or Dutch oven. Stir in flour, sugar, remaining ½ teaspoon salt and ⅛ teaspoon pepper. Slowly stir in tomato puree, remaining 1 cup water and tomatoes. Simmer over low heat, stirring constantly until sauce is smooth. Stand filled peppers upright in sauce, cover. Simmer on low heat until peppers are tender, about 1 hour. Serve with crusty French bread. May be made ahead and reheated. Freezes. Yield: 6 servings.

SICILIAN MEATLOAF
Dawn Liesmann

2	eggs, beaten	¼	teaspoon pepper
¾	cup soft bread crumbs	1	clove garlic, minced
½	cup tomato juice	2	pounds lean ground beef
2	tablespoons dried parsley	8	thin slices of ham
½	teaspoon dried oregano	1½	cups Mozzarella cheese, shredded
¼	teaspoon salt		

Preheat oven to 350 degrees. Combine first 8 ingredients. Stir in ground beef and mix well. On foil or wax paper, flatten beef mixture to about 10 x 12-inch rectangle. Lay ham down center of patty. Spread cheese over ham. Roll edge of patty toward center, overlapping slightly. Pat all edges firmly to seal in cheese. Invert into 13 x 9 x 2-inch pyrex dish. Pat to make sure there are no holes. Bake for 1 hour and let stand 15 minutes before cutting. Leftovers makes good sandwiches. Yield: 8-10 servings.

MEATLOAF CUPS
Gail Rucker

This was one of my prize-winning recipes when I was in 4-H. I still make my meatloaf in muffin cups because it cooks faster than a large loaf.

⅔ cup undiluted evaporated milk
1½ pounds ground beef
⅔ cup fine dry bread crumbs
¼ cup onion, chopped
¼ cup green pepper, chopped
2 tablespoons prepared mustard
1 teaspoon salt
¼ teaspoon pepper

Combine above ingredients in a bowl. Mix. Fill muffin cups ¾ full. Bake 12-15 minutes at 375 degrees. For small loaves bake for 20 minutes. Yield: 6 servings.

BARBECUED MEATBALLS
Norma Honeycutt &
Jewell Sultemeier

You will appreciate this recipe if you are a busy person. Meatballs can be made ahead and frozen. Thaw and add sauce. Store bought sauce can also be used. A few can be taken out for smaller meals or to add to spaghetti.

3 pounds ground beef
1 (12-ounce) can evaporated milk
1 cup oatmeal
1 cup cracker crumbs
2 eggs
½ cup onion, chopped
½ teaspoon garlic powder
2 teaspoons salt
½ teaspoon pepper
2 teaspoons chili powder
Sauce
2 cups ketchup
1 cup brown sugar
½ teaspoon liquid smoke or to taste
½ teaspoon garlic powder
¼ cup onion, chopped

To make meatballs, combine all ingredients (mixture will be soft) and shape into walnut-size balls. Place meatballs in a single layer on wax paper-lined cookie sheets; freeze until solid. Store frozen meatballs in freezer bags until ready to cook. To make sauce, combine all ingredients and stir until sugar is dissolved. Place frozen meatballs in a 13 x 9 x 2-inch baking pan; pour on the sauce. Bake at 350 degrees for 1 hour. Yield: 80 meatballs and 2½ cups sauce.

MEATBALLS WITH BROWN GRAVY

Cynthia Smith

Use a black cast iron Dutch oven or skillet to cook this. It never sticks unless your husband tries to help out as mine did once and cleaned mine. My husband decided my favorite black cast iron skillet needed cleaning. He spent hours meticulously chipping away at the 'crust' on the outside of the skillet. He couldn't understand why I was not happy with what he had done. Everything I cooked in that skillet for months, stuck. It took ages to build up that 'protective crust' again.

1 pound ground meat	¾ cup cracker crumbs
Salt and pepper to taste	1 heaping tablespoon flour
1 egg	1 tablespoon oil
½ cup milk	1 to 2 tablespoons flour
1 large onion, chop half and cut other half in rings	1 cup water
10 ounces fresh mushrooms, sliced, optional	1 teaspoon Kitchen Bouquet, optional

Mix meat with salt and pepper; beat egg with milk and add to meat mixture with chopped onion, mushrooms if desired and cracker crumbs. Shape into balls, flour, then flatten to about 1½-inch patties. Brown in oil. Remove browned meatballs to plate and pour out all but 1-2 tablespoons of drippings. Add flour to drippings, (use 1 tablespoon flour for each tablespoon of drippings), stirring counter clockwise until the flour is very brown but not burned. Add water and stir again, counter clockwise (to prevent steam from burning you as you stir). Put meatballs back into the skillet, add onion rings, and simmer covered for about 30 minutes. If gravy is too light, add a teaspoon of Kitchen Bouquet (I call it the cook's helper or cheater). Yield: 4 servings.

PORCUPINES

Bobbie Hale

I acquired this recipe when I lived in San Francisco in 1960. People usually balk at the name, but after one taste, they always come back for more. You may have to assure them you have not been out hunting porcupines in order to make it.

1 pound ground meat	½ teaspoon salt
1 medium onion, chopped	½ teaspoon garlic powder
½ cup long-grain rice	2¼ cups milk
¼ teaspoon black pepper	1 can cream of mushroom soup

Preheat oven to 400 degrees. In large mixing bowl, mix thoroughly ground beef, onion, rice, pepper, salt, garlic powder, and milk. Mixture will be soupy. Spoon into 7½ x 12-inch baking dish in the shape of balls. Spoon undiluted soup evenly over top. Bake for 1 hour, or until meat is done in the center. Good served with mashed potatoes. Yield: 4-6 servings.

BEAN BURGER STEW

Leah Mauck

We fix this when we go camping as it is easy to fix on an open fire.

1 pound ground beef	2 cups water
1 large onion, chopped	1 cup elbow macaroni
Salt and pepper to taste	1 cup water
1 tablespoon chili powder	1 (16-ounce) can pork and
1 (16-ounce) can tomatoes	beans

Brown meat, onion, and seasonings in large Dutch oven. Add tomatoes with juice and 2 cups of water. Cover and simmer for 30 minutes. Add macaroni and water. Cook 8-10 minutes or until macaroni is cooked. Add pork and beans and heat thoroughly. Yield: 4-6 servings.

MASS CASSEROLE

Margaret Dannecker

Called "Mass Casserole" because it was often served at church suppers following Mass at our Episcopal church and also because it served a "mass" of people! For smaller gatherings or family supper, freeze half for later.

2 pounds lean ground beef	1 pound sharp Cheddar <u>or</u>
1 onion, chopped	Mozzarella cheese, grated
1 clove garlic, minced	1 (8-ounce) package shell
1 (6-ounce) can tomato paste	macaroni
2 cans cream of mushroom	
soup	

Brown meat, onion, and garlic. Add tomato paste, mushroom soup and cheese. Cook and drain macaroni and add to other ingredients. Place in large casserole or 13 x 9 x 2-inch pan. Bake at 350 degrees for 15 to 20 minutes. Yield: 10-12 servings.

HOT GREEN PEPPER MEAT CASSEROLE   *Elnora Kneese*

This is a rich dish. Everyone enjoys it.

12 ounces spaghetti	1 teaspoon basil
1 pound ground beef	Salt and pepper to taste
½ onion, chopped	1 can cream of mushroom
2 tablespoons of oil <u>or</u> butter	soup
1 (8-ounce) can tomato sauce	1½ cups Velveeta cheese,
1 jalapeño pepper, chopped	grated
1 garlic clove, crushed	

Cook spaghetti according to package directions. Drain and set aside. Brown meat and onion in oil or butter until rather dry or drain off excess grease. Add the tomato sauce, pepper, garlic, basil, salt, pepper and soup. Mix well. Layer spaghetti, then meat mixture, then spaghetti, then meat again in a 12 x 8 x 2-inch casserole dish. Sprinkle cheese on top. Bake about 30 minutes at 350 degrees. Yield: 6 to 8 servings.

ROMAN HOLIDAY   *Mariallen Moursund*

1½ pounds ground beef	1 (17-ounce) can whole
1 pound pure pork sausage	kernel corn, drained
2 medium onions, chopped	1 (5¾-ounce) jar stuffed
1 clove garlic, chopped fine	green olives, chopped
1 tablespoon shortening	1 pound Cheddar cheese,
Salt and pepper to taste	grated and divided
1 (8-ounce) can tomato sauce	1 (4-ounce) can mushrooms,
2 cans tomato soup	drained and chopped
1 (7-ounce) box spaghetti	

Mix ground beef and sausage well or have butcher grind them together twice. Set aside. Sauté onions and garlic in shortening. Add meat mixture and brown slowly over low heat. Add salt and pepper generously. Simmer for 30 minutes. Add tomato sauce and soup and simmer for 1 hour. Cook spaghetti as directed on package; blanch when done with cold water. Add spaghetti, corn, olives, ½ cheese, and mushrooms. Mix well. Place in 13 x 9 x 2-inch baking dish. Bake 30 minutes at 325 degrees, sprinkle rest of cheese on top and cook another 30 minutes. Freezes well. May use more spaghetti if desired. Yield: 12 servings.

AUNT DORA'S SPAGHETTI
Janey Wiemers

Our neighbors in Alaska had a sister who never married. She didn't cook much but dearly loved to visit and be with the four nieces. This was the only dish she cooked which the girls loved. When I got the recipe it became a favorite for our family.

10-ounce package of spaghetti	1	soup can cold water	
1½	pounds ground beef <u>or</u> ground turkey	1	tablespoon onion, minced
2	teaspoons margarine	1	cup Cheddar cheese, grated
1	can tomato soup	Dash of salt, pepper and garlic powder	
1	can mushroom soup		

Cook spaghetti according to directions on the package. Break up spaghetti into smaller pieces as it is put into boiling water. Brown meat in the margarine. Mix the browned meat, spaghetti, soups, water, onion, and seasonings in a 13 x 9 x 2-inch casserole. Top with grated cheese. Bake at 350 degrees for 30 minutes. Yield: 8-10 servings.

SNOWIE TEETERS' ITALIAN SPAGHETTI
Ola Matus

2	pounds ground beef	1	(16-ounce) can Mexican style beans
1	medium onion, chopped		
1	can tomato soup	12	ounces spaghetti
1	can mushroom soup	1	cup Cheddar cheese, grated

Brown meat and onion in skillet. Set aside. Mix soups and beans together. Cook spaghetti as directed on package. In a large pyrex dish put a layer of spaghetti, a layer of meat and onion and a layer of soup mixture. Top with cheese and bake until hot and cheese is melted, about 30 minutes at 350 degrees. Yield: 6 servings.

HINTS:

Meat with no bone and little fat, allow ¼ to ⅓ pound per serving.

When choosing meat for grilling allow 4 ounces raw meat or 3 ounces cooked meat per serving.

A substitute for wine in cooking is half grapefruit juice and half grape juice.

HUSBAND'S DELIGHT CASSEROLE *Geneva Eubanks*

My sister-in-law, Dolly Bingham, received this recipe about fifteen years ago in one of those "Recipe Chain Letters." It came from a lady in Alabama.

1	(8-ounce) package cream cheese, softened	1	teaspoon sugar
2	cups sour cream	1	teaspoon salt
3	green onions, chopped		Dash of pepper
1½	pounds ground chuck		Dash of Worcestershire sauce
2	tablespoons margarine	2	(5-ounce) packages noodles
2	(8-ounce) cans tomato sauce	½	cup Cheddar cheese, shredded

In a bowl, mix cream cheese, sour cream, and onions. Brown the meat in margarine; add tomato sauce, sugar, salt, pepper, and Worcestershire sauce. Cook noodles according to package directions. In a 2-quart casserole put alternate layers of noodles, beef mixture and sour cream mixture, making last addition meat. Top with the cheese and bake at 350 degrees until brown, about 30 minutes. Yield: 8 servings.

CHOW MEIN CASSEROLE *Lucia Carbary*

1½	pounds ground beef	1	(16-ounce) can whole kernel corn, undrained
½	cup onion, chopped		
½	cup green pepper, chopped	1	(5-ounce) can Chow Mein noodles, soften with
1	egg, slightly beaten		enough boiling water
1	can Cheddar cheese soup		to cover
1	can tomato soup		

Brown meat, onion, and green pepper. Add egg, soups, corn, and noodles. Bake in 13 x 9 x 2 inch pan at 350 degrees for 45 to 60 minutes. If desired, leave out noodles and serve meat over dry noodles. Yield: 6-8 servings.

HINTS:

Marinate meat by placing marinade and meat in a plastic bag with zip top or twist tie. Set bag of meat in a plastic container. The marinade stays close to the meat and the container stays clean, but prevents disaster if the plastic bag tears.

To thicken roast gravy, add a grated Irish potato about thirty minutes before roast is done. — *Helen Mayfield*

WEST TEXAS STEW
Geneva Eubanks

This recipe came to me from a co-worker in Midland, Texas. It is good on a winter night with cornbread, butter and honey.

1½	pounds lean ground beef	1	(15-ounce) can Ranch
1	medium onion, chopped		Style beans
½	teaspoon salt	1	(12-ounce) can whole
Pepper to taste			kernel corn
4	medium potatoes, cubed	1	can tomato soup
2	cups water	1	(4-ounce) can mild green
1	(16-ounce) can stewed		chilies, chopped
	tomatoes		

Combine meat, onion, salt and pepper in large dutch oven. Cook on medium heat until meat is brown, stirring to crumble. Drain. Add potatoes and water. Cover and cook until potatoes are tender. Add all other ingredients and simmer 1 hour, stirring occasionally. Freezes. Yield: 6-8 servings.

BLACK-EYED PEA CORNBREAD
Daisy Cox

1	pound ground beef	¼	cup cooking oil
1	cup canned black-eyed	2	eggs, slightly beaten
	peas, drained	1	teaspoon salt
1	cup onion, chopped	½	teaspoon soda
¾	cup cream style corn	2	jalapeño peppers, chopped
1	cup cornmeal	1	cup Cheddar cheese,
½	cup flour		grated
1	cup buttermilk		

Brown meat and drain well. Break into small pieces. Add other ingredients in order given above. Mix well. Place in a 13 x 9 x 2-inch pan that has been well greased. Cook at 350 degrees for 45 minutes, or until done. Yield: 10 servings.

☆ ☆ ☆ ☆ ☆

HINT:

To retrieve a whole garlic pod that has been used to season stews; spear it first with a toothpick before putting it in the pot.

☆ ☆ ☆ ☆ ☆

CABBAGE ROLLS

Dorothy C. Lackey

½ yeast cake or package
2 tablespoons lukewarm water
½ cup milk
2 tablespoons butter
1 tablespoon sugar
½ teaspoon salt
1 egg, well beaten

3½ to 4 cups flour
1 pound ground beef
1 onion, chopped
½ teaspoon salt
½ teaspoon pepper
1 teaspoon caraway seeds
1 medium head cabbage, chopped

Dissolve yeast in warm water. Scald milk and add butter, sugar and salt. Let cool to lukewarm and add yeast mixture. Add egg. Add 2 cups flour and beat well. Add rest of flour to make a stiff dough. Let rise until double in bulk. Brown meat with onion, salt, pepper, and caraway seeds. Simmer. Drain off grease and add cabbage. Cook until cabbage is done. Cool. Roll dough to ⅛-inch thickness, cut 8 square pieces. Fill squares with mixture. Bring corners together. Lift with pancake turner to greased 13 x 9 x 2-inch cake pan. Let rise 1 hour. Bake at 350 degrees for about 20 minutes or until brown. Dot with butter and serve. Yield: 8 servings.

DEEP-DISH BEEF SQUARES

Thelma Elm

½ pound ground beef
½ cup dairy sour cream
⅓ cup mayonnaise _or_ salad dressing
½ cup sharp Cheddar cheese, shredded
1 tablespoon chopped onion

1 cup buttermilk baking mix
¼ cup cold water
1 to 2 medium tomatoes, thinly sliced
½ cup green pepper, chopped
Paprika

Heat oven to 375 degrees. Grease square baking dish, 8 x 8 x 2-inch. Cook and stir ground beef until brown; drain. Mix sour cream, mayonnaise, cheese and onion; set aside. Mix baking mix and water until soft dough forms. Pat in pan pressing dough ½ inch up sides. Layer beef, tomatoes and green pepper in pan; spoon sour cream mixture over top. Sprinkle with paprika. Bake until edges of dough are light brown, about 25-30 minutes. Yield: 5-6 servings.

SOUTH-OF-THE-BORDER LIVER   *Joycelyn Carter*

2 tablespoons flour	1 cup whole-kernel corn
1 tablespoon chili powder	1 cup canned tomatoes,
1 pound beef liver, cut into	chopped
2-inch pieces	¾ teaspoon salt
1 tablespoon vegetable oil	Dash pepper
½ cup onion, chopped	

Combine flour and chili powder; dredge liver strips in mixture to coat, being sure to use all mixture. In nonstick skillet heat oil over high heat; add onion and sauté until translucent, about 3 minutes. Reduce heat to medium, add liver, and cook, turning once, until lightly browned on all sides; stir in corn, tomatoes, salt and pepper. Reduce heat to low, cover, and simmer for 10 minutes. Yield: 3-4 servings.

SAUERKRAUT-CANADIAN BACON PIZZA   *Mary Earney*

There is a pizza and ice cream parlor in Iowa where the specialty is this pizza. We moved to Texas and really missed it so we began experimenting in an effort to recreate a HAPPY JOE'S SPECIAL PIZZA. This recipe comes close. It may sound awful, but it is delicious.

1 (6.5-ounce) package pizza	⅛ teaspoon each oregano,
crust mix	garlic powder and Parmesan
½ cup warm water	cheese
1 (16-ounce) can mild	½ to ¾ (14-ounce) jar pizza
sauerkraut	sauce, pepperoni flavor
· 8 to 12 ounces Mozzarella	Parmesan cheese, optional
cheese, shredded	
1 (5-ounce) package sliced	
Canadian bacon, cut into ¼ths	

Preheat oven to 375 degrees. Mix crust mix and water following package directions and set aside to rise. Soak kraut in water and rinse several times with cold water until kraut smell is gone or greatly reduced. Drain well and place in large bowl. Add Mozzarella cheese and bacon to kraut. Mix well and set aside. Pat out crust into greased 12-inch pizza pan, going up on sides of pan. Sprinkle crust lightly with oregano, garlic powder and Parmesan cheese. Bake crust for 5-6 minutes until partially baked. Remove from oven and spoon sauce onto crust until nicely covered. Add kraut mixture on top of sauce. The pizza will be thick. Return to oven for 10-15

56

minutes until crust is done and cheese is melted. Remove from oven; sprinkle with Parmesan cheese if desired and slice into 8 slices. Yield: 2-8 servings. **Note:** Don't let your family in the kitchen while preparing this pizza, because they may think all the stringy stuff is Mozzarella cheese. Mine did when they first ate it.

CABBAGE GOULASH
Jane Mills

1	pound pork sausage, hot if desired	1	(6-ounce) can tomato paste
1	pound ground chuck	2	tablespoons vinegar
1	large onion, chopped	1	tablespoon chili powder
1	(28-ounce) can tomatoes, chopped and drained	1	teaspoon garlic powder
		10	cups shredded cabbage, (1 large head)

In large pot, brown meats and onion; drain off fat. Add all ingredients except cabbage. Mix well, cooking at low heat 5 minutes. Add all of cabbage, stirring well. Simmer 15-20 minutes. Since my husband likes cabbage with a little crunch, I simmer it for 15 minutes. May be halved. Yield: 10-12 servings.

SAUSAGE JAMBALAYA
Cynthia Smith

Lip smacking good, I didn't say good for you, it is not fat free, I said it was goooood.

1	ring beef/pork smoked sausage	1	cup raw rice
¼	cup green onions, chopped	2	cups water
1	clove garlic, chopped		Salt and pepper to taste

Cut sausage into ¼-inch pieces. Cook in iron skillet slowly to brown well, add onions and garlic. Remove sausage from drippings; set aside. Add rice to skillet with meat drippings and stir until rice is dirty looking and brown. Do not burn. Add sausage mixture, water, salt and pepper and cook on low heat covered for about 20 minutes. Yield: 6 servings.

HINT:

Substitute spicy sausage when recipe calls for ground beef for a different taste.

SAUERKRAUT AND SAUSAGE　　　　　*Aline Slack*

1　pound link sausage	1　(16-ounce) can tomatoes,
1　clove garlic, minced	drained
½　cup onion, chopped	2　(16-ounce) cans sauerkraut,
½　bell pepper, chopped	drained
1　tablespoon vegetable oil	

Cut sausage in 2 inch pieces, boil and drain. Sauté garlic, onion and pepper in oil until tender. Add tomatoes, sausage and sauerkraut. Simmer covered for 15 to 20 minutes. Good with mashed potatoes. Yield: 4 to 6 servings.

SAUSAGE AND SPINACH LOAF　　　　　*Daisy Cox*

Even if you do not care for spinach, you will like this.

1　pound bulk sausage	1　(10-ounce) package frozen
¼　teaspoon salt	spinach, thawed and well
¼　teaspoon dried oregano	drained
½　teaspoon dried basil	2　cups Monterey Jack cheese,
1　pound loaf frozen bread	shredded
dough, thawed	

In a skillet brown sausage. Drain; sprinkle with salt, oregano and basil. Roll out bread dough to a 13 x 10-inch rectangle. Sprinkle meat on top of dough; place spinach on top of meat; top with cheese. Roll up from one of the long sides; seal seam and ends. Carefully place loaf on greased baking sheet. Bake at 350 degrees for 25-30 minutes or until crust is golden brown. Serve warm. Yield: 8 servings.

SAUSAGE STUFFED SWEET POTATO　　*Moline Lorenz*

A man in Temple, Texas, told me how to do this. I will always appreciate this recipe. I love to serve it with sauerkraut, pinto beans, and cornbread.

Sweet potatoes, large	**Pan sausage, mild or hot**

Wash potatoes. Slice one end off and core a hole according to size of potato as deep as you can without opening the other end. Make hole about the size of quarter or fifty-cent piece. Stuff the hole with raw sausage. Wrap potato in foil and bake in 350 degree until done, about 1 hour. When done, remove foil and cut potato in slices. It makes a very pretty plate. Yield: 1 potato will serve 2.

STUFFED PEPPERS

Susan Thomas

4 bell peppers
1 (16-ounce) can whole
  tomatoes
4 to 5 cups cornbread crumbs
  or 3 cups cornbread crumbs
  and 2 cups bread crumbs

½ cup onion, chopped
2 (3-ounce) or 1 (5½-ounce)
  can potted meat
1 egg
Salt and pepper to taste

Cut peppers in half, seed, and parboil 5-8 minutes. Pour tomatoes over crumbs. Stir to mix well; add onion, potted meat, egg, and seasonings. Mix well; fill pepper halves. Place in baking dish. Pour small amount of water in bottom of dish to prevent browning on bottom. Bake uncovered at 325 degrees until lightly browned. Yield: 6-8 servings.

MOM'S MACARONI DELIGHT

Thelma Elm

My mother was an excellent cook and she wrote some of her recipes in a theme book. This was her best macaroni dish and it was my favorite.

2 cups raw macaroni
¼ cup margarine
½ cup celery, chopped
½ cup ripe olives, chopped
2 tablespoons chili sauce
1 tablespoon water
1 teaspoon seasoned salt
¼ teaspoon Worcestershire
  sauce

1 cup smoked cheese, grated
1½ cups American cheese,
  grated
¼ cup cream
1 cup bread crumbs
2 tablespoons margarine,
  melted

Cook macaroni as directed on box. Melt margarine in saucepan; add celery, olives, chili sauce and water and simmer until tender. Add seasoned salt and Worcestershire sauce. Mix cooked macaroni, cheeses, and cooked seasonings together. Pour into a greased 8 x 8 x 2-inch pyrex dish. Pour cream over the top. Mix bread crumbs with melted margarine and cover top. Bake for 30 minutes at 350 degrees. Freezes well. Yield: 8 servings.

★ ★ ★ ★ ★

HINT:

Keep bacon drippings in a covered container in the refrigerator; use for browning meats, seasoning vegetables or making gravy.

VEGETARIAN SPAGHETTI SAUCE   *Margaret Dannecker*

When my younger daughter, Erin, became a vegetarian, it put her in grave danger of starvation at our house. So I adapted the family spaghetti and meatball sauce to create a version for her that also turned out to be a great diet pasta dish or lighter spaghetti sauce for those of us who like spaghetti even in the summer.

4 cups tomato juice	Pinch crushed red pepper
2 (6-ounce) cans tomato paste	½ green pepper, whole
1 (3-ounce) can mushrooms	1 teaspoon sugar
1 clove garlic, whole	1 teaspoon salt
1 small bay leaf	1 beef bouillon cube
Pinch rosemary	(unless you are a purist)
Pinch sweet basil	

Combine all ingredients in large saucepan and simmer over low heat for at least 2 hours. Remove garlic, green pepper and bay leaf when sauce is done. Serve over vermicelli or angel hair cooked pasta. Yield: 6-8 servings.

CHICKEN STUFFED WITH GRAPES   *Debbie Wiemers Hemphill*

1 (6-ounce) package Uncle Ben's Wild Rice mix	1 3-3½ pound broiler-fryer chicken
3 tablespoons margarine, melted	Salt
½ teaspoon crushed thyme	2 tablespoons soy sauce
⅛ teaspoon onion powder	2 tablespoons white wine
1½ cups green seedless grapes, halved	Additional grapes for garnish

Cook rice according to package. Add margarine, thyme, onion powder and halved grapes to rice and stir. Season cavity of chicken with salt. Place chicken, breast side up, on a rack of a shallow roasting pan. Stuff lightly with half of the rice mixture. Truss chicken and bake at 375 degrees for 1½ hours. Combine soy sauce and wine; use to baste the chicken during the last 30 minutes of baking. Put remaining rice mixture in a lightly greased 1-quart casserole and bake for 15 to 20 minutes at 375 degrees. Remove chicken to serving platter and spoon rice mixture around it. Garnish with additional grapes. Yield: 4-6 servings.

CHICKEN CONTINENTAL

Susan Thomas

3 to 4 pound frying chicken, cut up
⅓ cup flour
Salt and pepper
¼ cup oil
2 cans cream of chicken soup
2½ tablespoons grated onion
1 teaspoon salt

Dash pepper
1 tablespoon parsley flakes
⅛ teaspoon thyme
½ teaspoon celery flakes
2 cups water
2 cups Minute Rice
½ teaspoon paprika

Roll chicken in flour that has been seasoned with salt and pepper. Brown in oil on all sides. Set aside. Combine soup, onion and seasonings in saucepan; gradually add water, blend. Bring to a boil over medium heat, stirring constantly. Place rice in a shallow 2-quart casserole. Reserve 1 cup of soup mixture; pour remaining over rice. Stir just to moisten rice. Top rice with chicken pieces and pour remaining mixture over all. Cover with aluminum foil and bake at 375 degrees for 20-30 minutes. Sprinkle with paprika. Yield: 6 servings.

BAKED PARMESAN CHICKEN

Jody McCuiston

1 cup cracker crumbs
⅓ cup grated Parmesan cheese
¼ teaspoon ground oregano
¼ teaspoon pepper
Salt to taste

1 clove garlic, minced
¾ cup butter or margarine,
    melted, divided
1 fryer chicken, cut up

Combine cracker crumbs, cheese, oregano, pepper and salt; set aside. Lightly sauté garlic in 2 tablespoons butter; stir in remaining butter. Dip chicken in garlic butter; roll each piece in cracker crumb mixture. Place chicken in a 13 x 9 x 2-inch pan; sprinkle with remaining cracker crumb mixture, pour on remaining butter. Bake at 350 degrees for 55 minutes or until golden brown. Yield: 6 servings.

CHICKEN AND SQUASH

Susan Thomas

1 whole fryer, cut up
4 to 5 calabasa or any type of
    squash
1 onion, sliced
1 (16-ounce) can tomatoes, cut up

1 teaspoon cumin seed
1 teaspoon salt
1 teaspoon sugar
Pepper to taste

Brown chicken pieces in small amount of oil. When browned, add the rest

61

of the ingredients. Bring to a boil, reduce heat to simmer. Cover and simmer for 1 hour or until chicken is tender. Yield: 4-6 servings.

CHICKEN NOODLE CASSEROLE
Sallye Baker

This is good to serve a crowd.

5 pound hen, cut up
3 cups celery, chopped
2 cups onion, chopped
¾ cup parsley, chopped or
  ¼ cup dehydrated parsley
1 can tomato soup
1 (2.5-ounce) can mushrooms, sliced

1 (6-ounce) can giant olives, chopped or sliced
1 (2-ounce) jar pimiento, chopped
½ (5-ounce) bottle Worcestershire sauce
1 pound package noodles

Boil chicken until tender; season well, bone and cut into pieces. Into 2½ cups of the stock, boil celery, onion and parsley until tender. Drain and add to chicken. Then add soup, mushrooms, olives, pimiento and Worcestershire sauce. Place in refrigerator overnight to blend flavors. Next day, boil noodles and add to heated chicken. If too dry, use some of the remaining chicken stock. Yield: 15-20 servings.

CHICKEN-BEAN CASSEROLE
Joycelyn Carter

1 (16-ounce) can whole green beans, drained
3 cups cooked chicken, diced
½ cup water chestnuts, sliced
½ cup salad dressing
1 can cream of chicken soup

¼ cup onion, minced
¼ teaspoon curry
Red pepper and salt to taste
1 (2.8-ounce) can French fried onions, crushed

Place beans on bottom of a 8-inch square or 10 x 8 x 2 casserole. Place chicken on top of beans. Mix chestnuts, salad dressing, soup, onion, curry, red pepper and salt and spread mixture over chicken. Bake at 375 degrees until bubbly hot, about 20-30 minutes. Add crushed canned onions on top and bake 3-4 minutes more. Yield: 6-8 servings.

HINTS:

Substitute ground chicken or turkey for ground beef.

Use dental floss to tie a turkey or chicken, it will not tear the bird.

CHICKEN VEGETABLE BAKE

Angelia Stearns

1 large fryer, cut up	1 (8-ounce) jar cocktail onions
Flour	1 (3-ounce) can mushrooms,
1 tablespoon paprika	drained
1 tablespoon salt	3 to 4 tablespoons fat <u>or</u> oil
Salad oil	1 cup orange juice
2 cups carrots, sliced or	1 tablespoon brown sugar
chopped	¼ teaspoon ginger

Roll chicken in mixture of flour, paprika and salt. Brown chicken in salad oil. Spray a 13 x 9 x 2-inch pan with cooking spray. Line pan with carrots; add chicken, onions and mushrooms. Make gravy. Combine fat or oil, orange juice, sugar and ginger in skillet. When gravy thickens, pour over chicken. Cover with foil and bake 1½ hours at 350 degrees. Yield: 6 to 8 servings.

CHICKEN IN FOIL

Susan Thomas

Great for camping trips.

Favorite chicken pieces	¾ cup chopped onion, divided
Flour	1 can cream of mushroom
Hot oil	soup
1 potato per person,	1 soup can milk
peeled and diced	Salt and pepper to taste

Cut sheets of aluminum foil for each serving, about 15-inches long. Dust chicken with flour and brown in hot oil. Place individual chicken pieces on foil sheets. Top with potato and sprinkle with onions. Mix soup with milk. Spoon about ¼ to ½ cup of soup mixture over each serving. Sprinkle with salt and pepper to taste. Seal packets of foil, place on cookie sheet and bake in 350 degree oven for 1 hour and 15 minutes. To serve, place foil packet on individual plates and eat out of the foil. Be careful of the steam when you open the packets. Names can be placed on foil packets with a Magic Marker before baking, this makes it "fun." Yield: 5 or more servings.

HINT:

Freeze small portions of leftover meat or fowl until you have enough for a pot pie, curry or casserole.

☆ ☆ ☆ ☆ ☆

CHICKEN WITH 5 CANS SOUP　　　　*Geneva Eubanks*

My sister-in-law, Dolly Bingham serves this at family gatherings. It's wonderful!

3 to 5 (2 to 2½-pound) chickens,
　skinned and cut up
1　can cream of chicken soup
1　can cream of celery soup
1　can cream of mushroom soup

1　can cream of onion soup
1　can Cheddar cheese soup
1　soup can of water
Salt and pepper to taste

Layer chicken pieces in bottom of large casserole or heavy roaster with lid. Salt and pepper to taste. Mix soups and water in a mixing bowl and pour over chicken. Place in 350 degrees oven and cook for 1½ hours, or until chicken is still firm but tender. Serve with gravy over rice, wild rice or noodles. Any left over: remove chicken from bone to prevent discoloration, refrigerate. Heat later to serve over rice, noodles, toast or toasted English muffins . . . toasted twice to be really crisp. Serve with favorite vegetable and green salad or try applesauce with cinnamon or sweet/sour cole slaw or cranberry sauce. Yield: 20 or more servings.

CURRIED CHICKEN WITH LEMON　　　*Vanessa H. Luce*

A favorite, 335 calories.

2½　teaspoons curry powder
½　teaspoon salt, divided
Dash pepper
4　boned chicken breast
　　halves
1⅓　cups water
1　cup converted brand rice

2　teaspoons brown sugar
1　teaspoon dry mustard
Rind of lemon cut in small
　　pieces
2　tablespoons parsley
Juice of one lemon

Combine curry powder, ¼ teaspoon salt and pepper. Rub onto top and bottom of chicken breast, set aside. Combine remaining salt, water, rice, sugar, mustard and lemon rind in skillet; mix well. Bring to a boil. Arrange chicken over rice mixture. Cover tightly and simmer 20 minutes. Remove from heat. Let stand covered until all liquid is absorbed, about 5 minutes. Sprinkle with parsley and stir in lemon juice. Yield: 4 servings.

CHICKEN BREAST WITH ROSEMARY
Jewell Scott

2   whole chicken breasts,
skinned and split
¼   cup flour
Salt and freshly ground pepper
to taste
2   tablespoons olive oil
2   tablespoons butter
2   tablespoons fresh rosemary,
chopped or 1 tablespoon dried

4   garlic cloves
½   cup white wine
2   tablespoons fresh
lemon juice
2   tablespoons parsley,
chopped

Dredge chicken all over in flour seasoned with salt and pepper. Heat oil and butter in a heavy skillet large enough to hold chicken breasts in one layer. Add chicken, rosemary and garlic. Cook about 4 minutes or until pieces are nicely brown on one side. Turn and cook for 4 to 5 minutes until golden brown on other side. Do not cover. Pour off fat from skillet, leaving chicken, rosemary and garlic in skillet. Pour in wine and bring to a boil. Add the lemon juice and parsley. Cover closely and cook 3 minutes. Remove and discard garlic and serve immediately. Yield: 4 servings.

HEAVENLY CHICKEN
Joy Feuge & Martha Slack Piskorik

Don't count calories on this one – just great taste!

6   chicken breasts, boned
6   bacon slices
1   (6-ounce) package thin-sliced
smoked beef or 1 (4-ounce) jar
dried beef

1   can cream of mushroom
soup
1   (8-ounce) carton sour
cream

Wrap chicken with bacon. Put beef in bottom of casserole dish. Place wrapped chicken on top. Mix soup and sour cream and pour over chicken. Bake 3 hours uncovered at 275 degrees or covered for 2 hours at 350 degrees or until tender. Best served with rice. Other meaty pieces of chicken may be used. Yield: 6 servings.

HINTS:

Fresh garlic will retain it's sharp flavor up to four months.

For a small amount of grated onion, place onion pieces in garlic press.

ITALIAN CHICKEN
Susan Thomas

4   boned and skinned
    chicken breasts
Salt and pepper
½   cup flour
4   tablespoons olive oil
½   cup butter or margarine
1   cup fresh mushrooms, sliced

1   heaping tablespoon flour
¼   cup fresh chicken broth
¼   cup Marsala cooking wine
½   pint whipping cream
1 or 2 teaspoons thyme

Sprinkle chicken breasts with salt and pepper. Roll in flour. Melt margarine and olive oil in skillet until foam subsides. Brown chicken until done, turning occasionally. Remove from skillet and keep warm. Pour excess oil from skillet. To drippings, add mushrooms. Stir about 2 minutes. Sprinkle one heaping tablespoon flour over mushrooms, stir gently. Add chicken broth and cooking wine. Stir in whipping cream and add thyme. Simmer gently for 1 to 2 minutes. Pour over chicken breasts. Serve with spaghetti with garlic sauce or red sauce. Yield: 4 servings.

CHICKEN MONTEREY
Jewell Scott

Good with lemon rice and green salad.

6   chicken breasts, split, boned
    and skinned (12 pieces)
12 slices Monterey Jack cheese
2   cans cream of chicken soup
½   cup dry white wine
¼   teaspoon garlic powder, optional

Salt and pepper to taste
3 to 4 cups herb stuffing
    mix
½   cup butter or
    margarine, melted

Place breasts in a lightly oiled 13 x 9 x 2-inch baking dish. Top each breast with a substantial slice of cheese. Combine soup, wine and garlic powder. Pour over chicken. Salt lightly and pepper. Sprinkle with stuffing mix. Should be completely covered but not too thickly. Drizzle melted butter over stuffing. Bake at 350 degrees approximately 50 minutes. Yield: 8-12 servings.

HINT:

Chopped onions have the best flavor if they are browned in shortening before being added to casserole dishes.

PINEAPPLE HONEY MUSTARD CHICKEN   *Jewell Scott*

4 boneless, skinless chicken
   breast halves
Salt and pepper
2 large cloves garlic, pressed
1 teaspoon thyme, crumbled
2 teaspoons vegetable oil

1 (20-ounce) can sliced
   pineapple in juice,
   drain and reserve
1 tablespoon cornstarch
¼ cup honey
¼ cup Dijon mustard

Sprinkle chicken with salt and pepper. Rub with garlic and thyme. Brown in hot oil in nonstick skillet. Combine 2 tablespoons reserved juice with cornstarch, set aside. Combine honey and mustard; stir into skillet with remaining juice. Spoon sauce over chicken. Cover and simmer 15 minutes. Stir cornstarch mixture into pan juices. Add pineapple. Cook, stirring, until sauce boils and thickens. Yield: 4 servings.

CHICKEN AND BROCCOLI CASSEROLE   *Leah Mauck*

I got this recipe, along with many others, from Peggy Simpson, a long time family friend from Laredo and a wonderful cook.

8 chicken breasts
2 (12-ounce) packages
   frozen broccoli spears
1 can cream of mushroom
   soup
½ cup mayonnaise (not
   salad dressing)

½ cup chicken broth
8 slices of white bread, dried
½ cup margarine, melted
½ pound Cheddar cheese,
   grated

Boil chicken; reserve stock. Remove skin, bone and slice chicken. (Boneless chicken breasts may be substituted but increase amount to 10). Cook broccoli 3 minutes, drain, set aside. Mix soup with mayonnaise and chicken broth. Place broccoli spears in buttered 13 x 9 x 2-inch baking dish, cover with sliced chicken, top with soup mixture, and spread cheese over soup. Blend bread in blender. Place crumbs in skillet with margarine and gently brown, stirring constantly. Cover casserole with bread crumbs. Bake 30 minutes in 350 degrees oven. Yield: 12 servings.

CORNBREAD CHICKEN CASSEROLE   *Elnora Kneese*

1   (6-ounce) package   ½   cup celery, diced
    cornbread mix   ⅓   cup butter or margarine
2   thighs, 2 legs of chicken, or   2   eggs, beaten
    2 breasts, about 2–3 cups   ½   teaspoon pepper
1 to 2 cups chicken broth   1   teaspoon poultry
½   cup onion, chopped   seasoning

Bake cornbread mix according to package directions. Crumble when cool. Cook chicken with enough water to cover until tender, about 45 to 60 minutes. Reserve broth. Cool, bone and cut up meat. Brown onion and celery in butter. Add crumbled cornbread, eggs, pepper and poultry seasoning. Add chicken broth to moisten. Turn into shallow well greased 11 x 7 x 2-inch or 13 x 9 x 2-inch baking dish. Bake at 350 degrees for 30 minutes or until browned on top. Yield: 6-8 servings.

CHICKEN & DUMPLINGS WITH VEGETABLES   *Suzanne Law*

1   large chicken or hen   1   tablespoon dried parsley
6   cups water   2   tablespoons margarine
1   teaspoon salt   ¼   teaspoon celery seed
1   tablespoon minced onion   1   teaspoon pepper
2   cups flour   1   cup milk
1   teaspoon salt   1   cup frozen green peas
2   eggs   1   cup carrots, peeled and
½   cup milk   sliced
1   tablespoon instant chicken bouillon

In a large pot combine chicken, water, salt and onion and boil until done. Remove chicken, cool, bone, and cut into bite size pieces. Save broth. To make dumplings, mix flour, salt, eggs and ½ cup milk together to form a very stiff dough. Drop by teaspoonfuls into boiling chicken broth. Add boned chicken and remaining ingredients; boil 20 minutes, stirring occasionally. If broth is not thick enough, mix flour and water together and stir in. If broth is too thick, add more milk. Yield: 6-8 servings.

HINT:

A raw potato or sliced apple in anything that is too salty, soup or vegetables, will remove extra salt. Cook soup with raw potato a few minutes and remove and taste.

CRUNCHY CHICKEN CASSEROLE

Louise Gravenor

Mrs. Irene Grote and I used to share making this for the faculty luncheons. Since she was H.E. teacher and had the stove, I only had to furnish half the ingredients. Makes me feel guilty even now.

1 large broiler fryer	1 (8-ounce) can sliced
1 onion, chopped	water chestnuts, drained
1 can cream of chicken soup	2 tablespoons onions,
⅔ cup mayonnaise	minced
1 (4-ounce) can sliced	1 (16-ounce) can cut green
mushrooms, drained	beans, drained
1 cup cooked rice	Salt and pepper to taste
¾ cup celery, chopped	1 (8-ounce) box herb
1 cup chicken broth	stuffing mix, dry

Boil chicken and onion together until tender. Remove chicken, bone and cut into bite-size pieces. Place in large bowl and add everything except the stuffing mix. In a 11 x 14 x 2 greased casserole dish pour ½ of stuffing mix. Pour chicken mixture over mix. Top with remaining stuffing mix. Bake at 350 degrees for 30 minutes or until bubbly. Yield: serves 10-12 hungry teachers.

CHICKEN SALAD CASSEROLE

Aline Slack

2 cups boned chicken, diced	½ teaspoon pepper
3 hard cooked eggs, chopped	1 tablespoon lemon juice
1 can cream of chicken soup	½ cup mayonnaise
2 cups celery, diced	½ cup toasted almonds,
1 teaspoon minced onion	slivered
½ teaspoon salt	2 cups crushed potato chips

Mix all ingredients except potato chips. Place in 1–1½-quart casserole and cover with potato chips. Bake at 450 degrees for 15 minutes. Yield: 4–6 servings.

SAVORY CHICKEN SQUARES   *Dorothy C. Lackey*

These are delicious. One is a meal with a salad.

2 tablespoons margarine, melted	2 tablespoons milk
	¼ teaspoon paprika
1 (3-ounce) package cream cheese	1 (8-ounce) package Crescent Rolls
2 cups chicken, cooked and diced	*Topping*
	1 cup cream of chicken soup
1½ tablespoons pimiento, chopped	½ cup milk
	2 tablespoons croutons, crushed
3 tablespoons onion, diced	
¼ teaspoon salt	1 teaspoon poppy seeds
¼ teaspoon pepper	

Heat oven to 350 degrees. Mix margarine and cream cheese until smooth and creamy. Add rest of ingredients and blend. Open can of rolls and divide into 4 rectangles. Place ¼ of mixture on each. Fold corners and sides to form a square. Bake approximately 25 minutes or less until rolls are brown on top. Then heat soup and milk and pour over top. Sprinkle with croutons and poppy seeds. Yield: 4 servings.

EVIE'S CHICKEN SPAGHETTI   *Geneva Eubanks*

Received from my daughter-in-law Evie and often served when our family gathers. This is good served with a crisp salad and garlic French bread.

1 large fryer or stewing hen	2 teaspoons Worcestershire sauce
1 teaspoon salt	
1 teaspoon pepper	1 teaspoon Tabasco sauce, optional
1 large onion, chopped	
1 green bell pepper, chopped	1 (46-ounce) can V-8 juice
¾ of bunch celery stalks, chopped	1 (16-ounce) package spaghetti, break in 2-inch pieces
1 (7-ounce) jar diced pimiento	
1 (8-ounce) jar sliced mushrooms	1 pound Cheddar or Velveeta cheese

Boil chicken with salt and pepper until tender. Remove chicken. Cool, bone and chop. Strain broth, return to pot and add all ingredients except chicken, spaghetti and cheese. Simmer covered for one hour. Bring to a

70

boil and add chicken and slowly add spaghetti. Cook until spaghetti is done. Stir in cheese until melted. Serve hot. May be put in casserole and cheese put on top and heated in 350 degree oven for 20-30 minutes. Freezes well. Yield: 12–16 servings.

PUERTO RICAN STYLE GIZZARDS　　　*Dorothy C. Lackey*

If you like gizzards you will love these. They grow on you, like popcorn. The more you eat, the more you want.

1　pound chicken gizzards	2　medium onions, sliced
¾　cup vinegar	1　cup olive oil
2　bay leaves	

Pressure gizzards in salt water at 10-pound pressure for 25 minutes. Drain. Put vinegar in a skillet over medium heat, add bay leaves and onions. When the onions are transparent, remove from fire and add the olive oil. Put gizzards in a bowl and pour the onion mixture over them. Cover and let sit overnight. Yield: 4-6 servings.

TURKEY BAKE　　　　　　　　　　*Debbie Watson*

1 to 1½ pound turkey breast raw, sliced in serving sizes	Salt and pepper to taste Garlic powder to taste
4 to 6 medium potatoes, peeled, cut bite size	1　can cream of mushroom soup
2　pound carrots, peeled, cut bite size	1　can cream of chicken soup
2　onions, peeled and cut	Water

Place turkey in a 13 x 9 x 2-inch baking dish. Arrange vegetables around turkey; sprinkle with salt, pepper and garlic powder. Blend soups and pour over turkey and vegetables. May need to add a little water to cover. Cover dish with foil. Bake at 350 degrees for 3 hours. (Cut turkey across the grain to prevent tough meat.) Yield: 4-6 servings.

☆　☆　☆　☆　☆

HINT:

When you dress a wild turkey, cut up apples and celery and stuff turkey then freeze. When ready to bake, thaw and dispose of apples and celery before baking. This will rid the turkey of wild taste.

GROUND TURKEY LOAF
Juneth Watson

I adapted this from a ground beef recipe and did a lot of experimenting before I came up with the recipe. I learned not to leave out cheese, as the cheese "just makes it." Sometime in the 50s, it was published with my picture in The Farmer Stockman. *In 1989, my granddaughter, Jennifer Jenschke used the recipe in the Gillespie County 4-H Food Show and won a blue ribbon.*

1½ pounds ground turkey	1 tablespoon ketchup
½ cup milk	1½ teaspoons salt
1 egg, beaten	¼ teaspoon black pepper
1 cup saltine crackers, crushed	1 cup Cheddar cheese, grated
2 tablespoons onion, minced	Parsley, optional
1 teaspoon prepared mustard	

Mix all ingredients. Spoon into 9 x 5 x 3 bread pan that has been coated with a non-stick cooking spray. Cover and bake at 325 degrees for approximately 45 minutes to 1 hour. Garnish with parsley, if desired. Yield: 6 servings.

DRUGSTORE COWBOY CASSEROLE
Thelma Elm

1 pound ground turkey	2 beef bouillon cubes
½ green bell pepper, chopped	1½ cups hot water
1 cup tomato sauce	1½ cups cooked rice
Garlic to taste	4 ounces cheese, grated, divided
Chili powder to taste	

Brown meat, sauté green pepper, and add tomato sauce, garlic, chili powder and bouillon that has been dissolved in hot water. Stir in rice and ½ cheese. Pour into 1½-quart casserole dish and top with remaining cheese. Bake for 30 minutes at 350 degrees. Yield: 4 servings.

SEAFOOD HINT:
Two pounds of raw shrimp in shell will yield about a pound cooked and shelled.

TURKEY WIENERS AND BEANS WAIKIKI *Thelma Elm*

1 (20-ounce) can pineapple rings, drained, reserve juice	2 tablespoons vinegar
⅓ cup green bell pepper, chopped	1 tablespoon soy sauce
¼ cup onion, chopped	⅓ cup ketchup
1 (12-ounce) package turkey wieners, cut in chunks	⅓ cup brown sugar, packed
2 tablespoons butter or margarine	1 (31-ounce) can pork and beans
	1 (5-ounce) can Chow Mein noodles, optional

Cut pineapple into chunks, reserving 3 or 4 rings for garnish. Sauté green pepper, onion, pineapple and wiener chunks in margarine. Simmer 5 minutes, add pineapple syrup, vinegar, soy sauce, ketchup and brown sugar; heat until bubbly. Pour pork and beans into 2 quart casserole dish. Add pineapple mixture, stir gently to blend. Place reserved rings on top. Bake in moderate oven, 350 degrees, for 30 minutes. Serve with chow mein noodles. Yield: 6 servings.

PARMESAN BAKED FISH *Sally Gravenor*

This dish is too good to be so simple.

⅓ (12-ounce) box Ritz crackers (1 sleeve)	½ cup butter or margarine, melted
¾ cup grated Parmesan cheese	1 pound fish fillets
Salt	

Combine crackers and cheese in blender/processor. Add small amount of salt to butter. Dip fish in butter, then in cracker mixture. Place in greased 12 x 9 x 2 baking dish. Bake at 400 degrees for about 15 minutes. Can be prepared ahead of time, refrigerated, then baked for 20 minutes. (For extra flavor add ½ teaspoon each basil and oregano and ¼ teaspoon garlic powder.) Save any leftover cracker mixture for the next fish dinner. Yield: 4 servings.

☆ ☆ ☆ ☆ ☆

HINT:

For fillets: bone fish when you clean them. Skin may be left on one side to hold fish together.

☆ ☆ ☆ ☆ ☆

73

SHRIMP DIVINE
Cynthia Smith

2 cups fresh mushrooms, sliced
¼ cup butter <u>or</u> margarine
Dash salt and pepper
½ teaspoon Worcestershire sauce

1 pound shrimp, boiled and peeled
¼ cup white wine, any kind
1 cup sour cream

Cook mushrooms over low heat in butter for 10 minutes. Add next three ingredients and stir. Mix together the wine and sour cream and pour over the shrimp mixture. Heat thoroughly and serve over wild or white rice. Very delicious. Yield: 4 servings.

SHRIMP AND WILD RICE CASSEROLE
Cynthia Smith

1 can cream of shrimp soup
2 tablespoons green pepper, chopped
2 tablespoons onion, chopped
2 tablespoons margarine, melted
1 tablespoon lemon juice
1 (6-ounce) package long grain and wild rice cooked <u>or</u> 2 cups cooked white rice

½ tablespoon Worcestershire sauce
½ teaspoon salt
½ teaspoon black pepper
¾ cup American cheese, grated
1 pound or more shrimp, boiled and peeled, cut into small pieces

Mix all the above ingredients well. Pour into greased 1½ or 2 quart casserole and bake for 30 minutes at 350 degree or until cheese is bubbly. Use American cheese only; Cheddar is too coarse. Yield: 8 servings.

CRAB PINWHEELS WITH CHEESE SAUCE
Patricia J. Ripsom

1 (7½-ounce) can crab meat
¼ cup celery, finely chopped
2 tablespoons onion, finely chopped
2 tablespoons pimiento, finely chopped
1 tablespoon parsley flakes
2 to 4 tablespoons mayonnaise

½ teaspoon salt
¼ teaspoon pepper
1 recipe for biscuit dough
Sauce
2 tablespoons flour
2 tablespoons margarine
1 cup milk
1 cup Cheddar cheese, grated

Drain and slice crab meat. Combine with celery, onion, pimiento, parsley and enough mayonnaise to moisten. Add salt and pepper. Prepare biscuit

74

dough and roll out into a rectangle ½ inch thick. Spread crab mixture and roll up like a jelly roll. Slice ¾ inch thick. Place on a lightly buttered cookie sheet and bake 12-15 minutes at 450 degrees.

Sauce Blend flour and margarine in skillet. Gradually add milk to make a white sauce over medium heat. Stir constantly until slightly thickened. Add cheese and melt into white sauce until thick and smooth. Pour sauce over the crab pinwheels and serve. Yield: 8 servings.

SALMON CROQUETTES
Susan Thomas

1 (15½-ounce) can red salmon	1½ cups warm mashed potatoes
1 tablespoon fresh lemon juice	2 eggs
¼ teaspoon salt	2 teaspoons water
⅛ teaspoon pepper	2 to 3 cups saltine cracker crumbs

Drain and bone salmon, break up with a fork. Sprinkle with lemon juice and add salt and pepper. Stir in potatoes, ½ cup at a time, until well mixed. Roll into egg shaped rolls. Beat eggs and water together. Roll the salmon croquettes in the cracker crumbs, then the egg mixture and again in the cracker crumbs. Fry in deep fat until golden brown, drain. Serve with fresh lemon and ketchup, if desired. Yield: 6 servings.

AUNT ESTHER'S CHOPSTICK TUNA
Celia Grote

1 can cream of mushroom soup	½ cup salted, toasted cashews, chopped
½ cup water	¼ cup onion, chopped
1 (3-ounce) can Chow Mein noodles	1 (6½-ounce) can tuna packed in water, drained
1 cup celery, chopped	Dash black pepper

Blend soup and water. Add remaining ingredients and mix well. Place in greased 1-quart baking casserole dish and bake for 20 minutes at 375 degrees. May be doubled. Yield: 4 small servings.

✩　✩　✩　✩　✩

HINT:
Run hot boiled shrimp under cold water to ease the peeling job.

PERFECT TUNA CASSEROLE   *Thelma Elm*

This is one of my Mother's favorite fast recipes from Michigan. She prepared it for many years for our family.

1 can cream of celery soup	2 hard cooked eggs, sliced
¼ cup milk	1 cup cooked peas
2 (6½-ounce) cans tuna, drained and flaked	½ cup crumbled potato chips

In 1 quart casserole, blend soup and milk; stir in tuna, eggs and peas. Bake at 350 degrees for 25 minutes or until bubbly. Stir and top with potato chips. Bake another 5 minutes. Yield: 4 servings.

REYNOLD'S VENISON POT ROAST   *Joyce Ellis*

The meat melts in your mouth, it is so tender. If there are leftovers, cut the meat and vegetables in bite size pieces. Add the left over gravy and a little water and heat. This is an excellent stew. I usually double this recipe just to have the extra.

4 pounds venison roast, hind quarter	2 large onions, peeled and cut in ¼ths.
Salt and pepper to taste	Reynold's Oven Cooking Bag
Garlic powder to taste	*Gravy*
4 slices bacon	2 teaspoons cornstarch
8 medium potatoes, peeled and quartered	2 teaspoons water
1 pound carrots, peeled and halved	Juice from cooked venison, add water to make 3 cups
	Salt and pepper to taste

Wash and dry roast. Sprinkle with salt, pepper and garlic powder. Place in cooking bag. Lay bacon slices across roast. Place vegetables in bag and close bag with tie. Cut slits in top of bag according to cooking bag directions. Bake at 350 degrees for 1½ to 2 hours.

Gravy Mix cornstarch and water, set aside. Pour juice from venison in frying pan and heat to boiling. Add cornstarch mixture and season to taste. Stir until gravy is slightly thick. Yield: 10-12 servings.

VENISON STEAK AND NOODLES ITALIAN   *Beverly K. Voron*

I got this recipe from a friend when we lived in Wrangell, Alaska. She always used moose steak, but I love to use venison. Round or chuck steak may be used if the other is not available.

2 to 2½ pounds backstrap venison, cut into small pieces	1 teaspoon basil
¼ cup salad oil	½ teaspoon pepper
4 garlic cloves	1 cup water
1 cup beef bouillon	1 (8-ounce) can mushrooms
2 teaspoons bottled sauce for gravy	2 (9-ounce) packages frozen green beans
½ tablespoon salt	1 (16-ounce) package noodles
	3 beef bouillon cubes

About two hours before serving, tenderize meat with meat hammer. In Dutch oven over medium heat, brown garlic well in hot salad oil; discard garlic. Add meat and brown well on both sides. Add bouillon, sauce for gravy, salt, basil, pepper and water. Reduce heat to simmer, cover and cook for 1 hour and 15 minutes, adding more water if necessary. Add mushrooms and green beans; cover and simmer 20 minutes or until meat and green beans are tender. Cook noodles as label directs, but add bouillon cubes to boiling water. Drain. Place meat on serving dish. Carefully stir noodles into green beans and serve around meat. Yield: 8-10 servings.

VENISON STROGANOFF   *Christine Schulze*

2 to 3 pound venison hindquarter, cubed 1-inch	1 (3-ounce) can sliced mushrooms
1 large onion, chopped	Water
¼ cup vegetable oil	1 can cream of mushroom soup
1 package Lipton's onion soup mix	1 tablespoon ketchup, optional
	1 teaspoon Dijon mustard, optional

Sauté meat and onion in oil. Add soup mix, mushrooms and enough water to cover. Simmer for 1 hour. I usually simmer 2-3 hours adding more water as needed. Thicken with soup. Ketchup or Dijon mustard may be added for a different taste. Serve over rice, noodles or boiled potatoes. Yield: 8-10 servings.

Eat It — It's Good For You

Vegetables, Side Dishes

BARNWELL HOME AND HOSPITAL

Completed in 1913, the first hospital in Blanco County was built and operated by James Franklin Barnwell, M.D. The first floor was the doctors residence, while upstairs was a hospital with surgical room, where Dr. Barnwell and his wife Irene, performed the first caesarean operation in this part of the country, saving both mother and child. Always interested in improving the living standard and eliminating misery, he continued to serve in his professional capacity until his death in 1934.

ASPARAGUS-PEA CASSEROLE

Jewell Sultemeier

½ cup margarine, melted
6 slices of bread, toasted and
   crumbled
1 (20-ounce) can green peas,
   drained
1 (20-ounce) can cut
   asparagus, drained

1 (5-ounce) can water
   chestnuts, drained and
   chopped
1 can cream of mushroom
   soup
1 cup cheese, grated

Mix together the margarine and bread crumbs. In a greased 2-quart casserole dish layer the green peas, asparagus and water chestnuts. Stir the soup to remove lumps and pour undiluted over the vegetables. Cover with grated cheese and top with buttered crumbs. Bake at 350 degrees for 30 minutes. Yield: 8 servings.

GREEN BEAN CASSEROLE

Jeannette Stanton

2 (10-ounce) packages frozen
   green beans or 2 (16-ounce)
   cans green beans
½ cup onion, chopped
2 tablespoons butter

2 tablespoons flour
1 teaspoon salt
¼ teaspoon pepper
1 cup sour cream
1 cup sharp cheese, grated

Cook green beans. Sauté onions until tender in butter: add flour, salt and pepper. Fold in sour cream and drained green beans. Pour into a buttered 8 x 8 x 2 baking dish and cover with grated cheese. Bake at 350 degrees for 20 minutes. Yield: 8 servings.

FRENCH GREEN BEAN CASSEROLE

Mary A. Thurlkill

1 can cream of mushroom
   soup
1 (6-ounce) roll Kraft jalapeño
   cheese
2 (16-ounce) cans French cut
   green beans, drained

1 (5-ounce) can sliced
   water chestnuts, drained
Dash Worcestershire sauce
1 (2.8-ounce) can French
   fried onion rings

Heat soup and cheese and stir together until the cheese melts. Mix all ingredients except onion rings into soup mixture. Pour into a 1½-2 quart casserole and bake at 350 degrees for 30 minutes. Top with onion rings and bake 10 more minutes. Yield: 8 servings.

⇪ ⇪ ⇪ ⇪ ⇪ ⇪ ⇪

GARLIC GREEN BEANS
Jeanne Hudson

2 (16-ounce) cans French style green beans
1 tablespoon butter <u>or</u> margarine
⅛ teaspoon garlic salt
¼ cup butter <u>or</u> margarine

1 heaping tablespoon flour
1 cup milk
1 cup Cheese Whiz <u>or</u> Velveeta
¼ cup bread crumbs

Place beans and 1 tablespoon butter in sauce pan. Boil until liquid is low. Drain and sprinkle with garlic salt. In another saucepan over low heat melt ¼ cup butter, add flour and stir well. Add milk and cheese, when cheese melts pour over beans. Place in a quart size casserole and cover with bread crumbs. Brown in 400 degree oven for 20 minutes. Yield: 6-8 servings.

GREEN BEANS WITH TOMATOES
Aline Slack

2 pounds fresh green beans <u>or</u> 2 (16-ounce) cans green beans
2 tablespoons butter <u>or</u> margarine
½ cup onion, chopped
1 (14½-ounce) can tomatoes, drained and coarsely chopped

½ teaspoon crumbled dried tarragon
½ teaspoon salt
¼ teaspoon black pepper
Pinch sugar

Trim green beans and cut in 2-inch lengths. Cook until crisp-tender, drain or use canned green beans drained. Spread beans in a greased shallow 2-quart baking dish. Melt butter in a small skillet over medium heat. Add onion and cook 3 minutes. Stir in remaining ingredients and cook 10 minutes. Spoon over beans. Bake uncovered in a 375 degree oven for 15 minutes or until bubbly. May be refrigerated overnight before baking. Yield: 10 servings.

ITALIAN BEAN BAKE
Robin Taylor

2 (16-ounce) cans Italian green beans, drained
1 (8-ounce) can tomato sauce
1 tablespoon prepared mustard
2 teaspoons minced dried onion

⅛ teaspoon garlic salt
⅛ teaspoon pepper
½ cup Provolone cheese, grated

Combine all ingredients, except cheese, in casserole dish. Mix well and cover. *In conventional oven:* Bake at 375 degrees for 30 minutes. Uncover

and add cheese and bake until cheese is melted. *In microwave:* Cover and cook on HIGH 6 minutes, stirring and rotating once. Uncover and add cheese. Cook an additional 2 minutes on HIGH or until cheese melts. Yield: 8 servings.

JOSIE'S GREEN BEAN CASSEROLE
Josie Byars

¼ cup milk
1 can cream of mushroom
   soup
⅛ teaspoon black pepper
2 tablespoons diced pimientos

2 (16-ounce) cans green
   beans, drained
1 (3-ounce) can French
   fried onions, divided

Combine milk, soup, pepper and pimientos; pour over beans. Add ½ can onions; pour into 1½ quart casserole. Bake at 350 degrees for 20 minutes. Garnish with remaining onions. Bake 5 minutes longer. Yield: 6 servings.

WILMA'S MARINATED GREEN BEANS
Wilma Fawcett

1 (16-ounce) can long green
   beans
1 green pepper, sliced
1 medium onion, chopped
6 ribs celery, sliced thin

Scant ½ cup oil
½ cup vinegar
¾ cup sugar
1 teaspoon paprika

Carefully mix together beans, green pepper, onion, and celery in container with lid. Mix oil, vinegar, sugar and paprika and pour over other ingredients. Marinate in refrigerator overnight. Serve cold. Will keep for several days. Double recipe for a crowd of people. Yield: 4-6 servings.

TEXAS BEANS
Lee Caruthers

The best supper is a soup bowl of cooked rice with beans and juice spooned over, topped with lots of rat cheese (Longhorn or Cheddar) grated over top, then sprinkled with chopped onion.

1 pound of dried pinto <u>or</u>
   kidney beans
1 large onion, chopped
2 cloves garlic

1 teaspoon chili powder
1 piece salt pork, not too big,
   sliced down to rind or chopped
Salt and pepper to taste

Wash and pick beans, soak overnight in water to cover by about 1 inch. Next day, add more water to cover beans by 2 inches. Add onion, garlic,

81

chili powder and salt pork. Cook over low heat until beans are tender about 1½ to 2 hours. Yield: 8 servings.

MARY JANE'S BROCCOLI CASSEROLE   *Margaret Dannecker*

Even George Bush would eat his broccoli prepared this way. The recipe is from a dear friend in Panama City, Florida.

1 onion, chopped	1 (3-ounce) can mushrooms
⅓ cup butter	with liquid
2 (10-ounce) packages frozen	1 tube Kraft's garlic cheese
chopped broccoli	spread
1 can cream of mushroom	1 (2.8-ounce) can onion rings
soup	Slivered almonds

Sauté onion in butter in electric skillet. Place broccoli on top, cover and steam until tender. Add soup, mushrooms with liquid and cheese spread. Transfer to 11 x 8 x 2-inch casserole. Top with onion rings and slivered almonds. Bake at 325 degrees until bubbly about 15 minutes. Yield: 6 servings.

CORN DISH   *Olivia Weiershausen*

This makes a nice dish to serve with meat. It is very good to take for a crowd of people.

½ cup bell pepper, finely	3 eggs, well beaten
chopped	2 teaspoons sugar
½ cup celery, finely chopped	1 cup instant rice
½ cup onion, finely chopped	½ teaspoon salt
2 tablespoons butter	1 teaspoon pepper
1 (17-ounce) can cream style corn	½ cup Cheddar cheese,
1 (17-ounce) can whole kernel	grated
corn, undrained	1 (2-ounce) jar pimiento

Sauté pepper, celery and onion in butter, when clear add corn. Slowly add eggs. Stir in sugar, rice, salt, pepper and pimiento. Fold in cheese. Pour into a 3-quart casserole and bake 30 minutes at 300 degrees. Yield: 8–12 servings.

✧ ✧ ✧ ✧ ✧ ✧ ✧

EASY CORN CASSEROLE

Geneva Eubanks

This dish was brought to company potluck dinners and was always a favorite.

2 to 3 cans whole kernel corn, drained <u>or</u> 2 to 3 (10-ounce) packages frozen corn
1 (8-ounce) package cream cheese, softened

1 (4-ounce) can chopped mild green chiles
⅛ teaspoon pepper
2 tablespoons margarine

Mix all ingredients except margarine. Put in 1½ quart casserole sprayed with non-stick cooking spray. Dot with margarine and bake uncovered in 350 degree oven for 25 minutes or microwave until hot. Yield: 6 servings.

HOT CORN

Flora Cox & Suzanne Law

A very different corn casserole, a favorite at Thanksgiving and Christmas. Adds zest to the holiday meal and very good to make an every day luncheon guest say <u>ummm!</u>

¼ cup margarine
8 ounces cream cheese
½ cup milk
2 or 3 (12-ounce) cans white shoe peg corn, drained

2 tablespoons flour
2 jalapeño peppers, seeded and chopped
Dash garlic powder
Salt and pepper to taste

Melt margarine and cream cheese; stir in milk, corn, flour, peppers and seasonings. Bake in a 1½ quart casserole at 350 degrees for 20 minutes or until hot. Yield: 6–8 servings.

CORN SCALLOP

Leah Mauck

1 (17-ounce) can cream style corn
2 eggs, beaten
½ cup crushed crackers
¼ cup margarine, melted
¼ cup undiluted evaporated milk
¼ cup carrots, finely shredded
¼ cup green pepper, chopped

¼ cup pimiento, chopped
1 tablespoon celery, chopped
1 teaspoon onion, chopped
6 drops Tabasco sauce
½ teaspoon sugar
½ teaspoon salt
½ cup Cheddar cheese, shredded
Paprika

Combine all ingredients except cheese and paprika. Mix thoroughly and pour into 8 x 8 x 2-inch greased baking dish. Top with cheese and sprinkle with paprika. Bake at 350 degrees for 30 minutes or until mixture is set and top is golden brown. Yield: 6-8 servings.

WESTERN CORN ON THE COB
Mary A. Thurlkill

4 or 5 ears of corn
½ cup butter, softened
1 tablespoon prepared mustard
1 teaspoon prepared horseradish

1 teaspoon salt
Dash black pepper, freshly
   ground
Fresh parsley, finely chopped

Preheat oven to 450 degrees. Husk corn and strip off the silk; spread each ear with a little horseradish butter. Wrap each ear loosely in foil and bake for 20 to 25 minutes. May be baked over hot coals on the grill.

Horseradish Butter Combine butter, mustard, horseradish, salt and pepper; cream until light and fluffy. Spread on each ear of corn. Sprinkle the remaining Horseradish Butter with the parsley and serve with the cooked corn. Yield: ½ cup butter, 4-5 servings.

SPICY HOMINY CASSEROLE
Norma Honeycutt

A different version of Frito Pie with a wonderful taste of masa.

1 cup onion, chopped
4 cloves garlic, chopped
2 tablespoons bacon grease
   or vegetable oil
1 (16-ounce) can tomatoes
1 (8-ounce) can tomato sauce
1 cup water
Salt and pepper to taste

2 teaspoons chili powder
2 (15½-ounce) cans hominy,
   drained
½ to ¾ pound Longhorn
   cheese, grated
11 ounce bag of Fritos corn
   chips, divided

Sauté onion and garlic in bacon grease or oil; add tomatoes, tomato sauce, water, salt, pepper and chili powder. Add hominy and cook until mixed well. In a 13 x 9 x 2-inch baking dish add ½ hominy mixture, layer with ½ cheese and ½ corn chips; add rest of hominy mixture and sprinkle with rest of cheese. Bake 30 or 40 minutes at 350 degrees. Sprinkle corn chips on top before serving. Yield: 8-10 servings.

PARSLIED MUSHROOM PATTIES

Shirley Spurlock Rosson

3 eggs, slightly beaten	⅓ cup onion, finely chopped
3 cups mushrooms, coarsely chopped	1 tablespoon parsley flakes
½ cup flour	¼ teaspoon pepper
½ cup fine, seasoned bread crumbs	3 tablespoons cooking oil

Mix all ingredients except oil in a large bowl. Make into patties and fry 3 to 4 minutes on each side. Yield: 8 patties.

STUFFED MUSHROOMS

Mariallen Moursund

4 slices bacon, diced	1 (3-ounce) package cream cheese, softened
¼ cup onion, minced	
2 tablespoons green pepper, minced	1 pound fresh mushrooms
½ teaspoon salt	½ cup soft bread crumbs
½ teaspoon Worcestershire sauce	1 tablespoon butter or margarine

Cook bacon, onion and green pepper in microwave on HIGH for 4 minutes, stirring once. Pour off fat, stir in salt, Worcestershire sauce and cream cheese. Set aside. Wash and dry mushrooms and remove stems. Chop stems and add to bacon mixture. Stuff mushroom caps with bacon mixture. Set aside. Heat bread crumbs and margarine on HIGH 1 minute. Stir and press on top of stuffed mushrooms. Place in pyrex that fits microwave oven and cook on HIGH 1 to 2 minutes. Yield: 4-5 servings.

OKRA CASSEROLE

Moline Lorenz

This is Jeannie Gillmore's recipe from Madera, CA. Delicious served with pinto beans and cornbread.

2 eggs, beaten	⅓ cup onion, minced
2 cups cracker crumbs, divided	⅓ cup celery, minced
2 cups okra, fresh or frozen, blanched and well drained	⅓ cup green pepper, minced
	2 tablespoons bacon drippings
2 cups tomatoes, fresh or canned, cooked and drained	Margarine

Combine eggs and 1 cup cracker crumbs. Add other ingredients except margarine, mix well. Pour into an oiled 1½-quart casserole and top with remaining cracker crumbs and dot with margarine. Bake in 350 degree oven for 1 hour. Yield: 6 servings.

FRESH OKRA AND TOMATOES　　　　*Aline Slack*

1　clove garlic, minced	3　cups tomatoes, peeled
½　cup onion, chopped	and chopped
½　cup green pepper, chopped	¼　teaspoon dried whole
2　tablespoons butter or	oregano
margarine, melted	½　teaspoon salt
2　cups okra, sliced	½　teaspoon pepper

Sauté garlic, onion and green pepper in butter about 10 minutes or until tender. Add remaining ingredients and cook 5 minutes, stirring frequently. Yield: 4-6 servings.

JOHN'S OKRA PATTIES　　　　*Geneva Eubanks*

Many years ago I worked for John Stevenson who was then Sheriff and Tax Collector of Blanco County. He always loved to share vegetables from his carefully tended garden with friends. He gave this recipe to me and our family loves okra this way.

1　large egg, beaten	1　(10-ounce) package frozen
½　cup milk	cut okra or fresh
⅔　cup flour	Vegetable oil
1½　teaspoons salt	

Mix first 4 ingredients, add okra and stir. Put oil in large skillet and heat. Drop mixture by tablespoonfuls and fry until golden, turn and cook until done. (The batter will be like glue but when cooked the okra is not slimy). Yield: 12-15 3-inch patties.

EASY AU GRATIN POTATOES　　　　*Inez Steolyn Evavold*

2 to 3 tablespoons butter	1　tablespoon Miracle
1　tablespoon flour	Whip salad dressing
¾　cup milk	4　medium potatoes,
3 to 4 slices American cheese	boiled, sliced thin

86

Heat butter in skillet, add flour, stir. While stirring add enough milk to form thin sauce. Add cheese and salad dressing stirring until cheese melts. Add potatoes and coat with sauce. Place in 1½-quart greased baking dish and bake in 350 degree oven until lightly browned. Yield: 6-8 servings.

HOT POTATOES   *Jewell Scott*

Some of these potatoes will turn out crisp and some chewy, but all are delicious. The longer you bake them, the more they will crispen.

4 medium size baking potatoes, about 1 pound	**½ teaspoon black pepper**
¼ cup vegetable oil <u>or</u> melted butter <u>or</u> margarine	**½ teaspoon dried thyme, oregano, sage or basil, crumbled**
1 teaspoon salt	

Preheat oven to 450 degrees. Peel potatoes and cut into slices ⅛-inch thick. In a bowl thoroughly combine remaining ingredients; add potatoes; toss well. Place mixture in a 15½ x 10½ x 1-inch baking pan, spreading out slices so they overlap slightly. Bake, uncovered, for about 20 minutes. Yield: 4 servings.

JALAPEÑO POTATOES   *Sallye Baker & Celia Grote*

4 medium red potatoes	**¼ cup butter**
1 small bell pepper, slivered	**1 tablespoon flour**
1 (2-ounce) can pimientos	**1 cup milk**
1 jalapeño, seeded and chopped, optional	**½ (6-ounce) roll garlic cheese, grated or cubed**
6 slices bacon, cooked and crumbled, optional	**½ (6-ounce) roll jalapeño cheese, grated or cubed**
Salt and pepper to taste	

Boil potatoes in the jackets in salted water until tender. When cool to handle, peel, slice and layer in a buttered 2-quart casserole with bell pepper and pimiento; add jalapeño and bacon at this time if desired. Salt and pepper each layer. Melt butter in a sauce pan, add flour and stir until blended. Gradually add milk, stirring constantly. Add cheese and cook until melted. Pour over potatoes and bake at 350 degrees for 45 minutes to 1 hour. Yield: 6-8 servings.

CRISPY ROSEMARY POTATOES   *Jewell Scott*

6   large baking potatoes, about   1   teaspoon salt
3 pounds, peeled and sliced   1   teaspoon pepper
⅛ inch thick   1   cup Parmesan cheese,
⅓   cup olive oil   grated, divided
2 to 4 tablespoons fresh rosemary,
chopped <u>or</u> 2 to 4 teaspoons dried

Heat oven to 400 degrees. Grease sides of an 8 to 9½ inch spring form pan. Place on a greased jelly-roll pan. Mix potatoes, oil, rosemary, salt and pepper in a large bowl. Arrange about one third the potatoes in overlapping layers in the ring. Sprinkle with ½ cup cheese. Top with half the remaining potatoes and all the remaining cheese. Top with remaining potatoes. Bake 1 hour to 1 hour 10 minutes until top is golden brown and crisp. Let cool. To serve, run a thin knife around edge of potatoes. Remove pan sides. Slide a spatula underneath potatoes to loosen. Lift with 2 spatulas to serving plate. Let cool to room temperature. Yield: 6 servings, 316 calories.

JO'S SCALLOPED POTATOES   *Leah Mauck*

This recipe is from my neighbor friend, Jo Crone, who said she didn't have anything "special" to enter – so I am entering it for her! Believe me, it is great!

5   medium size potatoes   *Sauce*
¼   cup green onions, chopped   2   tablespoons butter
¼   cup bell pepper, chopped   2   tablespoons flour
½   (2-ounce) jar pimiento strips   2   cups milk
Jalapeño chopped, if desired   1   teaspoon salt
¼   teaspoon pepper
½   cup sharp Cheddar cheese

Peel potatoes and slice thin. Place half potatoes in greased 1½ quart casserole. Cover with ½ of onions, ½ bell pepper, ½ pimiento and jalapeños if desired. Repeat layer of potatoes and vegetables. *Cheese sauce:* Melt butter in saucepan; add flour and stir in milk, salt and pepper. Continue to stir until thickened; add cheese, stirring until cheese melts. Cover potatoes with cheese sauce. Cover and bake at 350 degrees about 45 minutes. Uncover and cook until brown. Yield: 6–8 servings.

SWEET POTATO BALLS SURPRISE

Cynthia Smith

I use Louisiana yams, they are sweeter.

2½ cups cooked <u>or</u> canned
  sweet potatoes <u>or</u> yams
¾ teaspoon salt
2 tablespoons brown sugar
Dash pepper
4 tablespoons margarine,
  melted, divided

½ cup miniature
  marshmallows
½ cup honey
1 cup pecans <u>or</u>
  walnuts, chopped

Mash sweet potatoes; add salt, sugar, pepper and 2 tablespoons margarine. Stir in marshmallows and chill. Shape into balls using ¼ cup mixture for each ball. In small heavy skillet combine 2 tablespoons melted margarine with honey, stir. Add the potato balls and roll around to coat well. Then roll balls in nuts, coat well. Place in a greased shallow pan and drizzle with any leftover honey/margarine mixture. Bake at 350 degrees for 15 to 20 minutes. Yield: 10 servings.

TRISH'S SWEET POTATOES

Patricia Bushnell

½ cup margarine
1 (20-ounce) can pineapple
  chunks with juice
6 cups brown sugar

1½ teaspoons ground cloves
7 to 8 large yams <u>or</u> sweet
  potatoes, peeled and cut
  in ½-inch slices

In medium saucepan over medium heat, melt margarine; add pineapple with juice. Gradually add brown sugar and cloves. Cook until sugar is dissolved. Place potatoes in a small roaster or Dutch oven; pour pineapple mixture over potatoes. Bake, uncovered, in a 375 degree oven for 1 hour or until tender. Yield: 20 servings.

ALINE'S RICE CASSEROLE

Aline Slack

1 small onion, chopped
1 (2-ounce) can mushrooms
2 cups raw rice

2 heaping teaspoons oregano
¼ cup margarine
3 cans beef consommé

Simmer first 4 ingredients in margarine for 20 minutes. Add consommé, cooking slowly until liquid is absorbed. Yield: 8 or more servings.

CECILIA'S HERBED RICE

Beverly K. Voron

When we first visited Bill's brother, Dan, in Tempe, Arizona, Cecilia served this wonderful vegetarian dish. I often serve it like this (although I don't usually have the kelp) but, it is also wonderful with ham cut up in small pieces and added to the rice and herbs.

3 or 4 green bell peppers
Water
1 cup long grain white rice, cook as directed on box
4 small carrots, chopped
2 medium onions, finely chopped
2 teaspoons dried parsley
½ teaspoon salt

½ teaspoon each of basil, oregano, paprika
⅛ teaspoon each of marjoram, thyme, kelp
2 tablespoons sesame seeds or chopped sunflower seeds
Several dashes cayenne pepper
2 tablespoons oil

Clean and hollow out peppers. Bake in 350 degree oven in a small amount of water for about 30 minutes; or microwave for 10 minutes. Sauté onions, carrots, salt and herbs in oil until tender. Add cooked rice and cayenne pepper. Stir. Fill pepper shells and serve. Yield: 3 or 4 servings.

FRENCH RICE RICHTER

Tish Richter

You wouldn't think a German named Richter could teach someone named Robichaux how to cook French rice but here it is. C'est bon!

1 can beef bouillon
1 can French onion soup
1 (2-ounce) jar mushrooms, sliced

¼ cup margarine, melted
1 cup long grain white rice, raw

Stir together all ingredients; place in 1½-quart oven proof dish and bake at 350 for 45 minutes, uncovered. Yield: 6-8 servings.

GENEVA'S RICE CASSEROLE

Geneva Eubanks

1 cup raw rice, long cooking
2 cans beef bouillon
1 small onion, diced
¼ teaspoon garlic salt

1 teaspoon Worcestershire sauce
¼ pound bacon, fried crisp and crumbled
2 tablespoons bacon grease

Combine all in a 1½ quart pyrex bowl and cook uncovered in 350 degree oven for 45 minutes. Yield: 4 to 6 servings.

LEMON RICE
Jewell Scott

2½ cups defatted chicken broth	2 tablespoons fresh dill, chopped
½ teaspoon salt	2 tablespoons butter or margarine
1 large clove garlic, bruised	Pepper to taste
1 cup long grain white rice	
1 tablespoon lemon peel, grated	

Bring broth, salt and garlic to boil. Add rice, return to boil; lower heat, cover, and cook 20 minutes. Take off heat, remove garlic clove, add lemon peel. Let set 5 minutes, covered. Add dill, butter and pepper. Water should be completely absorbed, if not, cook a little longer before adding dill and butter. Yield: 4-6 servings.

SPINACH LOAF
Leah Mauck

2 cups cooked spinach, chopped	2 tablespoons bacon drippings
2 eggs, well beaten	1 cup crushed saltine crackers
¾ cup Cheddar cheese, grated	1 tablespoon vinegar

Combine in order given. Place in greased 8 x 4 loaf pan. Bake at 350 degrees for 30 minutes. Yield: 6 servings.

SQUASH APPLE BAKE
Geneva Eubanks

1 large or 2 small butternut squash	½ cup brown sugar
2 baking apples	1 tablespoon flour
¼ cup margarine, melted	1 teaspoon salt

Cut squash in half lengthwise and remove seeds and pulp. Pare skin with vegetable peeler. Cut into ½-inch slices and put in ungreased baking dish. Core, peel and slice apples and layer over squash. Mix remaining ingredients and drizzle over squash/apples. Cover and bake at 350 degrees for 50-60 minutes or bake in microwave 20 minutes on HIGH or until tender. This is good served with pork chops or ham. Yield: 4-6 servings.

SUMMER SQUASH WITH RAISINS AND NUTS *Jewell Scott*

2	tablespoons oil	1	teaspoon allspice <u>or</u> nutmeg
3	onions, chopped		
10	to 12 small yellow crookneck <u>or</u> pattypan squash, about 3 pounds, medium diced	½	teaspoon cinnamon
		1	tablespoon honey <u>or</u> molasses
½	cup raisins		
½	cup nuts, almonds <u>or</u> pecans, chopped or slivered		

In a medium frying pan sauté the onions in oil until transparent. Add squash and sauté another couple of minutes. Lower heat, add raisins, nuts, spices, and honey or molasses. Sauté another minute or so to blend. Simmer 3-5 minutes. Yield: 6 servings.

STUFFED YELLOW SQUASH *Angelia Stearns*

I used this recipe when we had a garden with lots of fresh yellow squash. My children love it. When we moved and yellow squash couldn't be found in winter, I bought frozen yellow squash and layered it with the spinach mixture and it was wonderful, too!

4	medium yellow squash, peeled	1½	cups cooked rice
		⅓	cup Parmesan cheese, grated, divided
⅛	teaspoon salt		
1	(12-ounce) package frozen Stouffer's Spinach Souffle, thawed		

Boil whole squash for 4 minutes. Remove from water and allow to cool. Halve squash lengthwise and scoop pulp from squash. Chop pulp. Arrange squash shells in lightly greased baking dish and sprinkle with salt. Combine spinach, rice, squash pulp and half of the Parmesan cheese. Mix well and fill squash shells. Sprinkle remaining cheese on squash and bake at 350 degrees for 30 minutes. Yield: 8 servings.

HINT:

Any vegetable that grows under the ground start off in cold water, beets, carrots, potatoes, etc. Anything that grows above ground, start off in boiling water, beans, broccoli, greens, etc.

VEGETABLE PILAF
Holly Lawson

This is very good and very filling. If you have a bread machine that cooks rice this can be made in it.

4	tablespoons margarine	1½	cups regular long-grain rice
1	pound red potatoes cut in ½-inch cubes	1	(19-ounce) can red kidney beans, drained
3	green onions, cut into 1-inch pieces	1	cup frozen peas
2	medium carrots, diced	¼	cup Parmesan cheese, grated
3	cups water	½	cup Mozzarella cheese, shredded
½	teaspoon salt		
⅛	teaspoon pepper		
2	chicken-flavor bouillon cubes		

In 12-inch skillet over medium-high heat, place margarine to heat, then cook potato cubes, green onions and carrots stirring frequently until lightly browned, about 5 minutes. Add water, salt, pepper, and bouillon; heat to boiling over high heat. Add rice; return to boiling. Reduce heat to low, cover and simmer 20 minutes or until rice and vegetables are tender and all liquid is absorbed. Into rice mixture, stir beans, peas and cheeses; cook, stirring gently, until beans and peas are heated and cheese melts. Yield: 8 servings.

VEGGIE CASSEROLE
Leah Mauck

This recipe is from my sister, Elaine Mays. Great to take to reunions and potluck suppers or to serve with an oven baked brisket.

1	can cream of celery or cream of mushroom soup	½	cup green pepper, diced
½	cup sour cream	½	cup celery, diced
½	cup sharp Cheddar cheese, grated	½	cup onion, diced
		¼	teaspoon salt
1	(16-ounce) can French style green beans, drained	¼	teaspoon pepper
		1	cup Cheese Nips crackers, crushed
1	(16-ounce) can whole kernel corn, drained	½	cup butter or margarine, melted

Combine soup, cheese and sour cream, add vegetables. Pour into a 13 x 9 x 2-inch casserole. Mix crushed crackers with butter. Sprinkle on top. Bake 350 degrees for 30-35 minutes or until casserole is bubbly and crackers are lightly browned. Do not over cook! Yield: 8 servings.

Variation: VEGETABLE BEAN CASSEROLE   *Norma Honeycutt*

Mix 3 (16-ounce) cans green beans, drained; 1 (16-ounce) can whole kernel corn, drained; 1 small onion, chopped; 1 bell pepper, chopped; 2 tablespoonfuls pimientos, chopped; 1 can cream of mushroom soup; with 1 (8-ounce) carton sour cream. Pour into a 13 x 9 x 2-inch greased casserole. Melt ½ cup margarine and mix with ½ box Cheese Nip crackers, crushed. Sprinkle on top of casserole. Bake at 350 degrees for 35 minutes or until it bubbles good. Yield: 8 to 10 servings.

VEGGIE MEDLEY   *Aline Slack*

1   **bunch broccoli, cut leaving**   ½   **cup fresh**
    1-inch stem   **mushrooms, sliced**
1   **small head cauliflower, broken**   ¼   **cup butter or**
1   **medium zucchini, cut in**   **margarine, melted**
    ¼-inch slices   **Seasoned salt**
1   **medium green pepper,**   **Lemon pepper**
    ¼-inch strips

Place veggies in 9-10-inch round dish in circular fashion. Pour butter over veggies and sprinkle with seasoned salt and lemon pepper. Cover with plastic wrap and microwave on HIGH for 5 minutes or until crisp tender. **Variations:** Use yellow squash or combination of both; use ½ teaspoon garlic salt instead of seasoned salt; sprinkle with Parmesan cheese after cooking; may add quartered tomatoes after cooking. Yield: 6 servings or more.

MIXED VEGETABLE CASSEROLE   *Ethel Cone*

1   **(20-ounce) package frozen**   1   **cup mayonnaise**
    mixed vegetables   1   **medium onion, chopped**
1   **cup celery, chopped**   34   **Ritz crackers, crumbled**
1   **cup Cheddar cheese, grated**

Preheat oven to 350 degrees. Cook vegetables and celery until tender; drain. Place in 2-quart greased casserole. Combine cheese, mayonnaise and onion; mix thoroughly and spread over vegetables. Top with cracker crumbs. Bake for 30 minutes. Sometimes I do not precook vegetables and then they are crunchy. Yield: 8 servings.

94

VEGETABLE MEDLEY

Lee Caruthers

2 tablespoons vegetable oil, divided
1 medium potato, peeled and sliced
1 zucchini, scrubbed and sliced
1 medium onion, sliced
1 yellow squash, sliced

¼ small green cabbage, cut in wedges
1 large tomato, peeled and sliced
Salt and pepper to taste
¼ teaspoon basil
¼ teaspoon Mrs. Dash
½ cup water

Put about a teaspoon of oil in bottom of heavy saucepan with lid. Layer potato, zucchini, onion, squash, cabbage and tomato. Sprinkle each layer with little salt, pepper, seasonings and oil as you go. Add water, cover and cook on low heat until potato is done, about 30 to 40 minutes. Yield: 4-6 servings.

QUICK AND EASY ZUCCHINI CASSEROLE

Sheryl Kusy

When the first "Potluck on the Pedernales" was published, my Grandma Gipson gave me one for Christmas when I was thirteen years old. I have really enjoyed reading it and trying the recipes. Then I found out there was going to be a "Second Helping" and I could send in my favorite recipe. This is one I like very much given to me by my Grandma Shirley Hammack of Leander, Texas.

1 small onion, chopped
1 tablespoon oil
14 to 15 small zucchini squash
1 (14-ounce) jar Ragu spaghetti sauce

½ cup Mozzarella cheese, grated

Sauté onion in oil. Dice or slice zucchini and spread in 13 x 9 x 2-inch baking dish. Sprinkle onion over zucchini. Pour entire jar of spaghetti sauce over dish. Bake at 350 degrees for 30-40 minutes or until tender. Sprinkle cheese over casserole and place back in oven until cheese is melted. Cool 5 to 10 minutes. Serve and enjoy. Yield: 8 servings.

HINT:
Vegetables that grow under ground should be cooked covered and those grown on top of ground uncovered.

BAKED FRUIT
Dolores Fasel Bozeman

This recipe was the outstanding dish served at a Tasty-Luncheon many years ago in Louisiana. I added cherries to the original recipe. It has become a tradition that I serve it with our Christmas eve dinner. However it is great at any time of the year.

1 (16-ounce) can sliced peaches, drained
1 (16-ounce) can apricot halves, drained
1 (16-ounce) can pear halves, sliced and drained
1 (15¼-ounce) can pineapple chunks or tidbits, drained
1 (11-ounce) can Mandarin oranges, drained

1 (10-ounce) jar Maraschino cherries, drained
Lemon juice
Almond extract
2 cups Rice Chex, crushed
2 tablespoons brown sugar
¼ cup melted margarine
¼ teaspoon nutmeg
Dash of salt

Arrange fruits in 13 x 9 x 2-inch baking dish. Sprinkle with lemon juice and almond extract. Mix Rice Chex, sugar, margarine, nutmeg and salt. Sprinkle over fruit. Bake at 350 degrees for 30 minutes. Yield: 10-12 servings.

FRUIT BAKE
Gail Rucker

⅓ cup butter or margarine, melted
¾ cup brown sugar
4 teaspoons cinnamon
5 Maraschino cherries
1 (16-ounce) can pear halves, drained

1 (16-ounce) can peaches or apricot halves, drained
1 (15¼-ounce) can pineapple chunks, drained

Mix margarine, sugar and cinnamon. Layer fruit in 1½-quart casserole. Top with cherries and sugar mixture. Bake 1 hour uncovered at 325 degrees. Especially good served with baked ham. Yield: 6 to 8 servings.

HINTS:

Cooked dried fruits or fig preserves make a substitute for dates.

Baked apples keep their shape and look more attractive when cooked in a well-greased muffin tin.

HOT FRUIT
Sadie Sharp

Always looks impressive in a chafing dish.

2 (15½-ounce) cans mixed fruits	¼ cup butter **or** margarine
	½ cup brown sugar

Drain fruit and reserve juice. Melt butter and mix with sugar. Add fruit and enough juice to just cover. Simmer about an hour, adding juice when needed to keep it juicy but not watery. Yield: 6 to 8 servings.

SCALLOPED PINEAPPLE
Geneva Eubanks

1 (20-ounce) can unsweetened crushed pineapple	2 eggs, beaten until frothy
¾ cup sugar	¼ cup water, scant
2 tablespoons cornstarch	Cinnamon

Mix all ingredients and pour into buttered 1-quart casserole dish. Sprinkle cinnamon on top. Bake 1 hour at 350 degrees. Let cool slightly (watery when hot). Yield: 6-8 servings.

HINTS:

To freeze mushrooms, wash and dry quickly. Freeze in plastic bag. Do not thaw to use.

To remove the corn silks from corn on the cob, dampen a clean tooth-brush and brush downward on the cob to remove all strands.

Always cook okra quickly, as overcooking will result in a gummy texture.

1 pound of fresh okra pods yields about 2 cups sliced.

Sand and dirt can be removed from fresh vegetables by soaking in warm salted water 5 minutes.

To peel tomatoes; dip tomatoes into boiling water for 1 minute; then plunge them into cold water. The skin will slip off easily.

If you have an abundance of squash, try steaming, mashing and freezing any extra squash. Use it all year in recipes that call for pumpkin, like breads, cakes and pies.

Something From the Oven
Breads, Eggs, Cheese

GRIST MILL AND COTTON GIN

Soon after the origination of the town of Johnson City in 1879, James Polk Johnson built a steam powered cotton gin and grist mill on Town Creek. Principal crops in this area were corn and cotton. The corn ground at this mill was used to make the pioneer settlers favorite bread. In the early 1940s the gin was purchased by George Crofts and converted to a milling and grain operation which flourished until the late 1970s.

98

⇩ ⇩ ⇩ ⇩ ⇩ ⇩ ⇩

AUTUMN APPLE CAKES
Leslie Matus

This is a delicious treat that first-graders love! Also good served as pancakes.

2 apples, unpeeled, grated or	1 cup milk
1 cup chunky applesauce	1 teaspoon cinnamon
2 cups pancake mix	¾ cup brown sugar
2 eggs	½ cup vegetable oil

Mix all the ingredients except the oil. Mix until smooth. (Children love to help with the mixing process). Heat an electric skillet to about 325 degrees. Coat the cooking surface with about 1 teaspoonful of oil. Drop two tablespoonfuls of batter for each cake into the skillet. Fry two minutes on each side, or until golden brown. Recoat the cooking surface with oil and make the next batch. Drain thoroughly on paper towels. They should be eaten while warm. Yield: about 25.

SOUTHERN SALAD BISCUIT MUFFINS
Jewell Sultemeier

These delicious mini-muffins were served with salad at Castle Hill. My family says they are delicious just with butter.

2 cups flour	1 teaspoon salt
½ cup sugar	¼ cup margarine, cubed
1 tablespoon baking powder	¾ cup cold milk

Preheat oven to 350 degrees. Grease small size muffin pans and set aside. In a bowl combine flour, sugar, baking powder and salt. Mix well. Work the margarine into flour, mixing by hand until mixture resembles coarse cornmeal. Add milk to flour mixture stirring until just mixed. Drop spoonfuls of mixture into prepared muffin pans. Bake 10 to 15 minutes or until just browned. Yield: 24 muffins.

WHOLE WHEAT BISCUITS
Patsy Holloway

These good biscuits are lower in calories and fat.

1½ cups flour	3 tablespoons reduced
½ cup whole wheat flour	calorie margarine
1 tablespoon baking powder	¾ cup evaporated skim milk
½ teaspoon salt	Vegetable cooking spray

Combine first four ingredients, cut in the margarine with a pastry blender

until mixture resembles coarse meal. Add milk, stirring until dry ingredients are moistened. Turn dough out onto floured surface, knead one minute. Shape dough into 12 balls, place in an 8-inch square pan coated with vegetable spray. Flatten slightly and bake at 450 degrees for 10-12 minutes. Yield 12 biscuits.

ONE LOAF WHITE BREAD
Ima Hobbs

This recipe works in a bread machine making a large loaf. It is hard to resist cutting and slapping some butter on when it comes out of the oven. Best sliced for sandwiches when it is completely cool.

1¼	cups water	2	tablespoons sugar
1	package dry yeast	2	teaspoons salt
2	tablespoons oil	3	cups flour

Place water and yeast in bowl. Stir to dissolve yeast. Add remaining ingredients, mix well. Let rise until double. Punch down; let it rest 10 minutes, then make into a loaf. Place in greased 9 x 5 x 3-inch pan and let it rise again. Bake 45-50 minutes at 375 degrees. Heat may vary in different ovens. Yield: 1 large loaf.

DISHPAN WHITE BREAD
Merl Saxon

1	package dry yeast	5	teaspoons salt
6	cups lukewarm water	2	cups sugar
5	pounds flour	2½	cups Crisco

Dissolve yeast in water. Put flour in large dishpan; add salt, sugar and shortening. Mix all well getting shortening well mixed into flour, use hands. Add water with yeast mixture, stir. Mix and knead together well until you give out. Allow this to rise overnight. (I usually do this about 6:30 in the evening and next morning punch it down and knead it). Grease six bread pans, 9 x 5 x 3-inch, divide dough in six parts and shape into loaves. Put in pans, cover and allow to rise until about 2 in the afternoon. Bake in 350 degree oven for 30 to 40 minutes. Yield: 6 loaves.

HINT:
To make good yeast breads, it is essential to learn the "feel" of the dough. This takes experience.

BUTTERMILK BREAD

Anna Lou Felps & Ima Hobbs

Half recipe to make in bread machine.

6 cups unsifted flour, divided
3 tablespoons sugar
½ to 2½ teaspoons salt
¼ teaspoon soda

1 package dry yeast or
  1 tablespoon
1 cup buttermilk
1 cup water
⅓ to ½ cup margarine

Combine 2 cups flour, sugar, salt, soda and yeast. Heat buttermilk, water and margarine over low heat until warm. (Mixture will appear curdled.) Add to dry ingredients; beat two minutes at medium speed scraping bowl occasionally. Add 1 cup flour and beat on high 2 minutes. Stir in enough flour to make soft dough. Turn onto floured board and knead 8-10 minutes. Place in greased bowl; cover and let rise until double about 1 to 1½ hours. Punch down, turn onto lightly floured surface and divide in half; cover and let rest 10 minutes. Shape into 2 loaves and place in greased 8½ x 4½ x 2½-inch loaf pans. Let rise again until double, about 30 to 60 minutes. Bake in 375 degree oven for 35 minutes or until done. Remove from pans and cool on rack. Yield: 2 loaves.

NO FAIL FRENCH BREAD

Joan Shafford

This recipe comes from Oklahoma. Really quite easy to make. Can make individual sandwich rolls, Hoagie or sub-rolls. Our family, friends and neighbors really enjoy this bread.

2 packages active dry yeast
½ cup warm water
2 cups hot water
3 tablespoons sugar
1 tablespoon salt

⅓ cup shortening, melted
6 cups flour, divided
1 egg white, beaten
Sesame seeds or poppy seeds,
  optional

Dissolve yeast in warm water. In large glass mixing bowl combine hot water, sugar, salt and shortening and allow to stand until lukewarm. Add dissolved yeast and 3 cups flour. Beat with wire whisk until smooth and well blended. Add remaining flour to make a soft dough that can still be mixed with a wooden spoon. Leave spoon in batter and allow dough to rest 10 minutes. Stir batter down, let rest 10 minutes again. Repeat this process for a total of 5 times. Turn dough out onto a floured board and knead only enough to coat dough with flour so it can be handled. Divide dough in half. Roll each half into a rectangle 9 x 12-inches. Roll up jellyroll

101

style. Arrange each length-wise on large greased cookie pan, allowing room for both loaves or use pans, one loaf to a pan. Brush tops with a beaten egg white, then sprinkle generously with seeds if desired. With a sharp knife, slice diagonally about 3 to 4 times across the loaf and cover and let rise until double in size, about 30 to 60 minutes. Bake at 400 degrees for 35 minutes or until done. This can be made with a heavy duty mixer following same directions. For softer crust, brush with butter after taking out of the oven. Yield: 2 loaves.

BRAN BREAD
Viola Hoppe

4 cups warm water
1 package dry yeast
2 teaspoons salt
1 tablespoon sugar

2 tablespoons molasses, optional
1 cup All Bran or Bran Buds
2 tablespoons Crisco
9 cups flour

Mix water, yeast, salt, sugar and bran. Set aside until bran softens; then add Crisco and flour. Knead well on floured board. Let rise to double; punch down, let rise again. Make into 3 loaves and place in greased loaf pans. Let rise again. Bake at 350 degrees for 25 minutes or until loaf sounds hollow when tapped. Yield: 3 loaves.

HONEY WHOLE WHEAT BREAD
Ima Hobbs

2 packages dry yeast
1½ cups warm water
⅓ cup honey
¼ cup shortening
1 tablespoon salt

1¾ cups warm water
3 cups whole wheat flour
3 to 4 cups all purpose flour
Margarine or butter

Dissolve yeast in 1½ cups warm water in large mixing bowl. Stir in honey, shortening, salt and 1¾ cups water. Add whole wheat flour, beat until smooth. Mix in enough all purpose flour to make dough easy to handle. Place dough on lightly floured surface and knead until smooth and elastic, about 10 minutes. Place in greased bowl, turn greased side up. Cover and let rise in warm place about 1 hour. Dough is ready if indentions remain when touched. Punch down. Divide in half and form into 2 loaves. Place in greased 9 x 5 x 3-inch loaf pans, seam side down. Brush with margarine. Let rise until doubled. Bake 375 degrees until golden brown, about 40 to 45 minutes or when tapped there is a hollow sound. Remove from pans; cool on wire rack. Yield: 2 loaves.

BIT OF HONEY WHOLE WHEAT BREAD   *Ima Hobbs*

1	package active dry yeast	⅓	cup butter <u>or</u> margarine,
2½	cups warm water		softened
1	teaspoon salt	2½	cups all purpose flour
½	cup honey	2½	cups whole wheat flour
⅓	cup molasses	1½	cup medium rye flour

Grease 2 pans (9 x 5 x 3 or 8 x 4 x 3). In large bowl dissolve yeast in warm water, about 105 to 115 degrees. Lightly spoon flour into measuring cup, level off. Add salt, honey, molasses, margarine, 1½ cups flour, and whole wheat flour. Blend on low speed until moistened about 3 minutes. Stir in rye flour and ½ to 1 cup of all purpose flour. Stir until dough turns loose from sides of bowl. Turn out on lightly floured surface and knead until light and elastic, about 10 to 15 minutes. Place in greased bowl, cover loosely, let rise until light and doubled. Punch dough down several times to remove bubbles. Divide and shape into 2 loaves. Place in prepared pans, cover and let rise until doubled. Bake 35 to 45 minutes at 350 degrees. Remove from pan and cool on wire rack. Yield: 2 loaves.

EARLY COLONIAL BREAD   *Aline Slack*

½	cup yellow cornmeal	½	cup lukewarm water
⅓	cup brown sugar	¾	cup stirred whole wheat
1	tablespoon salt		flour
2	cups boiling water	½	cup stirred rye flour
¼	cup cooking oil	4¼ to 4½ cups sifted all
2	packages yeast		purpose flour

Combine first five ingredients. Cool to lukewarm, about 30 minutes. Soften yeast in water, add to meal mixture. Add first two flours (these flours pack so stir before measuring), mix well. Stir in last flour to make moderately stiff dough. Turn out on lightly floured surface and knead until smooth and elastic, 6 to 8 minutes. Place in greased bowl, turning once to grease surface. Cover and let rise until double, 50 to 60 minutes. Punch down, turn out on lightly floured surface and divide in half; cover and let rest 10 minutes. Shape into 2 loaves and place in greased 9 x 5 x 3-inch loaf pans. Let rise again until double; about 30 minutes. Bake in 375 degree oven for 45 minutes or until done. Top loaves with foil after 25 minutes if bread browns rapidly. Remove from pans and cool on rack: Yield: 2 loaves.

HEARTY OATS AND WHEAT LOAVES
Ima Hobbs

A wholesome bread for toast, sandwiches or dinner.

2 to 2½	cups all purpose flour, divided	½	cup margarine or butter
1	cup rolled oats	2	eggs, reserve 1 egg white
2	teaspoons salt	2	cups whole wheat flour
3	packages dry yeast	1	cup medium rye flour
1¾	cups water	1	tablespoon water
½	cup corn syrup	4	teaspoons sesame seeds, optional

Generously grease two 9 x 5 x 3 loaf pans. Lightly spoon flour into measuring cups, level off. In large bowl combine 1½ cups white flour, oats, salt and yeast. Blend well. In medium sauce pan heat water, corn syrup and margarine to 120 to 130 degrees. Add warm liquid to eggs and flour mixture. Blend at low speed until moistened about 3 minutes at medium speed. By hand stir in whole wheat flour and rye flour to form soft dough. Place on lightly floured board and knead in up to one cup all purpose flour until smooth and elastic, about 10 minutes. Place dough in greased pan or bowl, cover. Let rise until double, about 1 hour. Punch dough down. Divide into 2 balls. Allow to rest on counter covered with inverted bowl for 15 minutes. Shape into 2 loaves and place in the prepared pans. Cover, let rise in warm place until doubled, about 1 hour. Combine water and egg white. Brush on loaves, sprinkle with sesame seeds, if desired. Yield: 2 loaves.

HOLLYWOOD ROLLS
Joan Shafford

I've had many compliments on these rolls.

1	package dry yeast	½	cup shortening
¼	cup warm water	1	egg
1	teaspoon sugar	1	cup warm water
¼ to ⅓	cup sugar	4	cups flour
1	teaspoon salt		Butter, melted

Dissolve yeast in water and 1 teaspoon sugar. Put ¼ to ⅓ cup sugar, salt, shortening and egg in large bowl and cream well. Add yeast mixture, 1 cup water and flour. Mix well. Dough will be sticky. Put in greased bowl and let stand covered until double in size. Shape dough into rolls and place on a greased baking pan. Cover and let rise until double in size. Bake at 350 degrees for 15 minutes or until golden brown. Brush with melted butter. Yield: 20 to 24 rolls.

✧ ✧ ✧ ✧ ✧ ✧ ✧

JAN'S POTATO ROLLS

Elizabeth Sublett

This recipe was given to me by a good friend, Jan Vick. She is the wife of Pastor Vick, former pastor of Stonewall Trinity Lutheran Church. They are very good rolls.

1 cup boiling water	2 eggs, beaten
¾ cup shortening	1 package dry yeast
¼ to ½ cup sugar	¼ cup warm water
1 cup mashed potatoes	2 teaspoons salt
½ cup potato water	6 cups flour

Pour boiling water over shortening and sugar. When shortening is melted, add potatoes and potato water. When lukewarm add eggs and yeast that has been dissolved in ¼ cup water. Add salt and flour, mix well. Add flour until it doesn't stick to the hands. Let rise in warm place, usually 2 hours. Knead down and let rise again. Make into rolls. Bake at 375 degrees until light brown, about 15 to 20 minutes. Yield: 3 to 4 dozen.

QUICK AND EASY REFRIGERATOR ROLLS

Mary Dyer

This is the only recipe I use to make rolls because it does not require all the kneading, punching down and resting procedures that most recipes call for. May also be used to make bread, makes two small loaves.

½ cup sugar	1 package dry yeast
1¼ teaspoons salt	1 cup lukewarm water
¾ cup Crisco	6 cups flour
1 cup boiling water	¼ cup margarine, melted
2 eggs, well beaten	

Mix sugar, salt and Crisco in large bowl, pour boiling water over mixture, stir well and cool to lukewarm. Add eggs. Set aside. Sprinkle yeast over lukewarm water; let stand 5 minutes. Stir well and add to sugar mixture. Add flour gradually, mixing well after each addition. (Wooden spoon works well to stir this with.) When well mixed, cover with foil, refrigerate at least 2 hours, or overnight, if desired. Roll to ½ inch thickness, cut out and place in oiled baking pan. Brush with margarine and let rise in a warm place until doubled in size, about 2 hours. Bake in preheated 400 degree oven for 15 minutes or until lightly browned. Yield: 12 large rolls.

REFRIGERATED ROLLS

Oma Deike

Oma Deike was a wonderful cook in her day. She made delicious breads and doughnuts. She is now in a nursing home in Fredericksburg. She was a faithful member of the Pleasant Hill Home Extension Club. This recipe was submitted by Jewell Sultemeier.

2 packages dry yeast	2 eggs, well beaten
2½ cups warm water	8 to 8½ cups flour, divided
¾ cup shortening, melted	2½ teaspoons salt
¾ cup sugar	

Soften yeast in warm water, add shortening, sugar, eggs, 4 cups flour and salt. Stir and beat 1 minute. Stir in remaining flour, work in last 3 cups by hand. Cover tightly until needed in refrigerator overnight or when ready to use. Punch dough down, pinch off ⅓, cover and return remaining to refrigerator. Shape into rolls and place in a greased baking pan. Cover and let rise in a warm place until double in bulk. Bake 400 degrees for 15 to 20 minutes. Yield: 12 to 18 rolls for ⅓ of dough.

Pecan Coffee Ring

Glaze

½ cup butter	1 cup powdered sugar
⅔ cup brown sugar	¼ teaspoon vanilla <u>or</u> maple
1 tablespoon corn syrup	flavor
¾ cup pecans, finely chopped	1 tablespoon water

In a saucepan combine butter, brown sugar and corn syrup and cook over low heat until sugar dissolves. Set aside. On a well floured board, roll ⅓ dough to ¼-inch thick oblong. Spread sugar mixture evenly over dough; sprinkle with pecans. Roll up, jellyroll fashion, and seal edges. Shape in ring on cooking sheet. Place a greased custard cup in center of dough. With a sharp knife slash every 2 inches. Bake at 350 degrees for 30 minutes. For glaze: mix sugar, vanilla and water together and spread on ring while warm. Yield: 1 ring.

BASIC SWEET DOUGH

Joan Shafford

I've used this recipe for over twenty-five years. I found it in a recipe book compiled by the Altar Society of St. Francis Xavier Catholic Church of Enid, Oklahoma, in 1963. May be used for cinnamon rolls, kolaches, dinner rolls or frosted sweet rolls.

1	package dry yeast	½	cup sugar
½	cup warm water	1	tablespoon salt
2	cups milk	½	cup margarine
8	cups flour	2	eggs, slightly beaten

Soften yeast in warm water. Scald milk and cool to lukewarm. Mix flour, sugar, salt and margarine until consistency of coarse meal. Add milk, yeast mixture and eggs. Stir and knead until mixed to a soft dough. Place in greased bowl, let rise in a warm place until double in bulk, about 1½ to 2 hours. Punch down and let rise again until double in bulk, about 1 hour. Form into rolls. Let rise in warm place. Bake 375 for 10 to 15 minutes or until golden brown. Yield: 16 to 36 rolls depending on thickness.

CINNAMON ROLLS

Joan Shafford

Basic sweet dough, recipe above

1½	cups brown sugar, packed	1	cup raisins, optional
½	cup flour		*Glaze*
2	tablespoons ground cinnamon	1½	cups powdered sugar
1	cup butter <u>or</u> margarine	3 to 4	tablespoons milk
1	cup pecans, chopped, optional	½	teaspoon vanilla

Make basic sweet dough recipe above. Instead of making rolls; divide dough into two parts. Working with one portion at a time, place dough on lightly floured surface; roll dough in a rectangle, about 14 x 9-inches. Combine sugar, flour and cinnamon; cut butter or margarine in until mixture is crumbly. Spread ½ filling on dough; sprinkle with ½ of the pecans and raisins, if desired. Roll dough jellyroll fashion, starting at long side. Pinch seam to seal but do not seal ends. Cut roll into 14 1-inch slices. Place in greased 13 x 9 x 2 pan or in two 8-inch round cake pans. Repeat process with remaining dough. Cover and let rise in a warm place, free of drafts, 40 minutes or until rolls are doubled in bulk. Bake at 350 degrees for 20 to 25 minutes or until golden brown. Cool on wire rack. Powdered sugar glaze may be used if desired. Combine all ingredients; mix well and drizzle over rolls while warm. Yield: about 28 rolls.

DILL ROLLS

Cynthia Smith

These are similar to the rolls that were served at a restaurant in Fredericksburg, Texas, some years ago. They are delicious served with a big bowl of cheese soup.

1¼	cups wheat flour	2	tablespoons margarine
1¼	cups white flour	1	cup drained small curd
2	tablespoons sugar		cottage cheese
½	teaspoon salt	½	cup warm water
1	tablespoon onion, minced	2	packages active dry yeast
1	tablespoon dill weed <u>or</u>	1	egg, beaten
	seed		Margarine

Grease 2-inch muffin pans. Blend first 8 ingredients with a fork. Mix water and yeast in small bowl, let stand a few minutes. Mix in egg. Add the yeast mix to the flour mix. Beat thoroughly, cover and let rise until doubled in bulk. Beat dough down. Fill muffin cup half full, tap pans on counter to settle dough. Let rise until batter reaches the top of the cup. (I like to fill my cups ⅔ full and let the rolls rise over the cups, making gigantic rolls.) Bake at 350 degrees for 20 to 30 minutes. Yield: 12 rolls.

LILLIAN'S LUSCIOUS CORNBREAD   *Lillian Stewart*

I've made cornbread all my life, but this is the best I've ever made. It's very moist.

1	cup yellow cornmeal	1	cup sour cream
½	cup flour	2	eggs
½	teaspoon salt	½	cup milk
½	teaspoon soda	½	cup vegetable oil
1	tablespoon baking powder		

Combine dry ingredients. Blend together remaining ingredients and fold into dry mixture just until mixed. Do not over mix. Pour into greased muffin tins and bake at 400 degrees for 10 to 15 minutes. Yield: 12 muffins.

SAUSAGE CORNBREAD   *Euphenia Slack*

My son John says "A meal of pinto beans and sausage cornbread is the way to go!"

½	pound ground sausage	½	cup green pepper,
1	(6½-ounce) cornbread mix		chopped, optional
½	cup onion, chopped, optional		

Sauté sausage in an 8 or 9-inch iron skillet. Drain. Mix cornbread mix according to directions on package. Add sausage and blend. Add onion and green peppers if desired. Return to skillet and bake at 425 degrees for 20 to 25 minutes. Yield: 4 servings.

BEER HUSH PUPPIES *Thelma Ulrich*

The beer makes them light and fluffy.

Vegetable oil for frying	3 teaspoons baking powder
1½ cups yellow cornmeal	½ can beer, about ¾ cup
½ cup flour	1 small onion, grated
1 teaspoon salt	¼ cup jalapeños, chopped,
1 tablespoon sugar	optional

Start oil for deep frying. Mix meal, flour, salt and sugar. Add baking powder and pour beer directly on it. Stir, then add onion and jalapeños, if desired. Drop from a heaping teaspoon into hot oil, frying until brown. Puppies will turn over when touched, if done. Do not drop too many at one time. Yield: 3 to 4 dozen.

HUSH PUPPIES *Shirley Rosson*

This recipe was given to me by Maurine Adam.

1 cup flour	⅓ cup onion, chopped
1 cup cornmeal	Milk
4 tablespoons baking powder	Vegetable shortening for
½ teaspoon salt	deep frying
⅓ cup sugar	

Mix dry ingredients and onions together. Add enough milk to make mixture stiff enough to drop from a teaspoon into hot grease. (Crisco gives me best results.) Cook until brown and drain on paper towel. Yield: About 2 dozen.

CARROT PINEAPPLE BRAN MUFFINS *Cynthia Smith*

I made these heart healthy muffins for some Home Economists who stayed in my guest house. I also made some 'box' cookies for the cookie jar. They raved over the ordinary cookies, but didn't say much about the healthy muffins. I would suppose good takes precedence over healthy some time. They are good, though not too sweet. Only 92 calories and no fat! I serve these at my Bed and Breakfast/guest house.

109

1½ cups all purpose flour
1 teaspoon baking powder
½ teaspoon baking soda
½ teaspoon cinnamon
¼ teaspoon nutmeg
½ cup All Bran cereal
½ cup skim milk
1 egg white <u>or</u> egg substitute, beaten

2 teaspoons vanilla
4 tablespoons brown sugar
1 cup peeled carrots, shredded fine
1 cup crushed pineapple, undrained

Preheat oven to 400 degrees and spray 12 muffin cups with no stick vegetable spray or line cups with paper liners. In a large bowl whisk together flour, baking powder, baking soda, cinnamon and nutmeg. Set aside. To the cereal add milk, egg white, vanilla, brown sugar, carrots and pineapples and mix well. Pour into the dry ingredients and stir until moistened so that there is no dry flour left. Do not over beat. Batter will be lumpy. Spoon batter into prepared tins, fill to just under the top. Bake 400 degrees for 15-20 minutes until tops are rounded and golden brown. Toothpick inserted should come out clean. Remove from pan and cool on wire racks. Yield: 12 muffins.

CRUNCHY OAT & CRANBERRY MUFFINS *Genevia Bushnell*

¾ cup unsifted flour
¾ cup unsifted whole-wheat flour
1 cup oatmeal
½ cup light brown sugar
1 tablespoon baking powder
½ teaspoon salt

1 teaspoon ground cinnamon
1 cup fresh <u>or</u> frozen cranberries
¼ cup butter
1 cup milk
1 large egg

Preheat oven to 425 degrees. Grease 12 muffin cups. In a bowl combine dry ingredients and blend well. Toss the cranberries with 1 tablespoonful of dry ingredients and set aside. Melt butter. Remove from heat; stir in milk and egg. Stir butter mixture into dry ingredients and when well mixed, stir in cranberries. Spoon into muffin cups and bake until lightly browned for 15 to 20 minutes. Let stand 5 minutes before removing from tin. In place of cranberries ½ cup raisins and ½ cup nuts may be used. Yield: 12 muffins.

HINT:

To make lighter muffins, put greased pans in oven for a few minutes before adding batter.

SWEET POTATO MUFFINS

Lee Caruthers

2	cups sweet potatoes	1	teaspoon salt
½	cup butter	2	teaspoons cinnamon
½	cup shortening	3	teaspoons nutmeg
2	cups sugar	⅔	cup cold strong coffee
4	eggs	1	cup walnuts or pecans,
3½	cups flour		chopped
2	teaspoons baking soda		

Bake sweet potatoes until tender. Cool, peel, mash and set aside. Cream butter, shortening and sugar. Add eggs one at a time. Blend in potatoes. Sift flour, baking soda, salt with spices and add to creamed mixture alternately with coffee. Add nuts. Pour into 30 greased muffin tins. Bake at 375 degrees for about 25 minutes. Cool 10 minutes. Muffins freeze well. Yield: 30 muffins.

HEALTHY ZUCCHINI MUFFINS

Genevia Bushnell

124 calories per muffin, 0 cholesterol, 1 gram dietary fiber, 1.5 grams fat, 124 milligrams sodium. Will satisfy anyone's sweet tooth.

1	cup whole wheat flour	2	egg whites
1	cup all purpose flour	1	cup skim milk
4	teaspoons baking powder	2	tablespoons butter or
½	teaspoon salt		margarine, melted
1	cup sugar	1	cup zucchini, grated

Stir dry ingredients together. Beat the egg whites just until foamy. Add to it the milk and butter. Add the liquid ingredients and the zucchini to the dry ingredients, stirring just enough to moisten. Spray muffin tins with cooking spray or line cups with paper liners. Fill each of the 16 cups ¾ full. Bake 375 degrees for 15 to 20 minutes. Yield: 16 muffins.

HINT:

Most bread recipes state "about" followed by the number of cups of flour. Some flours absorb more liquid than others, it is difficult to give exact measurements for that reason. Too much flour results in a heavy loaf, is crumbly, and is dry with an off-flavor. Keep the dough on the soft side, but still easy to handle.

111

LEMON BREAD
Cynthia Smith

After trying out many recipes that freeze well and still taste wonderful for my Bed and Breakfast, I have settled on this to serve.

⅓	cup margarine, melted		Rind of one lemon, grated
1	cup sugar	½	cup almonds, walnuts,
2	eggs, beaten		or pecans, ground
1½	cups flour, sifted	½	cup milk
1	teaspoon baking powder		*Glaze*
1	teaspoon salt	½	cup powdered sugar
2	teaspoons lemon extract	½	teaspoon lemon extract
	Juice of one lemon (3 tablespoons)		Milk to thin

Mix margarine, sugar and eggs. Combine flour, baking powder and salt together, set aside. Stir lemon extract, juice, rind and nuts into milk. Add flour mixture and milk mixture alternately to egg mixture. Stir well. Pour into greased 9 x 5 x 3 loaf pan or two 7 x 4 x 2-inch or individual heart shaped pans. Fill pans ⅔ full for nice rounded loaves. Bake 350 degrees for 50 to 60 minutes for one loaf, 30 to 40 minutes for two loaves. Done when toothpick inserted in middle comes out clean. For glaze combine sugar and lemon extract with enough milk to thin. While hot, drizzle with glaze over top. Cool 10 minutes in pan before removing. Yield: 1 large loaf or 2 small loaves.

PEACH BREAD
Denise Luckenbach

Makes great muffins. It is very moist.

3	cups peaches, sliced	1	teaspoon cinnamon
6	tablespoons sugar	1½	cups sugar
2	cups flour	½	cup shortening
1	teaspoon baking powder	2	eggs
1	teaspoon soda	1	cup pecans, chopped
¼	teaspoon salt	1	teaspoon vanilla

Blend peaches and 6 tablespoons sugar in blender and puree. (Makes about 2¼ cups.) Combine flour, baking powder, soda, salt and cinnamon, set aside. Combine 1½ cups sugar and shortening; cream well. Add eggs and mix well. Add peaches and dry ingredients, mixing until moistened. Stir in nuts and vanilla. Spoon batter into 2 well greased and floured

112

9 x 5 x 3-inch loaf pans. (Very important to grease and flour pans.) Bake at 325 degrees for 40 to 50 minutes or until done. Cool 10 minutes in pan. Turn out on rack and cool completely. Freezes well. Yield: 2 large loaves.

APRICOT STRUDEL
Daisy Cox

2¼ cups flour	¾ cup coconut
1 cup sour cream	1 cup pecans, chopped
1 cup margarine	Powdered sugar for garnish
1 (16-ounce) jar apricot preserves	

Mix flour, sour cream and margarine well and refrigerate at least one hour. Divide dough in four equal parts. Roll each part into a 13-inch long by 8-inch wide piece. Use a little flour when rolling out on plastic wrap or wax paper; so you can flip it over as you turn it. Spread apricot preserves along the narrow side. Sprinkle with coconut and pecans. Roll up jelly roll fashion and seal ends. Place on ungreased cookie sheet and bake at 400 degrees for 30 minutes. Let cool and dust with powdered sugar, if desired. Slice diagonally. It is easy to double the recipe and prepare for freezer. Yield: 12 to 14 servings.

DANISH PASTRY
Beverly K. Voron

I always make these for breakfast at Community Church of the Hills after the Easter Sunrise Service. They were also a big seller when the church had the Granny Goose Bakery.

1 cup flour	**Glaze**
½ cup butter	4 tablespoons milk
2 tablespoons cold water	2 cups powdered sugar
1 cup water	2 tablespoons butter
½ cup butter	½ teaspoon almond flavoring
1 cup flour	Dash salt
1 teaspoon vanilla	½ cup pecans or almonds,
Dash salt	chopped
4 eggs	

Blend the flour and butter, add the water and stir with a fork. Use fingers to press into a ungreased jelly roll pan. Boil water and butter. Remove from heat and add flour, vanilla, and salt. Cool, then add eggs, beating well after each one. Spread on top of crust. Bake at 400 degrees for 20 minutes, reduce heat to 350 degrees and bake an additional 30 minutes.

Glaze: Mix all ingredients except nuts and spread over pastry as soon as it comes from the oven. Sprinkle with nuts. Yield: 15 or more servings.

APPLESAUCE COFFEE CAKE
Jewell Weirich

¼	cup shortening	1	teaspoon baking powder
½	cup sugar	¾	teaspoon baking soda
2	egg whites	¼	teaspoon salt
1	teaspoon vanilla	¼	teaspoon nutmeg
¾	cup dry high fiber oat bran cereal		*Filling and topping*
		1	cup chunky applesauce,
1	cup chunky applesauce		divided
1¼	cups flour	¼	cup sugar
1½	teaspoons cinnamon	¼	teaspoon cinnamon

Preheat oven to 375 degrees. Grease 8-inch square pan. Cream shortening and sugar in medium bowl until blended. Add egg whites and vanilla. Beat until smooth. Stir in oat bran and applesauce. Let stand 5 minutes. Combine flour, cinnamon, baking powder, baking soda, salt and nutmeg in separate bowl. Stir in oat bran mixture. Spread half of batter in pan. For filling and topping spread ¾ cup applesauce over batter. Combine sugar and cinnamon and sprinkle half over applesauce. Add remaining batter and repeat topping. Bake for 30 to 35 minutes. Cake is done when springs back lightly when touched. Serve warm. Yield: 9 to 16 servings.

LOU'S COFFEE CAKE
Louise Koch

2½	cups flour	1	teaspoon baking soda
1	cup brown sugar	1	cup buttermilk
¾	cup sugar	2	teaspoons cinnamon
1	teaspoon salt	½	cup nuts, chopped
1	teaspoon nutmeg		*Glaze*
1	cup vegetable oil	1	cup powdered sugar
1	egg, slightly beaten		2 to 3 teaspoons hot water

Combine first 5 ingredients well. Remove ¾ cup and set aside. To remaining ingredients add oil, egg, soda and buttermilk. Mix well. Grease and flour 13 x 9 x 2-inch pan. Pour batter into pan. Into ¾ cup dry mixture, add cinnamon and nuts. Sprinkle over batter and bake in 350 degree oven for 25 to 30 minutes. Glaze: mix sugar and water to make a thin icing. Pour over cake while cake is warm. Yield: 12 to 24 servings.

EGGS / CHEESE

PEACHY KEEN COFFEE CAKE

Elizabeth Sublett

1¾	cups all-purpose flour	1	egg beaten	
½	cup vegetable oil	2	teaspoons baking powder	
½	cup sugar	1	teaspoon vanilla extract	
½	teaspoon ground cinnamon	¾	teaspoon baking soda	
¼	teaspoon ground nutmeg	½	teaspoon salt	
¾	cup buttermilk	1	cup peach pie filling	

Preheat oven to 350 degrees. In large bowl mix together flour, oil, sugar, cinnamon and nutmeg until crumbly. Remove ½ cup flour mixture, set aside. Add remaining ingredients except pie filling, stir until just mixed. Pour batter into oiled and floured 8-inch square baking pan. Spoon pie filling evenly over top batter. Sprinkle reserve flour mixture over top of batter and filling. Bake 50 minutes or until tests done with wooden pick. Serve warm. Yield: 8 servings.

JALAPEÑO SQUARES

Robin Taylor

1 (11¼-ounce) jar sliced jalapeño peppers
1½ pounds mild Cheddar cheese, shredded
7 eggs

Grease 13 x 9 x 2-inch pan. Line bottom of pan with sliced jalapeño peppers. Beat eggs and add shredded cheese and mix well. Cover peppers with mixture. Bake at 375 degrees for 10 minutes on lowest rack in oven. Move to middle rack and bake an additional 25 minutes. Cool and cut into squares. Yield: 12-15 squares.

Variation: JALAPEÑO PIE *Maurine Smith*

Grease a 9-inch pie pan or square pan for bite size pieces. Cover bottom of pan with sliced and seeded jalapeño peppers. Press 10-ounces or more of grated cheese (any kind) on top of peppers. Beat 5 eggs until frothy, pour over cheese and bake at 350 degrees for about 30 minutes. Yield: 8–16 slices or 20 to 36 bite size pieces.

Variation: JALAPEÑO HE MAN QUICHE *Celia Grote*

Beat 6 eggs. Add 10-ounces Cheddar cheese, grated and 8-ounces Monterey Jack cheese, grated and 2 or 3 jalapeño peppers, chopped. Pour into a 12 x 9 x 2-inch greased pan. Bake 45 minutes at 350 degrees. Let sit 5 minutes before serving. Freezes well. Yield: 12 to 16 squares.

EGG BUTTER

Dorothy C. Lackey

Delicious when spread on biscuits or toast. This recipe was given to me by a friend many years ago.

¼ cup margarine	2 cups white Karo
2 eggs	2 tablespoons water
2 cups sugar	1 teaspoon vanilla

Melt and lightly brown margarine in a black iron skillet. Mix eggs, sugar, Karo and beat. Pour into browned margarine. Rinse bowl with water and pour into the skillet. Cook until slightly thickened. Add vanilla. Put in a bowl or jar when cool. Yield: 2 cups.

EGGS McMARGARET

Margaret Dannecker

My family's favorite "Special Sunday Breakfast or Brunch" recipe.

6 English muffins	⅛ teaspoon dry mustard
Butter	¼ teaspoon Worcestershire
6 slices Canadian bacon	sauce
6 poached eggs	Several drops Tabasco sauce,
Sauce	to taste
1 can Cheddar cheese soup	Milk

Divide, toast and butter muffins. Serve muffins topped with hot slice bacon, poached egg and cheese sauce. To prepare cheese sauce: heat undiluted soup in saucepan, add dry mustard, Worcestershire sauce and Tabasco sauce. Thin to desired sauce consistency with milk. Yield: 6 servings.

PAT'S EGG CASSEROLE

Patricia J. Ripsom

Nice to make ahead for company.

8 slices white bread without crust	1 pound bacon, cooked
6 eggs	and crumbled
1 teaspoon dry mustard	Onions, optional
3 cups milk	1 (3-ounce) can
½ pound Cheddar cheese,	mushrooms, optional
grated	Green peppers, optional
½ pound Swiss cheese, grated	Broccoli, optional

Cube bread and place in greased 13 x 9 x 2-inch baking dish. Beat eggs with mustard and milk. Pour over bread. Sprinkle the cheeses and bacon on top. Cover and refrigerate overnight. Next morning uncover and bake at 350 degrees for metal or 325 for glass for 45 minutes. Cool 10 minutes and serve. May add partially cooked broccoli, sautéed mushrooms, onions or green pepper. Yield: 8 servings.

EGG-SAUSAGE CASSEROLE
Lee Caruthers

1 pound ground sausage	½ teaspoon salt
2¼ cups milk	1½ cups Cheddar cheese,
8 to 10 eggs	shredded
1½ teaspoons dry mustard	3 slices white bread, cubed

Heat oven to 350 degrees. In large skillet, brown sausage, drain well; set aside. In large bowl place milk, eggs, mustard and salt. Beat 1 minute on medium speed of mixer. Stir in cheese, bread and sausage. Pour into greased 13 x 9 x 2-inch baking dish. Bake at 350 for 30-40 minutes until knife inserted into center comes out clean. Yield: 12 servings.

Microwave: Crumble sausage into large glass bowl; cover with plastic wrap. Microwave on HIGH for 5-6 minutes rotating ½ turn half way through cooking time; drain. Stir in remaining ingredients, blend well. Pour into 2 8-inch glass round pans. Cook separately. Microwave on DE-FROST for 15-18 minutes; stir and rotate ¼ turn every 3 minutes and on HIGH for 3 minutes.

POTATO BREAKFAST CASSEROLE
Susan Thomas

1 pound breakfast sausage	2 to 3 potatoes, diced <u>or</u> 1
1 medium onion, chopped	(20-ounce) bag frozen
1 can cream of mushroom	hash-browned potatoes
soup	1 cup sour cream
	1½ cups Cheddar cheese, grated

Crumble sausage in pan and brown with onion. Combine with remaining ingredients and pour into greased 13 x 9 x 2-inch casserole. Bake one hour at 350 degrees. Yield: 6 to 8 servings.

HINT:

Don't throw that stale bread away! Make croutons. Cut bread into cubes and toast at 250 degrees until golden; then toss with melted butter.

Your Just Desserts
Sweets, Cakes, Pies, Cookies, Candies, Ice Cream

BRYAN CONFECTIONERY

George Bryan was the proprietor of the confectionery business in this Johnson City street scene, about 1912. Ice cream, fountain cokes and ice cream sodas were popular treats enjoyed by young and old alike. This building, along with most others in this block, was destroyed by fire. Mr. Bryan rebuilt a new store of stone and sold general merchandise. Most recently, it was an antique and gift shop known as The Generation Gap, operated by Peggy Arbon.

118

APPLE CRISP

Evelyn Fuelberg

6   medium size apples, peeled, 1 cup sifted flour
    cored and sliced   ½ cup firmly packed brown
⅔ cup sugar   sugar
½ to 1 teaspoon cinnamon   ½ cup butter or margarine
2 to 4 tablespoons water

Place apples in a greased 13 x 9 x 2-inch casserole. Sprinkle sugar, cinnamon and water over apples. Mix flour, brown sugar, and butter until crumbly. Then sprinkle over top of apples. Bake at 350 degrees for about 45 minutes. Yield: 8 servings.

UNCLE BOB'S BREAD PUDDING

Joyce Penick Ellis

Best served warm with Cool Whip or whipped cream. Refrigerate if any left. Homemade donuts are best.

6 to 8 leftover donuts   ½ cup sugar
½ cup fruit cocktail, drained 2 cups milk
¼ cup raisins, optional   1 teaspoon vanilla
Custard   ½ teaspoon cinnamon
3   large eggs

Cut donuts in 8ths or smaller. Place in 12 x 6 x 2-inch Pyrex baking dish. Place fruit on top of donuts. Sprinkle on raisins. Mix custard ingredients until sugar is dissolved. Pour the custard over donuts, sprinkle cinnamon over mixture. More milk may be added to cover donuts if necessary. Place baking dish in larger pan. Pour water ½ way up side of donut dish. Place aluminum foil in shape of tent over donut mixture and bake at 350 degrees for 45 minutes. When knife inserted in custard comes out clean it is done. Yield: Serves 8.

WHISKEY SAUCE FOR BREAD PUDDING

Mary A. Thurlkill

½ cup margarine   1 egg, well beaten
1   cup sugar   1½ to 2 jiggers of whiskey

Cream margarine and sugar in top of double boiler. Place over hot water and heat until very hot and well-dissolved. Add egg and whip very fast so egg does not curdle. Let cool; then add whiskey.

To serve, put 1½ to 2 tablespoons of the warm Whiskey Sauce on top of Bread Pudding, and if desired, a dab of whipped cream.

119

OR: Put each serving of Bread Pudding on a broiler proof dish, add a serving of sauce on top, and heat in broiler until bubbly. Watch very carefully, as it will burn easily. Yield: about 1 cup.

CHERRY OR BLUEBERRY SQUARES   *Dolores Fasel Bozeman*

This is a family favorite. It is a quick and delicious dessert. I have been making it for more years than I can recall.

1 (11-ounce) package pie crust mix	¼ cup slivered almonds
	½ teaspoon cinnamon
¾ cup firmly packed brown sugar	1 (21-ounce) can cherry pie filling (<u>or</u> any flavor)

Combine pie crust mix, brown sugar, almonds and cinnamon. Mix well. Press half over bottom of well-greased baking pan 10 x 6 x 2. Spread pie filling over that. Spread remaining pie crust mixture on top and pat down firmly. Bake at 425 degrees for 20 minutes. Serve warm with ice cream. Yield: 12–15 servings.

CHOCOLATE COFFEE POTS de CREME   *Cynthia Smith*

Need a really special dessert? This one fills the bill and is quick; makes them think you went to a fancy cooking school!

1 (6-ounce) package semi-sweet chocolate morsels, not imitation
3 tablespoons sugar
1⅓ cups Half and Half
1½ tablespoons Kahlua <u>or</u> coffee flavored liqueur <u>or</u> extract
½ teaspoon instant coffee granules
3 egg yolks, beaten
1 teaspoon vanilla

Place chocolate morsels in a 1 quart glass mixing bowl, microwave on medium for 2 to 3 minutes or until chocolate is soft looking and shiny. Stir until smooth. Add sugar, stirring until dissolved. Using whisk, gradually stir in half and half. Microwave on HIGH 3½–4 minutes, stirring at 1 minute intervals. Combine Kahlua and coffee granules stirring to dissolve coffee. Add to chocolate mixture, stir well. Beat yolks with whisk. Gradually stir in hot chocolate mixture, stirring constantly. Stir in vanilla. Pour into stemmed glasses or custard cups, and chill 3 to 4 hours. Garnish with whipped cream. Yield: 4 very rich servings!

FLORINE'S EASY CREAM CHEESE CLOUDS   *Elizabeth Sublett*

I got this recipe from my sister Florine Bruns; they are so good and pretty.

1 (8-ounce) package cream cheese, softened	1 (21-ounce) can cherry pie filling
½ cup powdered sugar	½ cup pecans, chopped,
¼ teaspoon vanilla	optional
1 cup heavy cream	

Mix cream cheese, sugar, and vanilla at medium speed in electric mixer. Gradually add cream, mixing well. Whip until thickened. Using the back of a spoon, shape into 10 3½-inch shells. Place on waxed paper lined cookie sheet. Freeze 2 hours or overnight. When ready to serve fill with cherry pie filling. Sprinkle with chopped nuts if desired. Yield: 10 small pies.

CREAM CHEESE ROLL   *Jane Mills*

My sister-in-law had this recipe. She makes it for some of her nursing staff and there is never any left over.

2 packages crescent rolls	1½ cups sugar, divided
2 (8-ounce) packages cream cheese	2 teaspoons vanilla
	1 egg, separated

Preheat oven to 325 degrees. Use 13 x 9 x 2-inch pan. Unroll one package rolls and pat into the pan, coming up sides about 1 inch. Mix cream cheese, 1 cup sugar, vanilla and yolk of egg. Spread on crust. Roll out other roll, place on mixture, pinching edges. Beat white of egg, until frothy. Spread on top of crust. Sprinkle with reserved ½ cup sugar. Bake 25-30 minutes. Cool, then refrigerate. Yield: 12 to 16 squares.

ICE CREAM "CRUNCH" CAKE   *Aline Slack*

1 (12-ounce) package chocolate chips	6 cups crisp rice cereal
⅔ cup smooth peanut butter	1 gallon vanilla ice cream

Melt chocolate chips and peanut butter together in large pan; add cereal. Spread on cookie sheet and cool; break up cereal mixture into small pieces. Soften ice cream; fold in all but one cup of cereal mixture and spread in 10-inch springform pan. Use remaining 1 cup cereal mixture to make decorative topping, then freeze. Garnish with whipped cream and strawberries, if desired. Yield: 12 to 16 servings.

⇪ ⇪ ⇪ ⇪ ⇪ ⇪ ⇪

BEN'S JELLO   *Louise Gravenor*

This is not as sweet or stiff as regular Jello. Ben tries to use it as a substitute for Blue Bell!

1 (0.17-ounce) package Tropical Punch Koolaid, plain	2 envelopes of unflavored Knox gelatin
2 tablespoons Sweet and Low	Water to make 7 cups

In large bowl put Koolaid, Sweet and Low and gelatin. Add enough water to allow gelatin to begin to melt, stir thoroughly. Heat 2 cups water to almost boiling, add other mixture. Stir; when clear add cold water to make about 7 cups in all. Pour into individual 1 cup containers and refrigerate. Yield: 7 servings.

FORGOTTEN MERINGUE   *Pat Rumpf*

This is excellent to use for an open house. It may be prepared the night before, and when the sun dawns on your occasion the piece of resistance is ready to put on the serving plate! Cut like a cake. Fruit sauce will add color and flavor.

12 egg whites	1 teaspoon cream of tartar
3 cups sugar	1 teaspoon vanilla
1 teaspoon vinegar (white)	Pinch of salt

Grease well a 10-inch tube pan. Preheat oven to 450 degrees. Beat egg whites until stiff. "SLOWLY" add other ingredients, pour into a tube pan. When meringue goes into oven, turn oven off, and leave until cold or preferably overnight. No peeking! Yield: 20 servings.

POACHED MERINGUE   *Holly Lawson*

Sugar	*Peach sauce*
10 egg whites	3 cups peaches, peeled, sliced
½ teaspoon cream of tartar	3 tablespoons sugar
1 cup sugar	½ teaspoon cinnamon
	1 teaspoon lemon juice

Preheat oven to 350 degrees. Grease 12 cup bundt cake pan, sprinkle with sugar. Beat egg whites and cream of tartar in large mixing bowl until

foamy. Beat in sugar, 1 tablespoon at a time. Beat until soft peaks form. Pour into pan. Run knife through batter to let large air bubbles out. Place bundt pan in shallow 13 x 9 x 2-inch cake pan and place on rack in oven. Pour very hot water in cake pan 1 inch deep. Bake 45 minutes or until top is golden brown and meringue is set. Immediately, but gently, loosen meringue from edges of pan with knife and turn onto serving plate. Cool 30 minutes. Refrigerate uncovered up to 24 hours. Cut into wedges. Yield: 18 servings.

Peach sauce: Puree peaches, add sugar, cinnamon and lemon juice and mix well. Chill until serving. Use 2 to 3 tablespoons over each wedge of meringue.

MYSTERY PUDDING
Inez Steolyn Evavold

1 cup flour	1 (16-ounce) can fruit
1 teaspoon soda	cocktail and juice
¾ cup sugar	½ cup brown sugar
½ teaspoon salt	½ cup pecans, whole
1 teaspoon vanilla	

Mix first 6 ingredients together and put in a 9 x 9 x 2-inch pan. Top with the brown sugar and the pecans. Bake at 325 degrees for 35 minutes. I use the whole pecans but chopped may be used. Yield: 6 to 8 servings.

PUMPKIN SQUARES
Kittie Clyde Leonard

This recipe was given to me by Lela (Bill) Ivy; she served it at bridge.

1 (16-ounce) can pumpkin	½ teaspoon nutmeg
1 cup sugar	1 cup pecans, chopped
1 teaspoon salt	½ gallon vanilla ice cream,
1 teaspoon cinnamon	softened
1 teaspoon ginger	36 gingersnaps (16-ounce) bag

Combine pumpkin, sugar, salt, spices and pecans. Fold mixture into softened ice cream. Line bottom of 13 x 9 x 2-inch pan with half the gingersnaps. Top with half the ice cream mixture. Cover with another layer of gingersnaps. Add remaining ice cream. Freeze until firm, about 5 hours. Cut in squares and garnish with whipped cream and pecans. Yield: 12-15 squares.

RITZ CRACKER CAKE *Patty Casparis*

This recipe was given to me by my girlhood friend, Mary Lou Cobb Turner, who lives in Cadiz, Kentucky. This is a very rich dessert.

Crust
6 egg whites
2 cups sugar
60 Ritz Crackers, crushed
1 cup pecans, chopped
Filling
½ cup sugar
1 (8-ounce) package cream
cheese

½ teaspoon vanilla
1 (8-ounce) carton whipped
topping
1 (16-ounce) can fruit
cocktail, drained
1 (15-ounce) can crushed
pineapple, drained

Crust: Beat egg whites. Gradually add sugar, beating until stiff. Fold crackers and pecans into egg white mixture. Pour into a greased and floured 13 x 9 x 2-inch pan and bake at 350 degrees for 20 minutes only. Remove from oven and cool completely.

Filling: Cream sugar and cream cheese. Add vanilla and fold in whipped topping. Fold in fruit cocktail and pineapple. Spread over baked crust and refrigerate. Yield: 16 servings.

BRANDIED STRAWBERRIES *Jane Mills*

When this was served to me in Gaithersburg, Maryland, the elderly gentleman served it before he took a bunch of us out for dinner. It was hard to enjoy a full meal, since we had filled up on strawberries!! I would serve it as an after-dinner treat, where you wouldn't want a heavy, rich dessert.

Strawberries — fresh and ripe and in season
1 (3-ounce) package of lime Jello (not diet)
Small bottle of brandy

Clean strawberries, leaving stem on if possible. Let drain on paper towels, until super dry. This can be done ahead. When ready to serve, place small bowl with dry Jello on a large serving tray. Beside this, place another small bowl of brandy. Place strawberries all around the two bowls. Dip a strawberry into the brandy, then into the lime Jello and enjoy!! Yield: Depends on how many people you want to serve. It is hard to stop with just one!!

STRAWBERRY CHEESE SUZETTES
Inez Steolyn Evavold

Omelet

3 eggs
1 tablespoon water
½ teaspoon nutmeg, optional
1 tablespoon butter or
   margarine

Filling

1 (8-ounce) package cream
   cheese, cut in small pieces
1 (8-ounce) carton cottage cheese

¼ cup sugar
Rind and juice of 1 lemon

Sauce

1 (10-ounce) package frozen,
   strawberries, sliced and
   thawed
1 tablespoon lemon juice
¼ teaspoon almond flavoring

Omelet: Combine eggs, water and nutmeg and beat enough to blend. Put a 9-inch nonstick skillet over low heat. When hot, add butter to coat pan. Pour the eggs in pan. Shake pan forward and backward, pulling the eggs with a fork, letting the uncooked part run to the edges, until the whole is creamy.

Filling: Mix filling ingredients. When omelet is done spread filling over entire surface. Fold omelet and remove from pan to serving plate.

Sauce: Mix strawberries, lemon juice and almond flavoring. Spoon over omelet. Cut into 4 wedges. Yield: 4 servings.

ENGLISH TRIFLE
Leslie Matus

½ of an Angel Food cake,
   broken into 1-inch squares
¾ cup of strawberry jam
1 (3-ounce) package of
   strawberry gelatin
2 cups of water, boiling

1 (4.6-ounce) package of
   vanilla pudding mix
   (not instant)
3 cups milk
2 bananas
Whipped cream or Cool Whip

Cover bottom of 2½ quart trifle dish with angel food cake pieces. Spread jam evenly over cake. Dissolve gelatin in boiling water. Spoon hot gelatin over cake and jam. Prepare vanilla pudding mix with milk according to package instructions. Pour into dish while still hot. Refrigerate until cool and set. Best to leave in refrigerator overnight. Slice bananas over top of pudding. Cover with whipped cream and refrigerate until serving time. I like to use more gelatin than recipe calls for. Yield: 12-15 servings.

BUTTERMILK CAKE

Joan Shafford

I found this recipe in The Austin-American Statesman *newspaper several years ago. This cake is delicious served with strawberries and whipped cream or ice cream. My son, Billy Joe, requests this cake for his birthday because it is his favorite. It's a very moist cake.*

1	cup shortening	1	cup buttermik
½	cup margarine	½	teaspoon soda dissolved in
2½	cups sugar	2	tablespoons hot water
5	eggs	1	teaspoon almond extract
3	cups flour		

Cream shortening, margarine and sugar. Add eggs, one at a time and continue to beat. Add flour and buttermilk alternately using slow speed of electric mixer. Add soda mixture and almond extract. Pour into a greased and floured 14 x 11½ x 1½-inch pan. Bake at 325 degrees for 50 minutes. It may be baked in a greased and floured tube or bundt pan. Let cool in pan 10 to 15 minutes before turning out of pan. This cake does not need an icing.

Variation: YOGURT POUND CAKE *Peggy Arbon*
Dianne Mitchell Williams shared this recipe with me. She works in the Surgical Clinic at BAMC. Cream 3 cups sugar and 1½ cups butter or margarine together. Add 5 eggs, one at a time, beating after each addition. Add 1 cup vanilla or lemon yogurt, 1 teaspoon lemon and 1 teaspoon vanilla extract and mix well. Blend in 3 cups flour. Bake in a greased and floured tube pan at 350 degrees for 1 hour or until wooden stick tests clean.

Variation: SOUR CREAM POUND CAKE *Elizabeth Sublett*
This recipe came from my mother-in-law, Emmie Sublett, who made such good sour cream cakes. Sift 3 cups flour, ¼ teaspoon soda and ⅛ teaspoon salt. Cream 1 cup margarine or butter with 3 cups sugar. Separate 6 eggs. Add egg yolks, one at a time, beating until creamy. Add 1 teaspoon vanilla, 1 teaspoon lemon flavoring and dry ingredients alternately with 1 cup sour cream to creamy mixture. Beat egg whites and fold into mixture. Place in a greased tube pan. Bake at 300 degrees for 1 hour and 30 minutes. *Glaze:* Blend ¾ cup powdered sugar and juice of one lemon well. Pour over hot cake.

Variation: SOUR CREAM POUND CAKE *Thelma Ulrich*
Beat 1 cup softened butter about 2 minutes until creamy. Gradually add 3 cups sugar, beating 5 to 7 minutes. Add 6 large eggs, one at a time, beating just until the yellow disappears. Combine 3 cups flour and ¼ teaspoon baking soda and add to cream mixture alternately with 1 cup sour cream, beginning and ending with flour. Mix on low speed just until blended

126

after each addition. Stir in 1 teaspoon vanilla extract and 1 teaspoon almond extract. Bake 1 hour 20 minutes at 325 degrees until wooden pick comes out clean. Cool pan on wire rack for 10–15 minutes. Remove and let cool completely on wire rack.

BUTTERSCOTCH POUND CAKE
Theresa Casparis

No one suspects it's a mix. It has excellent taste, texture and appearance.

1 butter pecan cake mix	
2 (3¾-ounce) packages	*Caramel Icing*
butterscotch instant pudding	1½ cups brown sugar
1 cup water	½ cup white sugar
¾ cup oil	1 cup half and half
4 large eggs	3 tablespoons butter
1 teaspoon vanilla extract	<u>or</u> margarine
1 teaspoon butter flavoring	1 teaspoon vanilla

Cake: With mixer, mix all ingredients together until well blended. Preheat oven at 350 degrees. Grease and flour tube pan. Pour in batter and bake 45 to 60 minutes. Test for doneness. Do not over cook or cake will be dry. Pour caramel icing over cool cake.

Icing: Mix all ingredients together in a saucepan. Boil to soft-ball stage. Set aside until lukewarm. Beat until thick enough to ice cake. Yield: 10-inch tube cake.

BUTTERSCOTCH TORTE
Sallye Baker

This torte was served by the Home Economics teacher at a faculty meeting when I taught in Leander ISD in the Sixties. It is a beautiful dessert and delicious.

6 eggs, separated	3 tablespoons powdered
1½ cups sugar	sugar
1 teaspoon baking powder	*Sauce*
2 teaspoons vanilla	¼ cup water
1 teaspoon almond extract	¼ cup butter, melted
2 cups graham cracker	1 cup brown sugar
crumbs	1 tablespoon flour
1 cup nuts, chopped	1 egg, beaten
Frosting	¼ cup orange juice
2 cups whipping cream	½ teaspoon vanilla

Beat egg yolks well, slowly adding sugar; then baking powder and flavorings. Mix well. Beat egg whites until they hold stiff peaks; fold into yolk mixture. Fold in crumbs and nuts. Pour into two 9-inch pans, greased and lined with wax paper. Bake in slow oven 325 degrees for 30 to 35 minutes; cool 10 minutes, remove from pans. Frost when completely cool or wrap layers individually for freezing. Yield: 12 servings.

Frosting: Whip whipping cream, slowly adding powdered sugar. Spread between layers and over top.

Sauce: Add water to butter, blend in brown sugar and flour. Add egg, orange juice, and vanilla. Mix well. Bring to boil and cook until thickened. Cool thoroughly. Pour over whipping cream so sauce dribbles down sides.

CANDY CAKE
Josie Byars

4 cups coconut, cut up fine
2 pounds pitted dates
2 (14-ounce) cans sweetened condensed milk
1 teaspoon vanilla
About ¼ teaspoon salt

12 small green gum drops, whole
12 small red gum drops, whole
1½ pounds pecans, chopped
2 slices candied pineapple, (white), cut up

Mix well, line 2 8 x 4 x 3-inch bread pans with wax paper, pack in pan good (especially in corners of pan). Cook 1 hour in slow oven, 250 degrees. Yield: 2 loaf-size cakes.

LITE CHEESECAKE
Ruth Teague

This cake is delicious even without the graham cracker crust.

16 (2½-inch) squares graham crackers, made into crumbs
16 teaspoons diet margarine, softened
½ cup boiling water
1 (3-ounce) box sugar free lemon gelatin

2⅔ cups lite cottage cheese, divided
1 tablespoon lemon juice
1 (8-ounce) carton Lite Cool Whip

Mix crumbs and margarine. Place in an 8-inch pie pan and press around pan. Bake at 350 degrees for 4 to 5 minutes.

Place boiling water in blender, pour Jello over water. Blend until smooth

and Jello dissolves. Put in 1 cup cottage cheese. Blend until smooth. Add lemon juice and blend. Add rest of the cottage cheese and blend until smooth. Pour over Cool Whip and mix well. Pour into crust and chill until set. May be served with fruit topping. Yield: 8 servings with 54 calories per serving.

PARTY CHEESECAKES
Jewell Sultemeier

24 vanilla wafers
2 (8-ounce) packages cream cheese
1 (14-ounce) can sweetened condensed milk

3 eggs, separated
¼ cup lemon juice
¼ teaspoon salt
Your favorite preserves or pie filling

Preheat oven to 275 degrees. Place paper liners in muffin tins and put 1 vanilla wafer in each. Beat cream cheese until fluffy. Add milk and egg yolks. Beat until smooth. Stir in lemon juice. Beat egg whites with salt until peaks form. Fold egg whites into cream cheese mixture. Spoon into muffin tins until ¾ full. Bake 20 to 25 minutes. Let cool in paper liners by chilling several hours. (Can remove paper at this point.) Top cheesecakes with your favorite preserves or pie filling. Yield: 24 mini-cakes.

SMOOTH 'N LUSCIOUS CHEESECAKE
Ola Matus

18 (2½-inch) graham crackers
¼ cup sugar
¼ cup butter or margarine, melted
4 (3-ounce) packages cream cheese, softened
3 egg yolks
½ cup cream

½ cup sugar
2 tablespoons all-purpose flour
1 teaspoon lemon juice
½ teaspoon vanilla
3 egg whites, beaten until stiff but not dry

Crush graham crackers in blender or food processor. Add sugar and butter to crumbs. Mix and then press firmly into bottom and 2 inches up sides of 8-inch spring-form pan. Chill.

Combine soft cream cheese and egg yolks until smooth. Then add cream, sugar, flour, lemon juice and vanilla, beating with mixer until smooth. Fold in beaten egg whites. Bake until cake springs back when touched lightly in center, 50 to 60 minutes. Chill. Garnish with your favorite fruit topping, very good with cherry pie filling. Yield: 8 to 10 servings.

CHEESECAKE SUPREME
Dawn McNutt Keller

Sadie Sharp is my great aunt. My mother, Beth McNutt and I do a lot of entertaining and this cheesecake is served often. It really is easy to make and so good!!!

Crust
1½ cups all purpose flour
¼ cup sugar
1½ teaspoons lemon peel <u>or</u> almond flavoring
¾ cup butter
2 egg yolks, slightly beaten
¼ teaspoon vanilla
Filling
5 (8-ounce) packages cream cheese, softened
¾ teaspoon lemon peel <u>or</u> almond extract

¼ teaspoon vanilla
1¾ cups sugar
3 tablespoons flour
¼ teaspoon salt
4 large eggs
2 egg yolks
¼ cup whipping cream
Topping
1 pint sour cream
⅓ cup sugar
1 teaspoon vanilla

Crust: Combine flour, sugar, and lemon peel. Cut in butter until crumbly. Add egg yolks and vanilla. Mix well. Pat ⅓ of the dough on bottom of 10-inch spring form pan, (sides removed). Bake at 400 degrees about 8 minutes. Cool. Butter sides of pan, attach to the bottom. Pat remaining dough on sides of pan.

Filling: Beat cream cheese until creamy. Add lemon peel and vanilla. Combine sugar, flour, and salt. Gradually blend into cheese mixture. Add eggs and egg yolks, one at a time, beating after each addition, just to blend. Gently stir in whipping cream. Turn into crust lined pan. Bake at 450 degrees for 12 minutes. Reduce heat to 300 degrees and bake 55 minutes. Remove from oven. Cool for 30 minutes. Loosen sides of cheesecake from pan with knife. Cool about 4 hours at room temperature.

Topping: Mix sour cream, sugar, and vanilla thoroughly. Spread over cheesecake and refrigerate. Before serving remove sides of pan. Yield: 18 to 20 servings.

HINT:
Slip your hand inside a waxed or plastic sandwich bag and you have a perfect mitt for greasing your cake pan.

CHOCOLATE CHERRY CAKE   *Bernice K. Weinheimer*

I have not found anyone who did not come back for more or try to lick up the crumbs.

1 box plain chocolate <u>or</u> fudge cake mix	**Icing**
	1 cup sugar
3 eggs	⅓ cup milk
¼ cup milk	5 tablespoons margarine
2 teaspoons almond extract	6 ounces chocolate chips
1 (21-ounce) can cherry pie filling	1 cup pecans, chopped, optional

Mix first four ingredients together. Gently add cherry pie filling. Treat 13 x 9 x 2-inch pan with vegetable spray and pour cake batter in. Bake at 350 degrees for 25 to 30 minutes or until center is done.

Icing: Mix all ingredients in pot and cook over low heat until well blended. Add pecans if desired. Leave cake in pan and pour hot icing over cake right after taking out of oven. Serve from pan. Yield: 15 servings.

QUICK CHOCOLATE VINEGAR CAKE   *Patricia J. Ripsom*

This turns out a very good, but heavy cake.

3 cups flour, sifted	2 cups cold water
2 cups sugar	2 teaspoons vanilla
6 tablespoons cocoa	12 tablespoons salad oil
2 teaspoons baking soda	(¾ cup)
1 teaspoon salt	2 tablespoons vinegar

In a large mixing bowl put flour, sugar, cocoa, baking soda, and salt. Stir together by hand. Then add remaining ingredients in the order listed. Stir by hand until smooth. Pour into a greased 13 x 9 x 2-inch baking pan. Bake in moderate oven at 350 degrees for 30 minutes or until top springs back. Cool in pan on rack and frost if desired. Yield: 15 servings.

HINT:

For quick and easy flouring of a greased cake pan, keep flour in a large shaker and shake out the amount of flour needed.

131

HERSHEY CAKE   *Lillian Stewart*

This is really a premier chocolate cake. After eating this one, other chocolate cakes don't taste nearly as good. The cake is good enough by itself without the icing.

½	cup butter	2	teaspoons vanilla
2	cups sugar	7	Hershey candy bars, plain
4	eggs	*Icing*	
2	(5½-ounce) cans of Hershey syrup	½	cup butter or vegetable shortening (Crisco)
2½	cups flour	1	pound powdered sugar
¼	teaspoon salt	8	teaspoons cocoa
½	teaspoon soda	8	teaspoons liquid coffee
1	cup buttermilk		

Cream butter and sugar together. Add eggs, one at a time, beating after each. Add syrup. Sift together flour, salt and soda and add alternately with buttermilk and vanilla.

Melt candy bars in a double boiler and add to the batter mixture. Beat well. Bake for 1 hour 15 minutes in 350 degree oven in a greased and flour 10-inch tube pan.

Icing: Cream butter and add other ingredients alternately. Spread on cooled cake. Yield: 10-inch tube cake.

COCONUT POUND CAKE WITH SAUCE   *Margaret Bergman*

1	cup shortening	1	teaspoon salt
2	cups sugar	2	cups Angel Flake coconut
1	teaspoon vanilla	*Sauce*	
1	teaspoon butter flavor extract	1	cup sugar
		½	cup water
6	eggs	2	teaspoons coconut flavor extract
2	cups flour		

Cream shortening and sugar. Add flavors. Add eggs, 3 at a time. Mix well. (Use high speed with electric mixer.) Sift flour and salt together then add slowly to creamed mixture. Fold in coconut. Pour into 10-inch stem pan that has been sprayed with vegetable spray. Bake at 325 degrees for about 1 hour and 20 minutes until toothpick inserted in center comes out clean. When cake is done, remove from pan immediately. Brush sauce on with

pastry brush while cake is still warm. To improve moisture in cake freeze and let thaw. Yield: 10-inch tube cake.

Sauce: Mix all ingredients together, bring to a boil, and boil for 1 minute. Yield: about 1 cup.

CRUMB CAKE
Pat Rumpf

This recipe was received from an Austin friend. The pan size may be altered to 13 x 9 x 2-inch; cake will be thicker and baking time will be longer.

1	cup brown sugar	1	teaspoon baking powder
¾	cup granulated sugar	¾	teaspoon baking soda
1	teaspoon salt	1	egg
1	teaspoon cinnamon	1	cup buttermilk
2½	cups flour	1	cup chopped pecans or
¾	cup vegetable oil		walnuts

Mix first 5 ingredients in large bowl. Add oil and stir until well mixed. Set aside about 1½ cups of this mixture for crumb topping. Add next 4 ingredients to remaining mixture in order given. Pour batter into 10 x 15 x 2-inch greased and well floured pan. Spread reserved crumbs on top of cake, sprinkle nuts on top, and press lightly with spoon. Bake about 30 minutes at 350 degrees. Yield: 15 to 18 servings.

GRANNY'S EARTHQUAKE CAKE
Robyn Henderson

There was always so much love in my Granny's kitchen, maybe it was because my Grandfather always helped her. He fetched and handed her pans, bowls, mixers, ingredients and washed the dishes as she used them. I often thought how could a woman not love cooking when she always has such loving company. I always pass this hint to newlyweds . . . "Cook together, Pray together, Stay together."

1	cup coconut	1	(8-ounce) package
1	cup pecans, chopped		cream cheese
1	box chocolate or yellow cake mix,	1	pound package
	mix according to package directions		powdered sugar
½	cup butter or margarine, melted		

Grease and flour 13 x 9 x 2-inch pan. Sprinkle coconut and pecans on bottom of pan. Prepare cake mix. Pour over pecans and coconut. Melt butter, add cream cheese and powdered sugar and mix well. Spread over cake

133

batter. Bake at 350 degrees for 45 to 50 minutes or until done. Cool, cut in squares to serve. Yield: 15 to 18 servings.

BARBARA TAYLOR and MOLINE LORENZ also submitted this recipe. They both use a German chocolate cake mix.

FIG CAKE

Evelyn Fuelberg

2½	cups sugar	1	teaspoon cinnamon
¾	cup margarine	3	cups flour, sifted
3	eggs	1	teaspoon soda
1	teaspoon cloves	1	cup buttermilk
1	teaspoon allspice	2	cups fig preserves (1 pint)

Cream sugar, margarine, eggs, cloves, allspice, and cinnamon. Add flour with soda, then buttermilk and preserves. Bake in greased and floured 10-inch tube pan; 350 degrees for 1 hour. Yield: 10-inch tube cake.

BEST FRUITCAKE EVER!!

Gracie Wittkohl

This recipe was given to me by my sister-in-law, Eloise Caddell. It is a beautiful holiday fruitcake.

4	cups flour	1	pound candied cherries, cut in small pieces
1	heaping teaspoon baking powder	1	pound orange gumdrops, cut in small pieces
1	teaspoon salt	2	(2-ounce) bottles lemon extract
1	pound butter	1	(2-ounce) bottle orange extract
2	cups sugar		
6	eggs		
1	pound pecans, chopped		
1	pound candied pineapple, cut in small pieces		

Sift dry ingredients together in a large bowl. In mixing bowl cream butter and sugar. Add 1 egg at a time. Mix well. Add dry ingredients. Mix well and then add pecans, pineapple, cherries, gumdrops, and extracts. Put in 2 greased and floured 10-inch tube pans or in 1 large and 2 small loaf pans. Bake three hours at 250 degrees. Yield: 2 tube cakes or 1 large and 2 small loaves.

MYSTERY NO-BAKE FRUITCAKE   *Ruth Teague*

1   (2-layer) spice cake mix
4   cups (2 1-pound packages) candied fruit mix
½ cup red candied cherries, cut in half
½ cup green candied cherries, cut in half

1½ cups seedless raisins
1   cup pitted dates, chopped
4   cups pecan halves
1   package fluffy white frosting mix (Betty Crocker)

Make and bake cake according to package directions. Cool. Crumble into large bowl and add mixed fruit, cherries, raisins, dates and pecans. Make frosting according to package directions. Add to fruit, nuts and cake mixture. Stir with large spoon or toss with hands until mixture is damp and well blended. Pack tightly into foil-lined loaf pans or a 10-inch tube pan. Pat down with buttered hands until smooth. Cover with foil and chill in refrigerator at least 24-hours. Cake improves if stored longer. Cake should be kept refrigerated. Slice with sharp knife. Yield: 10-inch tube cake.

FUDGE RIBBON CAKE   *Annie Lee West*

Cheese Mixture
2   tablespoons butter
¼ cup sugar
1   tablespoon cornstarch
1   (8-ounce) package cream cheese
1   egg
2   tablespoons milk
½ teaspoon vanilla
Cake
2   cups flour
2   cups sugar
1   teaspoon salt
1   teaspoon baking powder
½ teaspoon soda

½ cup soft shortening
1½ cups milk, divided
2   eggs
4   ounces unsweetened chocolate, melted
1   teaspoon vanilla
Frosting
⅓ cup milk
¼ cup butter
1   (6-ounce) package semi-sweet chocolate pieces
1   teaspoon vanilla
2¼ cups powdered sugar, sifted

Cheese Mixture: Cream butter, sugar, and cornstarch. Add cream cheese; beat until fluffy. Add remaining ingredients and beat until creamy. Set aside.

Cake: Grease and flour 13 x 9 x 2-inch pan. Combine dry ingredients, add shortening and 1 cup milk; blend at low speed of electric mixer. Beat 1½ minutes. Add remaining ingredients and ½ cup milk; continue beating for

135

1½ minutes. Spread half of batter in prepared pan; spoon on cheese mixture, spreading carefully to cover. Top with remaining batter and spread to cover. Bake at 350 degrees for 50 to 55 minutes. Remove from oven when done and allow to cool. Frost with Chocolate Frosting.

Frosting: Bring milk and butter to a boil; remove from heat. Blend in chocolate pieces. Stir in vanilla and the confectioners sugar. Beat until smooth and spread on cake. Yield: 12–16 servings.

GINGERBREAD
Jewell Sultemeier

½	cup shortening	1½	teaspoons ginger
1	cup sugar	½	teaspoon cinnamon
2	eggs	¼	teaspoon nutmeg
3	cups flour	1	cup molasses
2	teaspoons soda	1	cup sour milk

Cream shortening and sugar. Add eggs, beat well. Mix and sift dry ingredients. Add to creamed mixture alternately with molasses and sour milk. Put into greased 10-inch tube pan or 13 x 9 x 2-inch pan. Bake at 350 degrees for 40 to 45 minutes. Yield: 15 servings.

ARLENE'S PEACH CUSTARD CAKE
Sallye Baker

1½	cups flour	½	cup sugar
½	teaspoon salt	½	teaspoon cinnamon
½	cup margarine	½	cup peach syrup*
1	(1 pound 14-ounce) can sliced peaches, drained reserving syrup*	1	egg, slightly beaten
		1	cup evaporated milk

In ½ quart bowl put flour, salt, and margarine. Mix with pastry blender until mixture looks like coarse meal. With back of spoon, press mixture firmly on bottom and half-way up sides of buttered 8-inch square pan. Arrange peach slices on crust in pan. Sprinkle over peaches a mixture of sugar and cinnamon. Bake in 375 degree oven for 20 minutes. Mix the peach syrup, egg and milk. Pour over peaches. Bake 30 minutes more, or until custard is firm except in center. Center becomes firm on standing. Yield: 9 servings.

PINEAPPLE SAUCE CAKE
Elnora Kneese

½ cup shortening
1 cup sugar
2 eggs, separated
1 drop almond extract
¼ teaspoon vanilla extract
¼ teaspoon lemon extract
¼ teaspoon soda
⅔ cup pineapple, crushed
1¾ cups flour, sifted
1½ teaspoons baking powder

¼ teaspoon salt
Coconut Pecan Frosting
1 cup evaporated milk
1 cup sugar
3 egg yolks
½ cup margarine
1 teaspoon vanilla extract
1⅓ cups coconut
1 cup pecans, chopped

Cream shortening with sugar. Beat in egg yolks. Add almond, vanilla, and lemon extracts. Stir in soda and pineapple. Combine dry ingredients and stir in. Beat egg whites until soft peaks form. Fold into cake batter. Pour into a 13 x 9 x 2-inch pan. Bake at 350 degrees for 22 minutes. Frost with Coconut Pecan Frosting. Yield: 15 to 18 servings.

Frosting: Combine milk, sugar, egg yolks, margarine, and vanilla in a saucepan. Cook on low fire. Heat until mixture thickens, stirring constantly. Takes about 12 minutes. Add coconut and pecans. Beat until frosting is cool and thick enough to spread. Yield: 2⅔ cups.

PLUM CAKE
Sally Gravenor

This cake is moist and keeps well. Nice served with a cup of spiced tea or coffee.

2 cups flour
2 cups sugar
2 teaspoons soda
1 cup oil
2 (4-ounce) jars plum baby food
3 eggs
Red food color if deeper color is
    desired

1 teaspoon cinnamon
1 teaspoon cloves
1 cup nuts, chopped
Glaze
¼ cup lemon juice
1 cup powdered sugar

Mix flour, sugar, and soda together. Add oil, plums and eggs. Mix well, then add spices and nuts. Pour into greased and floured 10-inch bundt pan. Bake at 350 degrees for 1 hour. Pour glaze over warm cake.

Glaze: Bring to boil lemon juice and powdered sugar for one minute. Pour over cake. Yield: 10-inch tube cake.

FIVE FLAVORS POUND CAKE
Katy Finch

1 cup margarine	5 eggs, well beaten
½ cup oil	Dash salt
3 cups sugar	*Glaze*
1 cup milk	½ cup sugar
1 teaspoon rum extract	¼ cup water
1 teaspoon butter flavoring	½ teaspoon rum extract
1 teaspoon lemon flavoring	½ teaspoon butter flavoring
1 teaspoon coconut flavoring	½ teaspoon lemon flavoring
1 teaspoon vanilla extract	½ teaspoon coconut flavoring
½ teaspoon baking powder	½ teaspoon vanilla extract
3 cups flour	

Cream margarine, oil and sugar until light. Add milk and flavorings and beat. Mix baking powder and flour, add alternately the eggs and flour into butter mixture. Add salt. Bake in greased and floured 10-inch bundt pan at 325 degrees for 1½ hours.

Glaze: Bring all ingredients to a boil. Stir until sugar is dissolved. Brush over hot cake. Yield: 10-inch tube cake.

LEMON POPPY SEED POUND CAKE
Elizabeth Sublett

1¾ cups sugar	⅔ cup milk
1 cup Wesson oil	⅓ cup lemon juice
1 tablespoon lemon rind, grated	1½ tablespoons poppy seeds
4 eggs	*Glaze*
2½ cups all-purpose flour	1 cup powdered sugar
2 teaspoons baking powder	2½ tablespoons lemon juice
½ teaspoon nutmeg	1 teaspoon lemon rind, grated
½ teaspoon salt	½ teaspoon poppy seeds

Heat oven to 350 degrees. In large bowl mix sugar, oil, and lemon rind until well blended. Add eggs and beat until mixture is thick and pale. In medium bowl combine flour, baking powder, nutmeg, and salt. In small bowl combine milk and lemon juice. Mix flour and milk mixtures alternately into oil mixture, beginning and ending with flour mixture. Beat until smooth, about 2 minutes. Stir in poppy seeds. Spoon batter in a 10-inch oiled and floured bundt pan. Bake for 1 hour or until cake tests done with wooden pick. Invert on a rack, cool in pan 10 minutes. Remove and cool completely. Yield: 12 servings.

Glaze: In a small bowl whisk together glaze ingredients until smooth. Spoon glaze over cake and serve.

JACK HORNER CAKE (PRUNE CAKE)   *Leah Mauck*

I think this recipe came from an Imperial sugar bag, as I have had it forever. I like it best made in a sheet pan. The frosting is something I came up with along the way.

1 cup boiling water	½ cup salad oil
1 cup dried prunes, chopped	3 eggs
2 cups sifted flour	1 cup nuts, chopped
1½ cups sugar	*Coffee Frosting*
1 teaspoon salt	¼ cup butter
1¼ teaspoons soda	2 cups powdered sugar
1 teaspoon cloves	2 tablespoons strong coffee
1 teaspoon cinnamon	1 teaspoon instant coffee
1 teaspoon nutmeg	

Pour boiling water over prunes. Let stand 2 hours. Preheat oven to 350 degrees. Sift dry ingredients together. Add prune mixture and remaining ingredients. Blend thoroughly 1 minute, then beat 2 minutes at medium speed. Pour into greased and floured pans, 2 9-inch pans or a 13 x 9 x 2-inch sheet pan. Bake for 30 to 35 minutes.

Frosting: Cream butter and slowly add sugar and coffee. Beat until smooth. Yield: 15 servings.

SAD CAKE   *Jane Mills*

This recipe was given to me by a very dear friend, Minnie Pilgrim. At one time, she had her own cafe and she had cooked at the hospital here in Johnson City, before retiring to half time work. She was an amazing lady and is missed by many . . .

2 cups Pioneer Biscuit Mix	2 teaspoons vanilla
2 cups brown sugar	4 eggs
2 cups pecans, chopped	

Put all ingredients into mixing bowl; mix well. Spray 13 x 9 x 2-inch pan with Pam. Bake at 350 degrees for 25 to 35 minutes. Yield: 16 to 20 servings.

SCRIPTURE CAKE

Gracie Wittkohl

If you want to feel specially blessed in spirit as well as body, try this cake. This cake batter ingredients all are found in the Bible.

Judges 5:25	1	cup butter
Jeremiah 6:20	2	cups sugar
Jeremiah 17:11	4	eggs, separated and beaten
1 Samuel 14:25	2	tablespoons honey
Judges 4:19	1	cup milk
1 Kings 4:22	3½	cups flour, sifted and divided
2 Chronicles 9:9	1	teaspoon cinnamon
	½	teaspoon nutmeg
	½	teaspoon cloves
Leviticus 2:13	½	teaspoon salt
Amos 4:5	3½	teaspoons baking powder
Nahum 3:12	2	cups figs, cut in small pieces
1 Samuel 30:12	2	cups raisins

Cream butter and sugar, add egg yolks, honey, milk, and 3 cups flour, spices, baking powder, and salt. Use remaining ½ cup flour to flour figs and raisins. Add egg whites before fruits and pecans are added. Bake in greased floured 10-inch tube pan at 350 degrees for 40 minutes. Yield: 10-inch tube cake.

TEXAS TORNADO CAKE

Ruth Teague

1½	cups sugar	1	cup nuts, chopped
2	eggs		*Icing*
2	cups fruit cocktail, including juice	½	cup butter
		¾	cup sugar
2	teaspoons soda	½	cup evaporated milk
2	cups all-purpose flour	1	cup coconut
¼	cup brown sugar		

Mix and cream together the first five ingredients. Pour into lightly greased and floured 13 x 9 x 2-inch cake pan. Mix brown sugar and nuts together and sprinkle onto the batter. Place in 325 degree oven for 40 minutes. Spread icing on cake while hot.

Icing: Boil the butter, sugar, and milk for 2 minutes; add coconut. Spoon icing over cake as soon as cake is removed from the oven. Yield: 12 to 15 servings.

TURTLE CAKE
Beverly K. Voron

This is the most often requested birthday cake in our family. It's much easier to leave it in the pan and serve from there. But I have successfully taken it out of the pan to frost with whipping cream and made more festive. It's an easy cake to make. The hardest part is unwrapping all those caramels!

1	(14-ounce) package caramels	1⅓	cups water
½	cup evaporated milk	3	eggs
1	package German chocolate	¾	cup butter, softened
	cake mix	1	cup pecans, chopped
1	cup semi-sweet chocolate chips		

Melt caramels in a double boiler with the milk. Combine cake mix and water, add butter and eggs in a mixing bowl, beat on low speed for 30 seconds. Pour half the batter in a greased 13 x 9 x 2-inch pan and bake at 350 degrees for 10 minutes. Then pour caramel mixture over the partially baked cake layer to within ½ inch of the edge. Sprinkle nuts and chocolate chips over the caramel. Pour the remaining batter over all and bake again at 350 degrees for 25 to 30 minutes until top springs back when touched. Cool and top with ice cream or whipped cream. Yield: 12 to 15 servings.

OZARK PIE-CAKE
Aline Slack

1	large egg	1¼	teaspoons baking powder
¾	cup sugar	1	cup apples, pared and diced
¾	cup flour	1	cup nuts, chopped
⅛	teaspoon salt	1	teaspoon vanilla

Beat egg, stir in sugar. Add flour, salt, and baking powder; stir about 1 minute. Add remaining ingredients and stir until well blended. Spread mixture into a greased 9-inch pie pan. Bake at 350 degrees for 30 to 35 minutes or until brown. Especially good with ice cream or whipped cream. Yield: 9-inch pie.

PUMPKIN PIE CAKE
Maxine Parrott

4	eggs, slightly beaten	½	teaspoon cloves
2	(16-ounce) cans solid	3	cups evaporated milk **or**
	pack pumpkin		light cream
1½	cups sugar	1	(2-layer) package yellow
1	teaspoon salt		cake mix
2	teaspoons cinnamon	½	cup margarine, melted
1	teaspoon ginger	1	cup pecans finely chopped

Preheat oven to 350 degrees. Grease a 13 x 9 x 2-inch or slightly larger baking pan. Beat eggs; add pumpkin, sugar, salt, spices, and milk. Pour into prepared pan. Sprinkle dry cake mix evenly over top. Drizzle with margarine and sprinkle nuts on top, pushing nuts slightly into batter. Bake in preheated oven for 1 hour and 20 minutes, or until done. Serve topped with whipped cream. Cut into squares. Yield: 12 to 15 servings.

APPLESAUCE CUPCAKES WITH ICING *Genevia Bushnell*

This cupcake is excellent and the icing is outstanding. Try this icing and you will never buy another canned icing. I have had this recipe for most of the forty years of my married life.

2½ cups sifted cake flour
1⅔ cups sugar
¾ cup applesauce
⅔ cup vegetable shortening (Crisco)
1 teaspoon salt
3½ teaspoons baking powder
½ cup thin tart applesauce
3 eggs
1 tablespoon orange rind, grated

Icing
2⅓ cups sifted powdered sugar
¼ teaspoon salt
1 egg
2 tablespoons water
¼ cup sugar
½ cup vegetable shortening (Crisco)
1 teaspoon vanilla

Measure into mixing bowl flour, sugar, applesauce, shortening, and salt. Beat at medium speed for 2 minutes. Stir in baking powder. Add tart applesauce, eggs, and orange rind. Beat at medium speed for 2 minutes. Spray muffin pans with a vegetable cooking spray. Fill muffin or cupcake pans half full with batter. Bake at 400 degrees for 15 to 20 minutes. Ice with Creamy Icing. Yield: 30 cupcakes.

Icing: Mix powdered sugar, salt, and egg. Set aside. Boil water and sugar for 1 minute, blend with sugar-egg mixture. Add vegetable shortening and vanilla. Beat until creamy.

CARROT CAKE ICING *Pat Rumpf*

1 (3-ounce) package cream cheese
1 (8-ounce) can crushed pineapple with juice

1 cup powdered sugar
½ cup pecans, chopped

Cream the cream cheese until smooth. Add the pineapple and sugar,

blend until smooth. Add pecans and stir in. Spread icing over cooled cake. Yield: enough for 1 cake.

J. C.'s FLAKY PIE CRUST
Ola Matus

1 crust 8-9-10-inch	*Double 8-9-inch*	*Double 10-inch*
1⅓ cups flour	2 cups flour	2⅔ cups flour
½ teaspoon salt	1 teaspoon salt	1 teaspoon salt
½ cup Crisco	¾ cup Crisco	1 cup Crisco
3 tablespoons cold water	5 tablespoons cold water	7-8 tablespoons cold water

Combine flour and salt in bowl. Cut in Crisco using pastry blender until all flour is blended in to form pea-size chunks. Sprinkle water, one tablespoon at a time. Toss lightly with fork until dough will form a ball. Flour rolling surface and pin lightly. Roll dough into circle. Trim one inch larger than upside down pie plate. Press into pie plate. For recipe calling for unbaked pie shell, follow directions given in that recipe. For baked pie shell heat oven to 425 degrees. Thoroughly prick bottom and sides with fork, about 50 times, to prevent shrinkage. Bake for 10 to 15 minutes or until lightly browned. If you want a flakier crust than this, freeze shortening in tablespoon-size chunks before processing.

ALGERITA PIE
Pat Althaus

'Algerita' is Hill Country for Agarita! This is a berry growing in the wild all over the hill country. You harvest them by placing a sheet under the bush and beating or shaking the bush with a stick. The berries fall down on the sheet. There is quite a bit of cleaning the berries, but worth the effort. Watch for snakes. They say, "under every agarita bush lies a rattlesnake."

⅔	cups sugar	2	tablespoons margarine
2	tablespoons tapioca	½	cup light cream
½	teaspoon cinnamon		Pastry for double crust
1	quart ripe algerita berries		9-inch pie

Combine the sugar, tapioca and cinnamon and spread half of it over the bottom crust. Add the algerita berries. Sprinkle the remaining sugar mixture over the top. Dot with the margarine and pour the cream over the top. Cover with the other pie crust. Make steam slits in top crust. Bake 375 degrees for 1 hour. Yield: 9-inch pie.

BUTTERSCOTCH PIE

Pat Althaus

This recipe came from the days when it was O.K. to eat egg yolks, cream and whole milk.

¾ cup white sugar	⅓ cup white sugar
5 tablespoons flour	1 tablespoon butter
¼ teaspoon salt	½ teaspoon vanilla
2 cups milk	1 baked 9-inch pie shell
3 egg yolks, beaten	½ cup whipping cream

Combine ¾ cup sugar, flour, and salt in top of double boiler. Add milk and egg yolks. Mix well. Place over rapidly boiling water. Cook 10 minutes, stirring constantly. Remove from fire and let stand over the hot water.

Caramelize ⅓ cup sugar by placing it in an iron skillet over medium heat. Stir until it is melted and straw blond color. Add at once to thickened mixture which is in the double boiler. Add butter and vanilla and mix well. Cool mixture and pour into cooked pie shell. Top with whipped cream at serving time. Yield: 9-inch pie.

EASY CHERRY PIE

Olivia Weiershausen

1 (21-ounce) can cherry pie filling	1 cup pecans, chopped
1 (14-ounce) can sweetened condensed milk	1 (8-ounce) carton Cool Whip
	2 (10-inch) graham cracker pie crusts
1 (20-ounce) can pineapple, crushed and drained	

Fold all ingredients in Cool Whip and put in pie crusts. Place in refrigerator to chill over night. Yield: 2 10-inch pies.

CORNMEAL CHESS PIE

Opal Francis

Very tasty and lemony.

3 eggs	6 tablespoons flour
2 cups sugar	½ cup lemon juice
½ cup butter, melted	1 teaspoon vanilla
3 tablespoons cornmeal	1 9-inch unbaked pie shell

Mix all ingredients together and pour into unbaked pie shell. Bake at 350

degrees until light brown on top and knife inserted into middle comes clean. About 1 hour. Yield: 9-inch pie.

CHOCOLATE CHIP COOKIE PIE
Angelia Stearns

½	cup butter <u>or</u> margarine	1	teaspoon vanilla
1	cup sugar	1	cup chocolate chips
2	eggs	1	cup pecans, finely chopped
½	cup flour	1	9-inch unbaked pie shell

In mixer, cream butter and sugar. Add eggs one at a time, mixing well after each addition. Add flour, and vanilla. Blend well. Remove from mixer. By hand, stir in 1 cup chips and pecans. Pour batter in unbaked pie shell. Bake in preheated 350 degree oven 40 to 45 minutes. Cool at least 1 hour before serving. Semi-sweet or milk chocolate chips can be used. Very rich, cut in small wedges. Yield: 8 to 12 servings.

EGGLESS CHOCOLATE PIE
Moline Lorenz

This pie won a blue ribbon in the Sacramento, California fair. It was given to me by Della Alcorn in Yreka, California, and it is delicious.

4	cups milk	½	cup butter <u>or</u> margarine
1	cup flour	1	tablespoon vanilla
2½	cups sugar	2	baked 9-inch pie shells
½	cup cocoa		Whipped cream or Cool Whip
¼	teaspoon salt		

Make a paste with milk and flour, adding other ingredients except butter and vanilla. Mix well. Cook over low heat until very thick. Add butter and vanilla. Cool and pour into pie shells. Cover top of pie with Saran Wrap so skim doesn't form. Top with whipped cream or Cool Whip. Yield: 2 9-inch pies.

CHERRY COBBLER
Ray Sultemeier

Especially nice for a February dessert, but it's good the year around.

1	cup flour	½	cup milk
1	cup sugar	1	tablespoon butter, melted
2	teaspoons baking powder	1	(16-ounce) can sour cherries

Combine flour, ½ cup sugar and baking powder, mix well. Blend milk and

margarine, stir into flour mixture until moistened. Pour batter into 9-inch square baking pan. Combine cherries and juice and remaining sugar in saucepan; heat. Pour hot sweetened cherries over batter. Bake in 350 degree oven for 30 minutes. Not very sweet, may add more sugar. Yield: 9 servings.

CHERRY-PEACH COBBLER
Judy Gipson

1 (21-ounce) can cherry pie filling
1 (21-ounce) can peach slices
1 can of 10 flaky biscuits

½ cup butter, melted
1 teaspoon cinnamon
¼ cup sugar
½ cup pecans, chopped

Mix cherry pie filling and peach slices. Pour in a 13 x 9 x 2-inch baking pan. Separate each biscuit into 3 parts. Place your butter in a dish. Set aside. Mix cinnamon and sugar and place in a small bowl. Place pecans in a small bowl. Dip each biscuit part in butter, then the cinnamon-sugar mixture, then pecans and layer on the fruit. Sprinkle any leftover butter, cinnamon-sugar mixture, or pecans over biscuits. Bake at 350 degrees for 25 to 30 minutes or until juices are hot and bubbly and biscuits are golden brown. For a fruit filled cobbler add 2 cans of peaches. Yield: 15 servings.

FRUIT COBBLER
Gwen Pickett

3 or more cups fresh fruit
1 tablespoon lemon juice
1 cup flour
1 cup sugar

1 egg, beaten
¼ cup margarine, melted
Cinnamon

Place fruit in an 11 x 8 x 2-inch baking dish. Sprinkle with lemon juice. Beat egg, add flour and sugar, stir until mixture resembles coarse meal. Spread over fruit. Drizzle margarine over topping. Sprinkle with cinnamon. Bake at 375 degrees for 30 minutes or until lightly browned. Serve warm. Yield: 6 servings.

HINT:
Slip a cookie sheet or a sheet of foil under a cobbler or fruit pie when baking in the oven in order to catch any run over.

COCONUT CARAMEL PIE
Peggy Green

¼ cup butter **or** margarine
1 (7-ounce) package flaked coconut
½ cup pecans, chopped
1 (8-ounce) package cream cheese, softened
1 (14-ounce) can sweetened condensed milk

1 (16-ounce) carton frozen whipped topping
2 baked 9-inch pastry shells
1 (12-ounce) jar caramel ice cream topping

Melt butter in large skillet. Add coconut and pecans. Cook until golden brown, stirring frequently; set aside. Combine cream cheese and condensed milk. Beat until smooth. Fold in whipped topping. Layer ¼ cup cheese mixture in each baked crust. Drizzle ¼th caramel topping on each pie. Sprinkle ¼th coconut mixture evenly over ingredients. Repeat layers with remaining ingredients, ending with nut and caramel mixture as topping. Freeze until firm. Let stand at room temperature for 5 or 10 minutes before slicing. Yield: 2 9-inch pies.

COCONUT CUSTARD PIE
Thelma Elm

2½ cups milk
½ cup granulated sugar
3 eggs
1½ teaspoons vanilla extract
½ teaspoon salt

¼ teaspoon ground nutmeg
1 cup shredded coconut
1 9-inch unbaked pie shell
Garnish: Cool Whip **or** whipped cream

In bowl combine milk, sugar, eggs, vanilla, salt, and nutmeg. Beat well to blend. Sprinkle coconut into pastry shell. Pour egg mixture over coconut. Bake at 425 degrees for 35 to 40 minutes or until knife inserted in center comes out clean. Cool. Serve garnished with whipped cream or Cool Whip. Yield: 9-inch pie.

MIXED FRUIT PIE
Jody McCuiston & Moline Lorenz

1 (20-ounce) can crushed pineapple
3 tablespoons cornstarch
1 (6-ounce) package strawberry gelatin
1 (20-ounce) package frozen sliced strawberries, thawed

3 or 4 bananas sliced
½ cup pecans, chopped, optional
2 prepared 9-inch pie shells
Cool Whip

Place pineapple and cornstarch in saucepan. Heat until it starts to thicken; remove from heat. Add gelatin, strawberries, bananas and pecans. Stir and pour into shells. Chill and then top with Cool Whip. Yield: 2 9-inch pies.

LEMON PIE
Flora Cox

¼ cup flour
2 tablespoons cornstarch
1 cup sugar
2 cups boiling water
2 or 3 egg yolks

Juice and grated rind of 1 lemon
1 tablespoon butter
¼ teaspoon salt
1 9-inch baked pie shell
Meringue

Mix the flour, cornstarch, and sugar. Add the boiling water, stirring the mixture as the water is added. Stir and cook over a low flame for 15 minutes. Beat egg yolks slightly. Pour a portion of hot mixture into the egg yolks and mix. Add this mixture to the hot mixture, stir, and cook over low flame until thickened. Remove from the flame; add the lemon juice, butter, and salt and mix well. Pour into baked crust. Cover with Weepless Meringue. Yield: 9-inch pie.

WEEPLESS MERINGUE
Flora Cox

This meringue was served on a delicious lemon pie to my husband and me by my niece who lives in Missouri. She said that her family expected her to make all pies for Christmas and Thanksgiving. I could see and taste why!!

1 tablespoon cornstarch
6 tablespoons sugar
½ cup water

3 egg whites
Pinch of salt
1 teaspoon vanilla

Combine cornstarch and sugar in small sauce pan and add water. Cook while stirring constantly until the mixture is thick and clear. Meanwhile beat egg whites to soft peak. Continue beating while pouring hot mixture over the beaten egg whites. Beat to stiff peaks — about 5 minutes. Add vanilla and spread on any custard pie. Brown in oven 325 degrees until light brown. Yield: Meringue for one 9-inch pie.

HINT:
Your frosting will look more professional if you first frost with a thin layer and let it set. Then apply a second coat of frosting.

PEACH PIE
Stella Smith

My aunt, Minnie Sultemeier, was an extremely good cook. Her coconut and peach pies were the best, not to mention the cherry cookies. When I started learning to cook I felt I just had to have her peach pie recipe. But she had no recipe, it was a handful of this and half a handful of that. One day as she prepared a pie, I stayed right at her side with a measuring cup . . . thus this recipe.

2	9-inch unbaked pie shells	½	cup cream or milk
4	cups peaches, peeled and sliced, divided	½	teaspoon almond <u>or</u> lemon flavoring
1¼	cups sugar		Pinch of salt
2	tablespoons flour		*Meringue*
¾	cup butter	4	egg whites
4	egg yolks, beaten	¼	cup sugar

In each pie crust place 2 cups of peaches. Mix together sugar, flour, butter, egg yolks, cream, flavorings, and salt. Divide mixture evenly and pour over peaches. Bake in hot oven at 450 degrees for 8 minutes, reduce heat to 350 degrees and bake 40 to 45 minutes or until done.

Meringue: Beat egg white with the sugar until stiff, divide and spread half over each pie. Bake until brown. Yield: 2 9-inch pies.

KIM'S PEANUT BUTTER & BANANA PIE
Olivia Weiershausen

This recipe is from my daughter-in-law and it is a good rich pie.

1	cup peanut butter	1	(4.6-ounce) package instant vanilla pudding
1	cup powdered sugar		
1	9-inch baked pie shell	2	cups milk
2	bananas	1	(8-ounce) carton Cool Whip

Take peanut butter and mix in the powdered sugar to make a crumbly mixture. Put in bottom of pie shell, reserving ¼ of the mixture, set aside. Slice bananas and put on the peanut butter mixture. Mix vanilla pudding with milk. Pour over bananas. Chill for 15 minutes. Top with Cool Whip and sprinkle rest of the crumbly mixture on top of the Cool Whip. Yield: 9-inch pie.

CREAM CHEESE PEANUT BUTTER PIE   *Juneth Watson*

This recipe was in Reader's Digest, *advertising dairy products. Quick, easy and good. It proved to be all of those and a recipe I use again and again.*

1 (3-ounce) package cream cheese, at room temperature	1 (8-ounce) carton frozen whipped dairy topping, thawed
½ cup smooth peanut butter	
1 cup powdered sugar	1 pre-baked graham cracker
½ cup milk	pie crust

In large bowl, with an electric mixer combine cream cheese, peanut butter, sugar and milk. Beat until smooth. Gently fold in whipped topping. Pour into pie shell. Freeze 4 to 6 hours. Thaw 10 minutes before serving. Yield: 8 servings.

BUTTERMILK PECAN PIE   *Delores Slayton Fenton*

1½ cups sugar	2 teaspoons vanilla
¼ cup flour	½ cup margarine, melted
½ cup buttermilk	1 cup pecans, chopped
3 eggs	1 9-inch unbaked pie shell

Mix sugar and flour. Add buttermilk and eggs, beat well. Add vanilla and margarine. Put pecans in bottom of the pie shell. Pour mixture over pecans. Bake at 350 degrees for 40 to 45 minutes. Yield: 9-inch pie.

Variation: BUTTERMILK PECAN PIE   *Jewell Sultemeier*
My family prefers this pie to regular pecan pie. Place ⅓ cup butter or margarine, 2 cups sugar, 3 rounded tablespoons flour, 1 cup buttermilk, and 1 teaspoon vanilla in blender. Blend until thoroughly blended. Mixer may also be used. Pour into a 9-inch unbaked pie shell and add ½ cup chopped pecans. Bake for 45 to 50 minutes at 350 degrees. Test by inserting toothpick into center, if it comes out clean pie is done. Place on rack to cool before serving. I always add 1 teaspoon of lemon juice. Yield: 9-inch pie.

HINT:
Pie plates need no grease. The crust has enough shortening to prevent sticking.

🦎 🦎 🦎 🦎 🦎 🦎 🦎

EGGLESS FUDGE PECAN PIE

Moline Lorenz

This pie is delicious and freezes well. I have made it for several years and it is always enjoyed.

½ cup butter	1 (5-ounce) can pet milk
3 tablespoons cocoa	2 cups sugar
¾ cup hot water	¾ cup pecans, chopped
½ cup flour	1 9-inch deep dish unbaked
¼ teaspoon salt	pie crust
1 teaspoon vanilla	

Preheat oven and cookie sheet to 350 degrees. In medium saucepan melt butter. Add cocoa and stir well. Add hot water and stir with wire whisk. Stir in flour, salt, vanilla, milk, and sugar. Stir until batter is smooth, mix in pecans. Pour in pie crust. Bake on cookie sheet for 50 minutes or until custard sets. Yield: 9-inch deep dish pie.

HEATH BAR ENGLISH TOFFEE PECAN PIE

Norma Honeycutt

This recipe is from the best pecan pie baker in Austin, Charles Wallace, and this pie is the best thing you will ever eat. Taste it and decide for yourself!

1 9-inch unbaked pie shell	4 tablespoons butter
3 original Heath English	or margarine, melted
Toffee Bars or Hershey's	½ cup sugar
Skor Bars	1 tablespoon vanilla
4 eggs, slightly beaten	1 cup pecans, coarsely
1 cup light corn syrup	chopped

Cover the bottom of a 9-inch pie shell with broken candy bars. In a mixing bowl, combine eggs, corn syrup, sugar, butter, and vanilla. Mix well and add pecans. Pour mixture over the candy bars in the pie shell. Bake at 350 degrees for 50 to 55 minutes, or until pie is done. Yield: 9-inch pie.

ORANGE-PECAN PIE

Dardanella Gipson

2 eggs, beaten	¼ cup orange juice
½ cup sugar	2 tablespoons flour
1 cup white corn syrup	¼ teaspoon salt
1 tablespoon grated orange	1 cup chopped pecans
rind	1 unbaked 9-inch pastry shell

151

Combine first 7 ingredients, beat at medium speed of electric mixer until blended. Stir in chopped pecans. Pour mixture into pie shell. Bake at 350 degrees for 55 minutes. Yield: 9-inch pie.

PRALINE PIE
Beverly K. Voron

This pie is so delicious and it doesn't taste like "just pudding and Cool Whip"!!

⅓ cup butter
⅓ cup brown sugar
½ cup pecans, chopped
1 9-inch lightly baked
   pie shell

1 (5½-ounce) package French
   vanilla instant Jello pudding
2½ cups milk
1⅓ cups Cool Whip

Combine butter, brown sugar, and nuts. Microwave or cook until butter is melted. Spread in bottom of lightly baked pie shell. Bake at 450 degrees for 5 minutes. Cool. Prepare pudding with 2½ cups milk as directed on package for pie. Measure 1 cup filling; set aside. Pour remaining filling into pie shell. Fold the rest of the filling with the Cool Whip and spoon over filling. Chill about 3 hours. Yield: 9-inch pie.

PUMPKIN PIE
Josie Byars

2 eggs
1 (16-ounce) can pumpkin
¾ cup sugar
3 tablespoons white Karo
1 teaspoon cinnamon
½ teaspoon ginger

½ teaspoon cloves
½ teaspoon nutmeg
1 teaspoon vanilla
½ teaspoon salt
¼ cup margarine, melted
1 9-inch unbaked pie shell

Preheat oven to 400 degrees. Slightly beat eggs and place in large bowl; mix in pumpkin until smooth. Mix in remaining ingredients. Pour into pie shell and bake 55 to 60 minutes. Yield: 9-inch pie.

BIG BOY STRAWBERRY PIE
Patricia J. Ripsom

A very cool and refreshing pie. You may add Cool Whip on top.

4 cups fresh strawberries
1 cup water
1 cup sugar
3 tablespoons cornstarch

½ cup water
1 (3-ounce) package
   strawberry Jello
1 9-inch baked pie shell

152

Wash strawberries and set aside. In a small saucepan combine water and sugar and bring to a boil. Make a paste of the cornstarch and ½ cup water. Stir into sugar/water combination. Cook on medium heat until thickened and turns clear. Takes about 5 minutes. Stir in ¾ package of the Jello. Cool a little, then add berries. Pour into the pie shell and refrigerate. For a softer filling use ½ package of the Jello.

Raspberries and raspberry Jello may be used. If the berries aren't very sweet, a little sugar may be used, but not too much or the berries become juicy. Yield: 9-inch pie.

STRAWBERRY-RHUBARB PIE *Sally Powell*

1 cup sugar	1 (10-ounce) carton frozen
⅓ cup flour	strawberries, thawed
4 cups rhubarb or more, cut	Butter <u>or</u> margarine
1-inch pieces	Sugar
1 9-inch double crust pastry	Cinnamon

Mix sugar and flour together in large bowl and then mix with cut-up rhubarb. Use a slotted spoon to lift out rhubarb and lay in bottom crust, then sprinkle with the remaining flour/sugar mixture in bowl. Evenly pour strawberries and juice over rhubarb and dot with butter or margarine. Cover with top crust; sprinkle with cinnamon and sugar and cut a few slits. Bake at 375 degrees for 45 to 50 minutes or until the rhubarb is soft. Yield: 9-inch pie.

A house should have a cookie jar for when it's half past three
    And children hurry home from school as hungry as can be.
There's nothing quite so splendid as spicy, fluffy ginger cakes
    And sweet milk in a cup.
A house should have a mother waiting with a hug,
    No matter what a boy brings home, a puppy or a bug.
For children only loiter when the bell rings to dismiss,
    If no one's home to greet them with a cookie and a kiss.

★　★　★　★　★

153

CHOCOLATE CHIP CREAM CHEESE COOKIES *Jan Christensen*

These cookies are better the next day.

2 (20-ounce) rolls chocolate chip cookie dough	2 eggs
2 (8-ounce) packages cream cheese, softened	1 teaspoon vanilla
	1 cup sugar

Spray 13 x 9 x 2-inch pan with vegetable spray. Put dough in freezer for one hour before slicing. Slice 1 roll of chocolate chip cookie dough and layer on bottom of pan. Pat to fill in holes. Mix cream cheese, eggs, vanilla, and sugar. Pour over layer of cookie dough. Slice, and quarter each slice of the remaining cookie dough roll and layer on top of cheese mixture. Bake at 350 degrees for 30 to 40 minutes until light brown. Cool 2 hours and cut into bars. May need to be refrigerated to cut easier. Yield: 2 dozen bars.

CINNAMON COFFEE BARS   *Emma Reue*

¼	cup soft shortening	¼	teaspoon soda
1	cup brown sugar	¼	teaspoon salt
1	egg	½	teaspoon cinnamon
½	cup hot coffee	½	cup seedless raisins
1½	cups sifted flour	¼	cup nuts, chopped
1	teaspoon baking powder		

Cream together shortening, brown sugar and egg. Stir in hot coffee. Sift dry ingredients together and add to sugar mixture. Blend in raisins and nuts. Spread in greased and floured 13 x 9 x 2-inch pan. Bake 15 to 20 minutes at 350 degrees. Glaze with powdered sugar glaze while hot, cut while warm. Yield: 12 to 15 servings.

DREAM BARS   *Ola Matus*

An old favorite!

⅓	cup butter or margarine, softened	2	eggs
		1	teaspoon vanilla
1½	cups firmly packed brown sugar, divided	½	teaspoon salt
		1	teaspoon baking powder
1	cup plus 2 tablespoons all-purpose flour, divided	1½	cups shredded coconut
		1	cup nuts, chopped

In large bowl of an electric mixer, beat butter and ½ cup sugar until creamy. With a fork, blend in 1 cup of the flour until mixture resembles fine crumbs. Press mixture firmly over bottom of a greased 13 x 9 x 2-inch pan, forming an even layer. Bake at 375 degrees for 10 minutes. Let cool in pan on a rack.

Wash and dry mixer bowl. Place eggs in bowl and beat until light and lemon-colored; then gradually beat in remaining 1 cup sugar. Beat in vanilla, remaining 2 tablespoons flour, salt, and baking powder. Stir in coconut and nuts until thoroughly combined. Pour coconut mixture over baked crust, spreading evenly. Return to oven and bake for 20 minutes or until topping is golden; then let cool in pan on a rack for 10 to 15 minutes. Meanwhile prepare orange butter frosting. Cut partially cooled cookies into bars about 1½ by 3 inches. Do not remove from pan. Spread frosting over cookies and let cool completely in pan. Don't frost cookies before cutting them. Store covered. Yield: 2 dozen.

Orange Butter Frosting

4 tablespoons butter **or** margarine	1 teaspoon grated orange peel
2 cups powdered sugar	Orange juice (about 2 tablespoons)
1 teaspoon vanilla	

In small bowl of an electric mixer, beat butter and sugar until creamy. Add vanilla and orange peel. Beat in enough orange juice, about 2 tablespoons, to make a good spreading consistency.

ENGLISH TOFFEE SQUARES   *Ola Matus*

Delicious and easy to prepare.

1 cup butter **or** margarine, softened	2 cups all-purpose flour
1 cup sugar	1 teaspoon cinnamon
1 egg, separated	1 cup pecans, chopped

In large bowl of an electric mixer, beat butter and sugar until creamy. Separate egg. Beat yolk into butter mixture. Stir together flour and cinnamon; add to butter mixture, blending thoroughly. Spread dough evenly over bottom of a greased 15 x 10 x 2-inch rimmed baking pan. Beat egg white lightly, then brush over dough to cover evenly. Sprinkle pecans over top; press in lightly. Bake at 275 degrees for 1 hour or until firm when lightly touched. While hot, cut into 1½ inch squares. Let cool in pan on a rack. Yield: 5 dozen.

155

OATMEAL CARAMELITAS
Beverly Voron

These are rich but, oh so gooood! They were a big seller at the Granny Goose Bakery the Community Church of the Hills had for awhile.

2	cups flour	6	tablespoons flour
2	cups quick oatmeal	1½	cups caramel ice cream
1½	cups brown sugar		topping
1½	cups butter, melted	1	cup pecans
¼	teaspoon salt	2	cups chocolate chips

Mix flour, oatmeal, brown sugar, butter, and salt and put half of the mixture in the bottom of a 13 x 9 x 2-inch pan. Press down with fingers. Bake at 350 degrees for 10 minutes. Mix flour and caramel topping and spread over bottom layer. Sprinkle nuts and chocolate chips over caramel topping, crumble remaining half of the oatmeal mixture over the top. Bake at 350 degrees for 40 minutes. Yield: 24 bars.

HOLIDAY ORANGE SLICE COOKIES
Gracie Wittkohl

Friends and their recipes are special and this cookie recipe from a friend in Savay, Texas, has become a part of my holiday baking.

4	eggs	2	cups flour
1	pound brown sugar		*Glaze*
1½	cups orange slice candy, cut, diced and floured	4	tablespoons milk
		1	tablespoon butter
2	cups coconut <u>or</u> pecans <u>or</u> both	1½	cups powdered sugar
		1½	teaspoons vanilla

Beat eggs, add sugar, beat again until creamy, add floured orange slices and nuts. Add flour. Put a thin layer of dough in 2 11 x 8 x 2-inch baking pans. Bake in a slow oven 275 degrees for 20 to 30 minutes or until brown.

Glaze: Bring milk and butter to a boil. Add sugar, mix well. Stir in vanilla. Spread on cookies while still hot. Cool, cut in squares. Yield: 30 bars.

HINTS:

Let cookies cool completely before storing.

Store soft and chewy cookies in an airtight container and crisp cookies in a jar with a loose-fitting lid.

SQUARE DANCE SQUARES   *Lee Caruthers*

½ cup cocoa	1 cup coconut, divided
1½ cups flour	1 pound box powdered sugar
2 cups sugar	½ cup evaporated milk
4 eggs, beaten	1 teaspoon vanilla
1 cup margarine, melted	1 (7-ounce) jar
1¾ cups pecans, chopped, divided	marshmallow cream

Sift first 3 ingredients into a big bowl. Stir in eggs, add margarine, and 1 cup pecans. Pour into greased jelly roll pan. Bake 20 minutes. While baking make topping. Stir together ½ cup coconut, powdered sugar, milk, and vanilla. When baking is finished, remove from oven at once and spread marshmallow cream on top. Then spread topping over cream. Pat in remaining coconut and pecans. When cool cut into small squares. Yield: 24 bars.

Variation: FUDGE DREAM BARS   *Olivia Weiershausen*
This was in the PEC paper in 1944. All children love it. Melt 1 cup margarine with ⅓ cup cocoa over low heat. Beat 4 eggs well with 2 cups sugar. Add 1½ cups flour, dash of salt and 1 teaspoon vanilla extract. Pour batter into a greased 13 x 9 x 2-inch or jelly-roll pan. Bake at 350 degrees for 20 to 25 minutes. *Filling:* Cut ½ pound of large marshmallows into 4 pieces and place marshmallows on top of warm cake. Return cake to oven to melt marshmallows. Mix ¼ cup margarine, ⅓ cup cocoa, 1 (16-ounce) box powdered sugar and enough milk to spread over marshmallows. Cut into 24 squares when cool. Yield: 24 bars.

WHOLE WHEAT RAISIN BARS   *Jean Everson*

½ cup shortening	½ teaspoon baking soda
1 cup brown sugar	½ teaspoon nutmeg
1 egg	½ teaspoon cinnamon
1 cup whole wheat flour	1 cup cold coffee
1 cup flour	2 cups raisins
½ teaspoon baking powder	

Cream shortening, add sugar and egg. Sift together dry ingredients and add to creamed mixture with coffee until well mixed. Add raisins. Pour into well greased 13 x 9 x 2-inch pan. Bake for 15 minutes at 375 degrees. When cool sprinkle with powdered sugar. Cut into bars. Yield: 16 to 24 bars.

WHOLE WHEAT ALMOND BUTTER COOKIES   *Jean Everson*

1 cup butter	1 teaspoon baking soda
1½ cups sugar	½ teaspoon salt
3 eggs	½ teaspoon cinnamon
2 teaspoons almond extract	½ teaspoon nutmeg
1½ cups whole wheat flour	½ cup almonds,
2 cups white flour	chopped, optional

Cream together butter and sugar, add eggs and extract. Sift together dry ingredients. Add to first mixture. Stir in almonds if desired. Drop onto well greased cookie sheet. Bake 6 to 8 minutes at 375 degrees. Yield: 6 to 8 dozen.

BACHELOR BUTTON COOKIES   *Helen Mayfield*

½ cup margarine	½ cup maraschino
¾ cup brown sugar	cherries, chopped
1 egg	2½ cups flour
1 cup coconut, shredded	1 teaspoon baking soda
¼ cup walnuts, chopped	⅛ teaspoon salt

Preheat oven to 350 degrees. Cream margarine, add sugar and cream well. Beat egg and add to sugar mixture. Add coconut, walnuts, and cherries. Blend well. Mix flour, baking soda, and salt. Add flour mixture to first mixture very gradually. If mixture seems a little too thick, add a few drops of milk. Drop by teaspoonfuls on greased baking sheet. Bake about 15 to 20 minutes at 350 degrees. Yield: 3 dozen.

GREAT CHOCOLATE CHIP COOKIE   *Elizabeth Sublett*

This is my favorite chip cookie.

2½ cups flour	1 teaspoon vanilla
1 teaspoon baking soda	2 eggs
½ teaspoon salt	2 cups semi-sweet
1 cup butter or shortening, softened	chocolate chips
¾ cup sugar	1 cup nuts,
¾ cup brown sugar, packed tight	chopped

Heat oven to 375 degrees. In bowl stir together flour, baking soda, and salt. In large bowl, beat butter, sugars, and vanilla until creamy. Add eggs,

beat well. Gradually add flour mixture and beat well. Stir in chips and nuts. Drop by teaspoonfuls onto ungreased cookie sheet. Bake 9 to 11 minutes or until lightly browned. Cool slightly. Remove from cookie sheet onto wire rack. Cool completely. Yields: 6 dozen cookies.

COWBOY COOKIES
Adelia Felps

Years ago on a trip to Arkansas I found this recipe in an old cookbook; came home and made them with a little modernization. They have been a hit ever since. I usually freeze one half in freezer bags. But watch out, this doesn't keep them from disappearing right out of the freezer.

2 cups margarine	2 cups cornflakes
2 cups sugar	1 cup pecans, chopped
2 cups brown sugar	1 (6-ounce) package
4 eggs	chocolate chips
2 tablespoons vanilla	1 (6-ounce) package peanut
4 cups flour	butter chips
2 tablespoons soda	1 cup coconut
2 cups oatmeal	

Melt margarine in microwave. Add sugars and cream together, add eggs and vanilla, mix well and set aside. Mix remaining ingredients together in large bowl; add creamed sugars and egg mixture, mixing well. Drop by heaping teaspoonfuls on ungreased cookie sheet. Bake at 350 degrees for 10 to 15 minutes. Allow cookies to slightly cool on sheet before removing. Yield: 8 dozen cookies.

Variation: BUFFALO CHIP COOKIES
Pat Althaus
Cream together 2 cups margarine, 2 cups white sugar, 2 teaspoons vanilla, 2 cups brown sugar and 4 eggs. Sift together 4 cups flour, 2 teaspoons baking soda, 1 teaspoon salt, and 2 teaspoons baking powder. Add the dry ingredients to the creamed mixture a cup at a time. Mix in 2 cups oatmeal, 1 (12-ounce) package chocolate chips, 2 cups Post Toasties, and 1 or 2 cups pecans or walnuts, chopped. Put on a greased cookie sheet using an ice cream scoop for a whopper of a cookie! Bake at 350 degrees for 12–15 minutes. Yield: about 4 dozen large cookies.

HINT:
Freshly grated lemon or orange zest adds zip to all cookies.

FRUIT DELIGHT COOKIES   *Carmen Tulloch*

This recipe came to me in the teachers lounge at the Belton school in which I taught music. I started making these instead of making a fruit cake and people really enjoyed them.

1 cup butter	1½ pounds dates, chopped
1½ cups sugar	½ pound candied cherries,
2 eggs	chopped
2½ cups flour	½ pound candied pineapple,
1 teaspoon salt	chopped
1 teaspoon soda	1 pound pecans, chopped
1 teaspoon cinnamon	

Cream butter and sugar, add eggs and beat well. Add dry ingredients and mix well. Add fruit and nuts. Mix well. This is a very stiff batter and I use my hands to mix it thoroughly. Drop by rounded tablespoonfuls on a greased cookie sheet. Bake at 350 degrees for about 12 minutes. Yield: 6 dozen cookies.

GOLD RUSH COOKIES   *Helen Mayfield*

Accept a compliment, enjoy it, but only half believe it.

2 tablespoons butter	1 cup flour, sifted
1½ cups chocolate chips	1 teaspoon vanilla
1 (14-ounce) can sweetened condensed milk	1 cup nuts, chopped

Melt butter and chocolate chips in double boiler. Add milk. Then stir in flour, vanilla, and nuts. Mix well and chill. Drop by teaspoonfuls on well greased cookie sheet. Bake at 325 degrees for 15 minutes. These cookies will not seem done, but they are. Frost with your favorite chocolate frosting. These are almost like candy. Yield: 2 to 3 dozen.

IMPERIAL COOKIES   *Jan Christensen*

1 cup butter (Do Not Substitute), softened	½ teaspoon white vinegar
¾ cup sugar	1 teaspoon vanilla
½ teaspoon baking soda	1½ cups flour

Mix in mixing bowl in order given, mixing after each addition. Mix until

160

well blended. Drop by teaspoonfuls on greased cookie sheet. Do not flatten. Bake at 275 degrees for 25 to 30 minutes. Cookies will be light colored. Sprinkle with sugar or colored sugar prior to baking if desired. Yield: 3 dozen cookies.

"IN-A-HURRY" COOKIES   *Pat Althaus*

2 cups flour	1 egg
1 cup brown sugar	½ cup milk
2 tablespoons shortening (Crisco)	¼ teaspoon salt
	½ cup raisins <u>or</u> nuts <u>or</u>
2 teaspoons baking powder	coconut, <u>or</u> any combination

Mix ingredients in order given. Mix until well blended. Drop by teaspoonfuls on a greased cookie sheet. Bake at 375 degrees for 12 to 15 minutes. Spices may be added if desired. Yield: 4½ dozen cookies.

NO BAKE COOKIES   *Joy Feuge*

When working for Texas Employment Commission in Fort Worth, our local office newsletters offered an opportunity to share recipes. This is from one of my closest friends and neighbors, Jo Ann Bell.

2 cups sugar	2 cups graham
1 (5-ounce) can evaporated milk	cracker crumbs
½ cup butter or margarine	1 cup nuts, chopped
1 teaspoon vanilla	1 cup flaked coconut
1 (7-ounce) jar marshmallow cream	

Combine sugar, milk, and butter in large pan. Place over medium heat and cook to soft ball stage (230 to 234 degrees). Remove from heat, add vanilla and marshmallow cream, stirring until cream is melted. Add remaining ingredients, mixing well. Drop by teaspoonfuls onto wax paper. Cool completely. Yield: about 4 dozen cookies.

HINT:

To tint coconut; place 1 cup of coconut into a pint jar. Add a few drops of cake coloring to 1 to 2 tablespoons water. Add coconut, cover jar and shake well to distribute color.

☆   ☆   ☆   ☆   ☆

161

⌂ ⌂ ⌂ ⌂ ⌂ ⌂ ⌂

NO SUGAR COOKIES
Dorothy C. Lackey

This recipe is great for diabetics, as it has NO sugar in it.

1 cup raisins	1 teaspoon baking soda
½ cup apples, chopped	1 teaspoon vanilla
½ cup dates, chopped	1 cup quick-cooking oats
1 cup water	2 eggs, beaten
½ cup margarine	¾ cup nuts, chopped
1 cup flour	

Boil first 4 ingredients for 3 minutes on low heat. Cool slightly. Add rest of ingredients. Mix well. Refrigerate over night. Drop by teaspoonfuls on a greased cookie sheet. Bake at 350 degrees for 10 to 12 minutes. Yield: About 2½ dozen.

HEALTHY OATMEAL COOKIES
Gwen Pickett

1 cup flour	½ teaspoon cinnamon
½ cup sugar	2 egg whites
½ teaspoon salt	⅓ cup Karo light or dark
½ teaspoon baking powder	corn syrup
1 cup quick oats	1 tablespoon vanilla
½ teaspoon baking soda	½ cup raisins

In large bowl combine dry ingredients. Stir in egg whites, corn syrup and vanilla until well mixed. Add raisins. Batter will be stiff. Drop by rounded teaspoonfuls on cookie sheets sprayed with Pam. Bake at 375 degrees for 10 minutes or until firm. Do not over bake. Yield: 2½ dozen.

CHUNKY OATMEAL CHIP COOKIES
Bernice K. Weinheimer

½ cup butter or margarine, softened	4 eggs, large
	1 teaspoon vanilla
1 (18-ounce) jar chunky peanut butter	6 cups quick-cooking oatmeal
	2½ teaspoons baking soda
1½ cups sugar	1 cup semi-sweet chocolate
1½ cups brown sugar, firmly packed	chips

Beat together butter and peanut butter until fluffy. Gradually add sugars, beating well. Add eggs, one at a time and beat well. Add vanilla. Combine oats and baking soda; add to butter mixture, mixing well. Stir in chocolate

162

chips. Drop by teaspoonfuls onto ungreased cookie sheet. Bake at 350 degrees for 9 to 10 minutes. Cool on cookie sheets 5 minutes; remove to cool. This makes a big batch. Freeze half and enjoy the rest! Yield: 7 dozen cookies.

Variation: MONSTER COOKIES   *Josie Byars*
In a mammoth bowl, mix together ⅓ pound (½ cup plus 1½ tablespoons) margarine, 1⅓ cups brown sugar, 1⅓ cups white sugar, 4 eggs, 1 pound peanut butter, 6 cups uncooked oatmeal, and 2½ teaspoons baking soda. Stir in 1 (6-ounce) package of semi-sweet chocolate chips and 1 pound plain M&M's. Preheat oven to 350 degrees. Plop batter by tablespoonfuls about 4-inches apart onto an ungreased cookie sheet. Bake 10 to 12 minutes. Cool briefly on rack and gobble. Yield: about 4 dozen large cookies.

OATMEAL PUDDING COOKIES   *Opal Wierich*

1¼	cups flour	2	eggs
1	teaspoon baking soda	3½	cups oats
1	cup butter <u>or</u> margarine	1	cup raisins
¼	cup sugar	1	cup nuts, chopped
¾	cup brown sugar		
1	(3-ounce) package vanilla instant pudding mix		

Mix flour with soda. Combine butter, sugars, and pudding mix in bowl. Beat until smooth and creamy. Add eggs. Gradually add flour mixture, oats, raisins and nuts. Drop onto ungreased cookie sheet. Bake 10 to 12 minutes at 375 degrees. Yield: 6 dozen cookies.

SWEDISH OATMEAL COOKIES   *Dena Heider*

⅓	cup sugar	1	egg
¼	cup butter <u>or</u> margarine	½	teaspoon vanilla
1	tablespoon light corn syrup	¾	cup flour
½	cup chopped, blanched almonds	½	teaspoon soda
⅛	teaspoon almond extract	½	teaspoon salt
½	cup shortening	1½	cups quick cooking
½	cup sugar		oatmeal (uncooked)
½	cup firmly packed brown sugar		

Combine sugar, butter or margarine and corn syrup in a small saucepan and bring to a boil. Remove from heat and stir in almonds and almond extract. Set mixture aside.

In a large mixing bowl, cream shortening, gradually add sugars beat-

ing well at medium speed of the electric mixer. Add egg, vanilla, and beat well. Combine flour, soda, and salt. Add to creamed mixture beating well. Stir in quick cooking oats. Drop dough by rounded teaspoonfuls onto ungreased cookie sheets. Bake at 350 degrees for 8 minutes. Remove from oven, place ½ teaspoon of almond mixture in center of each cookie. Return to oven and bake an additional 6 to 8 minutes or until browned. Remove cookies to wire rack to cool completely. Yield: about 4 dozen.

CYNTHIA'S PARTY PINEAPPLE COOKIES — Cynthia Smith

I call these Party Pineapple cookies, because they are so delicious you want to share them with a lot of people. If I wasn't helping to put together this cookbook, I'd keep this recipe a secret! These cookies get rave reviews all the time.

1	cup sugar	1	teaspoon soda
1	cup brown sugar		Pinch of salt
1	cup shortening		*Icing*
2	eggs	¼	cup margarine
1	(20-ounce) can crushed	¼	cup boiling water
	pineapple, juice and all	½	teaspoon almond extract
1	teaspoon vanilla	1	pound powdered sugar
4	cups flour		

Cream sugars and shortening, add eggs and mix. Add rest of ingredients. Drop by teaspoonfuls onto ungreased cookie sheet. Bake at 375 degrees until just golden. Cool cookies on a wire rack and then ice them.

Icing: Melt the margarine in the boiling water, add the almond and powdered sugar. Beat together. If it is too runny just add more powdered sugar. Hint: Using a fork stick each cookie on the underside and just touch the cookie to the icing or place them on a wire rack with a cookie sheet underneath and drizzle the icing over the cookies. Leave cookies on wire rack until icing dries. Yield: 8 dozen silver dollar sized cookies.

SOUR CREAM DROPS — Margaret Dannecker

These cookies take some time to make, as does any iced cookie, but they always win raves. They were served to a visiting group of tour operation owners several years ago. Later the group's guide from the Department of Commerce called and said everyone wanted the recipe; she would fax it to them if I would send it to her. So the recipe ended up being faxed all over the U.S. and to Canada. They've been served at so many receptions for visitors to our area that we almost decided to rename them the Hospitality Cookies.

164

½ cup vegetable shortening
    (Crisco)
1½ cups brown sugar
2   eggs
1   cup sour cream
1   teaspoon vanilla
2¾ cups flour
½ teaspoon soda
1   teaspoon salt

1   cup pecans, chopped
Brown Sugar Icing
1   cup butter (Do NOT
    Substitute)
4   cups powdered sugar,
    sifted
2   teaspoon vanilla
4   tablespoons hot water

Mix shortening, brown sugar, and eggs thoroughly. Stir in sour cream and vanilla. Sift together flour, soda, and salt and add to first mixture. Stir in pecans. Drop by teaspoonfuls on greased baking sheet. Bake in 375 degree oven for 8 to 10 minutes, until set. When cool, top with icing. Yield: 5 dozen cookies.

Icing: Melt butter and brown sugar until caramel colored. Blend in powdered sugar and vanilla. Add hot water and blend until all of the butter is absorbed. If the icing starts to separate before you're finished icing cookies, add a teaspoon more of hot water and stir well. Do not add more powdered sugar.

BEST COOKIE EVER   *Leslie Matus*

1   cup of butter, softened, no
    margarine
1   cup of sugar
1   cup of brown sugar
2   eggs
1   teaspoon vanilla extract
2   cups all-purpose flour
2½ cups uncooked oatmeal

1   teaspoon baking soda
1   teaspoon baking powder
½ teaspoon salt
1   (12-ounce) bag of chocolate
    chips
1   (8-ounce) Hershey bar,
    grated
1½ cups of nuts, chopped

Preheat oven to 375 degrees. In a large bowl, cream together butter, sugar and brown sugar. Mix in eggs and vanilla extract. Mix in flour, oatmeal, baking soda, baking powder, and salt. Add remaining ingredients and mix together. Roll dough into small balls (no larger than ping pong ball size) and place about 2 inches apart on lightly greased cookie sheets. Bake for 6 minutes, 7 at most. Yes, that's enough; we want them to be moist and chewy. Yield: Approximately 5 dozen cookies.

MELTAWAY CHOCOLATE BALLS   *Leah Mauck*

Natzalie Pfluger used to make these for our Tuesday morning get-together when we lived in Austin. She didn't have a name for them so we came up with this name, as they really do melt in your mouth. They are so good.

1¼	cups margarine	½	cup cocoa
⅔	cup sugar	2	cups flour
1	teaspoon vanilla	⅛	teaspoon salt
¾	cup coconut		Powdered sugar

Cream margarine and sugar until fluffy. Add vanilla, then sifted dry ingredients, mix well. Add coconut. Refrigerate for at least 6 hours. Roll into 1-inch balls, place on ungreased cookie sheet. Bake at 300 degrees for 20 minutes. Cool on wire rack, then roll in powdered sugar. Yield: 3 to 4 dozen cookies, depending on size of ball.

CHOCOLATE CRINKLE COOKIES   *Genevia Bushnell*

A family favorite. I like to make this recipe at Christmas.

½	cup corn oil (Mazola)	2	teaspoons vanilla
4	(1-ounce) squares un-	½	teaspoon salt
	sweetened chocolate, melted	2	cups flour, sifted
2	cups sugar	2	teaspoons baking powder
4	eggs	1	cup powdered sugar

Mix oil, chocolate, and sugar. Blend in 1 egg at a time until well mixed. Add vanilla. Stir in salt, flour, and baking powder. Chill several hours or overnight. Heat oven to 350 degrees. Drop teaspoonfuls of dough into powdered sugar. Roll around and shape into balls. Place about 2 inches apart on greased baking sheet. Bake 10 to 12 minutes. Yield: about 4 dozen.

HINTS:

Chop a bar of good-quality chocolate by hand for lush chocolate chip cookies.

Because water is whipped into reduce-calorie margarine, it does not work well in baked products.

166

CELIA'S CHOCO-SNICKS

Celia Grote

The children needed cookies for school. I was in the process of making Snickerdoodles when I was told . . . they needed to be CHOCOLATE COOKIES! I quickly added the cocoa . . . thus Choco-Snicks were created and they are good.

1	cup shortening	1	teaspoon soda
1½	cups sugar	½	teaspoon salt
2	eggs, beaten	½	cup cocoa
2¾	cups flour	3	tablespoons sugar
2	teaspoons cream of tartar	1	teaspoon cinnamon

Cream shortening and sugar. Add eggs and mix well. Add flour, cream of tartar, soda, salt, and cocoa to the creamed mixture. Chill one hour. Roll into small balls. Roll balls in mixture of sugar and cinnamon. Bake at 350 degrees about 8 to 10 minutes or until lightly browned. Yield: 6 dozen cookies.

BLUE RIBBON GINGER SNAPS

Ima Hobbs

1½	cups shortening	2	teaspoons baking soda
2	cups sugar	2	teaspoons cinnamon
2	eggs	2	teaspoons cloves
½	cup molasses	2	teaspoons ginger
4	cups flour, sifted		

Cream shortening and sugar together. Beat in eggs, add molasses. Mix dry ingredients together. Mix 2 mixtures together thoroughly. Roll into 1 inch balls, dip in sugar, and place on baking sheet 2 inches apart. Bake at 375 degrees for 15 to 18 minutes. Yield: 9 to 10 dozen cookies.

FREEZER OATMEAL COOKIES

Debbie Wiemers Hemphill

I often cut off just a few to bake, fixing them gradually over the whole 3 months.

1½	cups flour	2	eggs
1	teaspoon baking soda	1	teaspoon vanilla
½	teaspoon salt	3	cups quick-cooking
1	cup margarine		oats, uncooked
1	cup sugar	1	cup pecans, chopped
1	cup brown sugar, firmly packed		

Combine and stir together flour, baking soda, and salt, set aside. Cream margarine in a large electric mixer bowl. Gradually add both sugars to margarine, beating well at medium speed. Add eggs and vanilla to this mixture, beating well. Add flour mixture, mixing well. Stir in oats and pecans. Divide the dough in half and wrap each half in wax paper. Place in freezer for 1 hour or until the dough can be shaped into a 12-inch roll. Freeze the dough at least six hours. Unwrap dough rolls and cut into ¼ inch slices. Bake at 375 degrees for 12 minutes or until light brown. Cool on wire racks. This dough may be frozen for up to 3 months. Yield: about 7 dozen cookies.

PFEFFERNUSSE COOKIES   *Jewell Sultemeier*

This cookie is a favorite of my grandson, Dr. Mark Wallis. This particular recipe is a good keeper, in fact, it improves with age.

4	cups sugar	1½	teaspoons black pepper
3	cups honey	1	teaspoon cloves
1	cup butter	1	teaspoon anise
6	eggs, well beaten	1	teaspoon cinnamon
1½	cups cold coffee	5	pounds flour
1	tablespoon baking soda		Powdered sugar
2	teaspoons baking powder		

Bring sugar, honey, and butter to a boil and let cool. Add rest of ingredients in order given, adding flour to make soft dough. Chill dough, roll out and cut with a 1½ inch round cookie cutter. These cookies roll out very easy. Bake at 450 degrees until firm. Remove from oven and shake in powdered sugar. For more of a sugar coating, shake again in sugar when cool. Yield: 27 dozen cookies.

RITZ CRACKER COOKIES   *Jane Mills*

This recipe comes from a friend, from a friend! The friend is Frances Stastney, and her friend is Velma Goertz, who both live in Austin. Velma does not remember where the recipe originally came from. It's a super recipe and oh so easy to make. BET YOU CAN'T EAT JUST ONE!!!

1	(14-ounce) can Eagle Brand milk	*Frosting*	
1	cup dates, chopped	1	(3-ounce) package cream cheese, softened
1	cup pecans, chopped	⅓	cup margarine
1½	sleeves of Ritz crackers	1½	cups powdered sugar
		1	teaspoon vanilla

Preheat oven to 325 degrees. Cook and stir over medium heat, the milk and dates, until very, very thick. Stir constantly to prevent scorching. Remove and add pecans, stirring well. Immediately spread on Ritz crackers. Place on cookie sheet and bake 6 to 8 minutes. Remove and cool completely. Prepare frosting mix, mixing until very smooth. When crackers are completely cooled, frost and then store in refrigerator. Yield: about 5 dozen.

SNICKERDOODLES   *Pat Rumpf*

This recipe was given to me by Ann Hudson.

1	cup shortening	1	teaspoon soda
1½	cups sugar	2	teaspoons cream of tartar
2	eggs	½	teaspoon salt
2¾	cups flour		

Cream shortening and sugar. Add eggs; beat well. Sift flour, soda, cream of tartar and salt. Add to cream mixture; mix well. Shape into balls the size of a walnut, about 1-inch. Place 2 inches apart on greased cookie sheet. Bake at 400 degrees for 6 to 10 minutes or until lightly brown. Cool on wire rack. Yield: 4 dozen.

Variation: Add 1 teaspoon of vanilla. Roll balls in 2 tablespoons sugar and 1 teaspoon of cinnamon before baking.

SUPER SUGAR COOKIES   *Anna Lou Felps*

From Martha D. Strothers, a Tour Director with Traveling Texans.

1	cup margarine	1	teaspoon baking soda
1	cup vegetable oil	4	cups flour
1	cup granulated sugar	1	teaspoon cream of tartar
1	cup powdered sugar	1	teaspoon salt
1	teaspoon vanilla		Granulated sugar for final step
2	eggs		

In a large bowl combine margarine, vegetable oil and granulated sugar; beat until creamy. Add powdered sugar, vanilla, and eggs; mix well. In a small bowl, sift together baking soda, flour, cream of tartar and salt. Add to other ingredients and mix well. Cover dough and refrigerate at least two hours. Roll dough into 1-inch balls and roll in granulated sugar. Flatten on lightly greased cookie sheet. Preheat oven to 350 degrees and bake until edges are light brown, about 12 minutes. Let cool slightly before removing from cookie sheet. Yield: 4 dozen.

ALMOND BARK RICE KRISPIES
Olivia Weiershausen

These are easy to fix, good for rich snacks for a party or at home.

1	(20-ounce) package almond bark	1	(3½-ounce) can coconut
3	cups Rice Krispies cereal	½	cups pecans, chopped
		1	teaspoon vanilla

Melt almond bark, then add cereal, coconut, pecans, and vanilla. Lay foil on table and drop mixture by teaspoonfuls on foil. They set in a hurry and are ready to eat or to take along. Yield: about 4 dozen.

BUCKEYES
Daisy Cox

While visiting Ohio last summer, we encountered this recipe on post cards and other material. It is fitting since Ohio is nicknamed the Buckeye State, because of the Buckeye trees.

3½	cups powdered sugar	½	cup melted margarine
2	cups crunchy peanut butter	1	(12-ounce) package chocolate chips
3	cups Rice Krispies cereal, slightly crushed	¼	stick paraffin

Mix together the sugar, peanut butter, cereal and margarine. Roll into balls and refrigerate one hour to firm up. Melt chocolate chips in paraffin over hot water. Dip balls in chocolate with toothpicks, leaving a small portion of the ball exposed, like a buckeye. Place on wax paper to cool. These also freeze well. Yield: 36 to 40 buckeyes.

HINT:
Always preheat oven at least 10 minutes before baking.

BUTTERSCOTCH CANDY

Neatta Cade

This was given to me one Christmas from Millie Revel of Homestead, Florida.

| 2 | (8-ounce) packages | 4 | cups Post Toasties |
| | Butterscotch Bits | 1½ | cups peanuts |

Melt Butterscotch Bits over water, use a double-boiler or use microwave. When melted pour over Post Toasties and peanuts. Mix, spoon with teaspoon on to wax paper. Makes a bunch.

AUNT BLANCHE'S FUDGE

Lillian Stewart

Aunt Blanche Dodgen from Littlefield, Texas, always came with her husband J.D., for hunting season each year. In between hunting trips, Blanche would be in the kitchen cooking up one good thing after the other. This fudge has always been a family favorite. When the children were in school I made this many, many times for class fund raisers. Lately it has been selling well at Lights Spectacular booths! The secret to the fudge is to stir it long enough at the end before dropping it onto the wax paper. It needs to begin to thicken. I don't put the pecans in the fudge, but put a half on top of each piece.

4½	cups sugar	18	ounces semi-sweet
1	(12-ounce) can evaporated		chocolate chips
	milk	1	pint jar marshmallow cream
¾	stick butter	1	pound whole pecans

Mix sugar, milk and butter and bring to a boil and boil for 5 minutes, slowly, stirring constantly. Pour this mixture over the chocolate chips and marshmallow cream. Mix well. Keep stirring until it begins to thicken. Drop on wax paper to harden in size pieces you desire. Put a pecan half on each piece. Yield: 30 to 40 pieces.

RICHARD'S HAWAIIAN FUDGE

Geneva Eubanks

This is an original recipe given to me by Richard Montgomery of Midland, Texas. I had the pleasure of working for him eight years. He liked to cook gourmet dishes and was excellent at making candies. At Christmas he would give each employee a container filled with various confections. His Hawaiian Fudge was my favorite. He created this recipe because his grandmother made a similar candy during his childhood.

3 cups sugar
1 cup sour cream
Scant ½ cup milk
4 tablespoons butter or
   margarine, divided
1 teaspoon pineapple extract

½ cup candied pineapple,
   finely diced
¼ cup slivered almonds
¼ cup macadamia nuts,
   chopped

In heavy saucepan combine sugar, sour cream, milk and 2 tablespoons butter. Cook until candy thermometer reaches 234 degrees. Remove from heat and stir in 2 more tablespoons butter and pineapple extract. Put saucepan in cool water and stir until pan is cool enough to touch and candy thickens some. Add the candied pineapple, almonds, and macadamia nuts and mix thoroughly. Pour into a buttered 13 x 9 x 2-inch dish. Cut in pieces when cool. Yield: 3 dozen 1½ inch pieces.

CHEWY PECAN PRALINES

Bernice K. Weinheimer

1 cup brown sugar
1 cup white sugar
1 cup white Karo
1 (14-ounce) can sweetened
   condensed milk

½ pound butter
3 cups pecans
1 teaspoon almond extract
1 teaspoon vanilla

Combine brown sugar, white sugar, Karo, milk and butter. Stir over low heat. Boil, stirring constantly until it forms a soft ball when dropped in a cup of cold water. Take off burner and add pecans, almond and vanilla extracts. Stir until thick and drop by spoonfuls onto a buttered platter. Yield: a bunch.

MICROWAVE CARAMEL POPCORN

Robin Taylor

1 cup brown sugar
½ cup margarine
¼ cup white Karo syrup

¼ teaspoon salt
½ teaspoon baking soda
6 quarts popped popcorn

Roll down the sides of a large brown paper grocery bag and spray inside with vegetable cooking spray. Put the popcorn into the bag. Combine the brown sugar, margarine, Karo syrup, and salt in a microwave safe dish. Cook on HIGH for 2 minutes. Stir and microwave an additional 2 minutes. Immediately add baking soda and stir. Pour mixture over popcorn in bag and quickly stir until mixture coats all popcorn. Put bag in microwave and heat on HIGH for 1½ minutes. Remove and stir and return to micro-

wave. Heat on HIGH an additional 1½ minutes. Stir once more and heat on HIGH for 45 seconds. Cool and break apart and enjoy! Yield: 6 quarts.

BANANA NUT ICE CREAM
Norma Honeycutt

Lots of calories, but so good; you can walk around the block after you have enjoyed a bowl! A lot of people do not like the taste of raw eggs in their ice cream, so I have always looked for recipes that did not contain eggs. This is a very good one that always seems to go over very well.

2 (14-ounce) cans sweetened condensed milk	½ cup sugar
	1 cup pecans, chopped
½ gallon milk	1 teaspoon vanilla
8 to 10 bananas, mashed	

Mix and pour in 1 gallon ice cream freezer, do not fill to the top. Prepare according to ice cream freezer directions. Yield: 1 gallon ice cream.

Variation: NUTTY BANANA ICE CREAM *Adelia Felps*
Combine 2 (14-ounce) cans sweetened condensed milk, 1 pint whipping cream, 1 pint Half and Half, 1 tablespoon vanilla, 4 large mashed bananas and 1 cup pecans, chopped. Place in gallon freezer container and add whole milk until ¾ full. Stir. Freeze according to manufacturer's directions. Yield: 1 gallon.

LOW FAT VANILLA ICE CREAM
Gwen Pickett

4 egg whites	1 (12-ounce) can evaporated skimmed milk, chilled
¼ cup corn oil or Canola oil	
3 cups skimmed milk	Dash salt
1½ cups sugar	1 tablespoon vanilla

Combine egg whites and oil in a large heavy saucepan. Blend thoroughly with a whisk. Add milk and sugar to the egg whites and cook over low heat until mixture begins to coat a metal spoon. Remove from heat and chill. Add evaporated milk, vanilla and salt to the chilled mixture. Blend well and freeze in a 2 quart freezer. Yield: 2 quarts.

☆ ☆ ☆ ☆ ☆

HINT:
If your pralines do not harden as they should, fold them into softened vanilla ice cream for praline ice cream.

DIABETIC HOMEMADE ICE CREAM   *Angelia Stearns*

My father has always been involved with selling ice cream. When he found out he was diabetic, he was wonderful and stuck to his diet always. So I decided to try various recipes and come up with something he could enjoy. His doctor approved and we all enjoy the ice cream! (Well almost; my kids still prefer Blue Bell, but this recipe comes pretty close!)

6 cups skim milk	1 (8-ounce) container frozen
1 (5-ounce) package Estee	lite whipped topping, thawed
Fructose (natural sweetener)	1 (5¼-ounce) package sugar
1 (12-ounce) can skim	free vanilla **or** chocolate
evaporated milk	pudding mix

Combine all ingredients in a large mixing bowl; beat at medium speed of an electric mixer until well blended. Pour mixture into freezer can of a 5-quart hand-turned or electric freezer. Freeze according to manufacturer's instructions. Let ripen 1 hour. Yield: 5 quarts.

HINTS:

To prevent nuts or fruit from sinking to the bottom of cake or bread, shake them in a bag with a small amount of flour to dust lightly before adding to batter.

For even slices, cut a whole cake in half, then quarters, then into the desired number of slices. Wrap unfrosted cakes in plastic wrap, not foil.

Fruit cakes or pound cakes are easier to slice when they are cold.

A quick frosting can be made by adding a bit of chocolate syrup to prepared whipped topping.

A chocolate bar placed on top of hot cake and spread over cake can be used for a quick frosting.

Add a finishing touch to pies; garnish with an ingredient used in the pie, such as lemon slices on a lemon pie.

Melting Pot
A Culinary Blending of Cultures . . .

THE PEARL HOTEL

In the 1880s, James P. Johnson had a two-story hotel built near Town Creek and named it for his daughter, Pearl. Mr. Johnson's vision for the future was that Johnson City become the county seat. Over the years, many a weary traveler or itinerant worker has found respite in the hotel, as did those coming on business, after it became the county seat. In 1928 Mrs. Dave Adams purchased and remodeled the building and named it Adams Hotel. The dining room was the heart of the hotel, serving home-cooked meals. Over the years, banquets were held, school was kept and town hall meetings were held here. Mr. Kent Smith presently owns the building.

175

LOS TRES BOBOS – FRIED SQUASH *Leah Mauck*

This recipe was a well kept secret for over three years – but was finally shared with Ellie Rucker, who passed it on in the Austin American-Statesman. *It is a mess to make, but well worth the effort. I usually make up a large batch, freeze on cookie sheets, then fry them as needed.*

6 to 8 squash, zucchini <u>or</u>
  yellow (sliced lengthwise)
Dry Batter
3 cups flour
1 cup biscuit mix (cheapest
  in store)
1 tablespoon black pepper

1 teaspoon garlic salt
Wet Batter
1 egg
2 cups buttermilk
½ cup biscuit mix
½ cup ice water
1 tablespoon oregano

Dip slices in batters – going from dry to wet and back to dry. Fry at 350 degrees in vegetable oil until golden brown, (probably 20 to 25 seconds). Yield: A bunch.

TACO SALAD / MEXICAN PARTY DIP *Holly Lawson*

When all of our family gets together, we make this – there is never any left!

2 (16-ounce) cans refried
  beans
2 jalapeño peppers,
  seeded and chopped
Salt and pepper to taste
4 to 5 avocados, peeled,
  seeded and mashed
3 teaspoons lemon juice
Salt and pepper to taste
1 cup sour cream

3 tablespoons salad dressing
1 (1.62-ounce) package
  enchilada sauce mix
1 green onion, chopped
3 medium tomatoes, chopped
½ cup chopped black olives
1 (8-ounce) package
  Cheddar cheese, grated
2 (10-ounce) packages
  tortilla chips

Mix beans, jalapeños, salt and pepper. Spread on a 12-inch round platter. Mix avocados, lemon juice, salt and pepper. Spread mixture over beans, leaving about ½-inch showing on edge. Mix sour cream, salad dressing and enchilada sauce mix. Spread over avocado layer, leaving ½-inch avocado mix showing. Layer onions, tomatoes, black olives, with each layer smaller than the previous layer. Sprinkle thin layer of cheese over all. Serve with tortilla chips. This whets the appetite of 14 to 20 people.

MEXICAN CHEESE SOUP

Cynthia Smith

This is husband tested, a winner and real easy to put together.

2½	cups water	1	(13-ounce) can condensed
1	medium tomato, peeled		cream of potato soup
	and finely chopped	1	(13-ounce) can condensed
2	green chilies, seeded		creamy onion soup
	and cut into strips	1	(8-ounce) package
1	small garlic pod, diced		Monterey Jack cheese,
¼	teaspoon pepper		grated
1	(13-ounce) can evaporated milk		

In a 3 quart saucepan, combine water, tomato, chili peppers, garlic and pepper. Bring to boil, reduce heat and cover. Simmer for 5 minutes. Blend in evaporated milk and soups which have been stirred together. Heat through. Divide cheese evenly among the soup bowls. Spoon the hot soup over the grated cheese. Serve at once. Cheese may be stirred into the pot rather than into individual bowls if you like. If you would like this hot, use jalapeño peppers. Yield: 8 1-cup servings.

CHILI SOUP

Dorothy C. Lackey

This is real good in the cold weather.

1	pound ground meat	1	(16-ounce) can tomatoes,
1	medium onion, chopped		chopped
2	(10¾-ounce) cans	1	cup Rotel tomatoes with
	Minestrone soup		green chilies
2	(16-ounce) cans Ranch Style beans		

Brown meat with onion. Pour off any fat. Add rest of the ingredients. Simmer for about 25 minutes. Yield: 6 to 8 servings.

TACO SOUP

Paula Lee & Maurine Smith

2	pounds lean ground meat	1	(1.25-ounce) package
1	onion, chopped		Ranch Style dressing
1	(16-ounce) can yellow hominy	2	(16-ounce) cans whole
1	(16-ounce) can Ranch Style		tomatoes, chopped
	beans	2 to 3 cups water	
1	(4-ounce) can chopped chilies	½	(10-ounce) can tomatoes
1	(1.25-ounce) package taco mix		with green chilies

177

Brown meat and onion. Add rest of the ingredients and simmer for 15 to 30 minutes. Adjust tomatoes with chilies to taste. Good as a soup or served over a baked potato. Yield: 8 or more servings.

CHICKEN ENCHILADA SOUP

Bernice K. Weinheimer

1   dozen corn tortillas
1   to 1½ cups vegetable oil
1   small onion, chopped
1   clove garlic, crushed
2   tablespoons vegetable oil
1   (4-ounce) can chopped
     green chilies, undrained
1   (14½-ounce) can beef
     broth, undiluted
1   (10¾-ounce) can chicken
     broth, undiluted
1   (10¾-ounce) can cream of
     chicken soup, undiluted

1   (6¾-ounce) can chunk-
     style chicken
1½   cups water
1   tablespoon steak sauce
2   teaspoons Worcestershire
     sauce
1   teaspoon ground cumin
1   teaspoon chili powder
3   cups (12-ounces) Cheddar
     cheese, shredded
Paprika

Cut 6 tortillas into ½-inch strips; set aside. Cut remaining tortillas into triangles. Fry in hot oil until crisp; set aside. Sauté onion and garlic in 2 tablespoonfuls hot oil in a Dutch oven. Add next 10 ingredients; bring to a boil. Cover, reduce heat and simmer 1 hour. Add tortilla strips and cheese; simmer, uncovered, 10 minutes. Sprinkle with paprika and serve with reserved tortilla chips. To save time, use no-salt tortilla chips instead of frying your own. Yield: 8 cups.

SPANISH SAUCE

Leah Mauck

Double the recipe and freeze in 1 cup containers. It can be used with chili rellenos, flautas, chicken enchiladas, or as a side dish with most Mexican dinners. Hot green chilies may be used if desired.

3   tablespoons shortening
1   medium onion, chopped
2   cloves garlic, crushed
2   cups tomatoes, peeled and chopped

1   cup chicken broth
1   (4-ounce) can chopped
     mild green chilies

In shortening, sauté onion and garlic, until clear. Add remaining ingredients and simmer until thickened. Yield: 2 to 3 cups.

178

MEXICAN CHEF SALAD
Suzanne Law

My mother, Ola Matus, used to fix this salad on Thursday nights when we were growing up. Dad had Lions Club and this was easy to fix and a treat for us.

1 onion, chopped	1 (10-ounce) bag Doritos
4 tomatoes, chopped	chips
1 head lettuce, chopped	1 large avocado, sliced
4 ounces Cheddar cheese, grated	1 pound ground meat
1 (8-ounce) bottle Catalina	1 (15-ounce) can kidney
dressing	beans, drained

Chop and mix together onion, tomatoes and lettuce. Toss with cheese and dressing. Crush chips and add, then add the avocado. Brown meat, draining well and add beans. Simmer 10 minutes. Add to salad and serve immediately. Yield: 6 to 8 servings.

CHILIES RELLENOS
Leah Mauck

This is one of our favorite dishes. Even though it is time consuming, it is well worth the effort. We usually have this for very special occasions. I think it came from a clipping from the Austin American-Statesman. *I know this is easier than dipping in a batter before frying.*

12 fresh green chilies	½ teaspoon salt
(Pablano peppers)	½ teaspoon ground cumin
1 pound ground beef	¼ teaspoon oregano
1 medium onion, chopped	(optional)
1 clove garlic, minced	12 egg roll wrappers
2 cups Cheddar cheese,	Vegetable oil
shredded	Picante sauce

Place chilies on baking sheet; broil 3 to 4 inches from heat. Turn often with tongs until chilies are blistered on all sides. Immediately place chilies in plastic bag; fasten securely and let steam 10 to 15 minutes. Remove peel from chilies; slit open and remove seeds. Cook beef, onion and garlic until meat is browned. Drain. Add cheese and seasonings, stirring well. Fill chilies with meat mixture. Place chilies diagonally off center on each egg roll wrapper, folding over chili. Fold sides over; brush edges of egg roll wrapper lightly with water. Roll up and press edges together to seal. Heat vegetable oil to depth of 4 to 5 inches in large saucepan. Place 2 to 3 filled rolls in hot oil and fry 30 seconds on each side until golden; drain chilies. Serve with picante sauce, beans and rice. Yield: 12 servings.

179

ENCHILADAS PICANTE

Pat Rumpf

This came from a man who enjoys spicy food. It may easily be made spicier or toned down.

½ cup chopped green onions,
    with tops
2   tablespoons butter <u>or</u>
    substitute
6   ounces Monterey Jack
    cheese, shredded

¾ cup sour cream
½ (10-ounce) can tomatoes
    with chilies (Rotel)
9   flour tortillas, about 9
    inches in diameter

Sauté onions and tops slowly in butter. While stirring, add cheese until melted. Add sour cream and tomatoes. Dip tortillas into mixture and stack in a shallow baking pan, slightly larger than diameter of tortillas, possibly an iron skillet. Pour any remaining mix over the top of stack. Bake at 250 degrees for 20 to 30 minutes, until bubbly. Cut into pie shaped pieces. Yield: Serves two enthusiastic eaters!

CHILI RELLENO CASSEROLE

Moline Lorenz

This recipe came from Linda Alcorn of Clovis, California.

1   (27-ounce) can green chili
    strips, <u>or</u> whole, cut and
    seeded
1   pound Monterey Jack
    cheese, grated

1   pound Cheddar cheese,
    grated
4   eggs
3   tablespoons Bisquick
1   cup milk

In a casserole dish 9 x 13 inches, layer ½ can of green chilies. Sprinkle Monterey Jack cheese over peppers. Layer rest of green chilies, then sprinkle Cheddar cheese over peppers. Whip eggs with milk and add Bisquick. Pour over chilies and cheese. Bake 350 degrees for 40 minutes. Serve with a vegetable salad and garlic bread and other Mexican dishes. Yield: 6 to 8 servings.

HINTS:

Wear rubber gloves when handling chiles if you have sensitive skin; they are as fiery to touch as they are to taste.

Use two or three sticks of gum in a jar of flour or meal to keep out weevils and bugs.

180

MEXICAN STEW
Sally Gravenor

This has long been a favorite of my daughter, Diann, and she always requests it when she comes for a visit.

1½	pounds stew meat, cut in cubes	1	(16-ounce) can tomatoes
4	teaspoons oil	1	teaspoon salt
1	onion, chopped	¼	teaspoon pepper
1	large clove garlic, minced	1	(11-ounce) can whole kernel corn
2	tablespoons chili powder	2	cups water

Brown meat on all sides, then add onion and garlic. Cook a few minutes, then add chili powder. Stir to coat the meat. Add tomatoes, salt, pepper, corn and water. Simmer for 1 hour or until meat is tender. Yield: 6 to 8 servings.

BEEF ENCHILADAS
Thelma Ulrich

2	pounds ground beef	15	corn tortillas
1	(16-ounce) can Wolf Brand chili	1	small onion, finely chopped
3	ounces Chili Quik	1	pound Velveeta cheese, sliced
4	cups water		

Brown beef, then add chili, Chili Quik and water. Cover and simmer for approximately 30 minutes. Soften corn tortillas in chili mixture, one at a time. Then place 2-3 tablespoonfuls chili mixture on each tortilla. Roll up and place in a 13 x 9 inch dish. Sprinkle onion over enchiladas and then cover with remaining chili mixture. Top with Velveeta cheese slices. Bake 400 degrees until cheese is thoroughly melted. Yield: 6 to 8 servings.

QUICK ENCHILADA CASSEROLE
Evelyn Francis

1	pound ground meat	10 to 15	flour or corn tortillas
1	package McCormick Chili Mix	3	cups grated Cheddar cheese
1	can tomato soup	½ to ¾	cup onion, finely chopped
2	soup cans water		

Make chili sauce by browning ground meat in Dutch oven. When brown, sprinkle in chili mix. Stir to mix and then add soup and water. Stir and cook approximately 10 minutes. Set aside 1 cup sauce.

In a 13 x 9 x 2-inch dish, spread about ½ cup sauce on bottom of dish. Place a layer of tortillas on bottom, cover with sauce, sprinkle on ½ of onion and ½ of cheese. Make another layer of sauce, onion and cheese. Pour 1 cup sauce over top. Bake in 400 degree oven for about 30 minutes. Yield: 6 to 8 servings.

SOUR CREAM ENCHILADAS   *Mary Dyer*

1 pound ground beef	½ cup milk
½ cup chopped onion	1 (8-ounce) carton sour
1 teaspoon garlic powder	cream
1 teaspoon ground cumin	2 tablespoons vegetable oil
½ teaspoon salt	12 corn tortillas
¼ teaspoon black pepper	2 cups sharp Cheddar
1 tablespoon chili powder	cheese, shredded, divided
1 can cream of mushroom	1 (2.2-ounce) can ripe
soup (do not dilute)	olives, drained and sliced

Sauté ground beef and onion in skillet; drain. Add garlic powder, cumin, salt and pepper and chili powder. Set aside. Combine and heat soup and milk over medium heat until bubbly. Remove from heat, add sour cream and blend. Set aside. Heat oil to 375 degrees and fry tortillas 3 to 5 seconds, turning, or just until softened. Drain on paper towels. Place 2 heaping tablespoonfuls ground beef on each tortilla and 1 tablespoonful shredded cheese on top of beef. Roll and place seam side down in 13 x 9 x 2 baking dish. Pour sour cream mixture over rolled tortillas. Cover with foil and bake at 350 degrees for 25 to 30 minutes. Sprinkle with 1 cup cheese, then sliced olives, return to oven uncovered for 5 minutes to melt cheese. Yield: 6 servings.

WHITE ENCHILADAS   *Flora Cox*

This delicious Mexican dish was served to Bill and me at an "after the ball game get together" of friends at Phillips, Texas by Mrs. Joel Lynch.

1 can cream of mushroom	1½ pounds ground meat
soup	1 (8-ounce) can taco sauce
1 can Cheddar cheese soup	1 (4-ounce) can green
1 (8-ounce) carton sour cream	chilies, chopped
cream	12 flour tortillas

Mix together the soups and sour cream. Place half of mixture in a 13 x 9 x 2

182

pan. Brown beef, drain, and add taco sauce and chilies. Warm tortillas and place meat mixture on tortillas and roll up. Place rolled tortillas on top of mixture in pan. Pour remaining soup mixture over the tortillas. Bake at 350 degrees until bubbly. Yield: 6 servings of 2 enchiladas each.

ENVUELTOS
Susan Thomas

Sauce
¾ cup onion, chopped
3 tablespoons oil
1 (16-ounce) can tomatoes, chopped
1 teaspoon salt
1 teaspoon sugar
1 teaspoon cumin seed
1 teaspoon cornstarch

1 tablespoon water
Meat
1 pound ground beef
1 cup onion chopped
1 teaspoon salt
1 tablespoon cumin seed
10 to 12 corn tortillas
Sour cream, optional

Make sauce first, before preparing meat and let simmer. Sauté onion in oil; add tomatoes, salt, sugar and cumin seed. Simmer 5 minutes then mix cornstarch and water; add to mixture stirring well. Simmer until thickened. Brown beef with onion and salt. Add cumin seed, stir and keep warm. Soften tortillas in hot oil. Place 3 to 4 tablespoonfuls of the meat mixture in each tortilla. Roll and place seam side down in 11 x 7 x 2-inch baking dish. Pour the sauce over rolled tortillas. Bake at 350 degrees for 20 minutes. Top each roll with 1 to 2 tablespoonfuls of sour cream. Yield: 4 to 6 servings.

MEXICAN DISH
Jody McCuiston

1 pound ground meat
1 can cream of chicken soup
1 can cream of mushroom soup
1 (4-ounce) can green chilies, chopped

4 ounces taco sauce
½ pound Longhorn cheese, grated
1 (9-ounce) package Doritos

Brown meat; drain. Mix meat, soups, chilies and taco sauce together. Line 2 quart oven-proof dish with half of Doritos, pour half of meat mixture over chips, layer again with other half of chips then meat mixture and top with cheese. Bake at 350 degrees for about 30 minutes. Yield: 6 to 8 servings.

HINT:
Substitute cottage cheese for ricotta. Cottage cheese yields a more moist product, while ricotta is cheesier in taste.

MEXICAN MEATBALLS
Cynthia Smith

1 pound ground beef	1 can Nacho Cheese soup
½ cup onion, chopped	¾ cup clear chicken broth
½ cup Fritos, crushed	¼ teaspoon garlic powder
½ (1.25-ounce) package taco seasoning (dry)	¼ teaspoon cumin
	2 cups cooked Fideo noodles
½ teaspoon pepper	<u>or</u> 2 cups cooked rice
2 tablespoons vegetable oil	

Mix ground beef with chopped onion, crushed corn chips, seasonings and pepper. Shape into 30 one-inch meatballs. Brown in skillet with little oil. Remove balls and drain, spoon off the remaining fat in skillet. Add soup, broth, garlic, and cumin to pan and return the meatballs at this time. Cover and simmer for ten minutes, serve hot over cooked Fideo noodles or rice. Yield: 4 to 6 servings.

SPANISH MEATLOAF
Joan Winters

This recipe came from my best friend's mother when I was growing up. She served it to us on special occasions and it has remained a favorite of my own family.

1 (16-ounce) can tomatoes	½ large bell pepper, chopped
1 pound lean ground beef	1 teaspoon salt
½ pound pork sausage	2 slices whole wheat bread
1 egg, beaten	6 saltine crackers
1 small onion, chopped	Pepper to taste
2 medium jalapeño peppers, chopped	

Drain tomatoes and retain liquid. Mix together meats, egg, tomatoes, onion and pepper. Wet bread and crackers and mix in with above ingredients. Form into a loaf and put into 11 x 7 x 1½-inch pan. Pour the saved tomato liquid on top of meatloaf, add 1 cup of water to pan and keep a little water in the pan all the time the meatloaf is baking. Bake in 350 degree oven for 1 hour and 15 minutes. Yield: 6 to 8 servings.

☆ ☆ ☆ ☆ ☆

HINT:
Washing eggs before storing removes the coating that prevents the entrance of bacteria. Wash just before using.

CHEESE TACO PIE
Cynthia Smith

1 pound ground beef	1 (9-inch) baked pie shell
1 medium onion, chopped	2 cups Cheddar cheese,
1 (1¼-ounce) package taco	shredded, divided
seasoning mix	1 cup Fritos, crushed
¾ cup water	Lettuce, shredded for garnish
1 (16-ounce) can refried beans	Tomatoes, chopped for
1 (8-ounce) jar taco sauce, divided	garnish

Cook beef with onion, stirring to crumble and brown the meat; drain. Add taco seasoning mix and water, stir well. Bring to boil, reduce heat and simmer for 20 minutes, uncovered. Combine refried beans with ⅓ cup of liquid taco sauce. Spoon half of bean mixture in bottom of cooked pastry shell. Top with half of meat mixture, half of cheese and half of Fritos. Repeat layers. Bake at 400 degrees for 20 to 25 minutes and top with the rest of liquid taco sauce and sprinkle with lettuce and tomatoes. Yield: 6 servings.

IMPOSSIBLE TACO PIE
Lucia Carbary

1 pound ground beef	1¼ cups milk
½ cup onions, chopped	¾ cup Bisquick baking mix
1 (1¼-ounce) envelope	3 eggs
taco seasoning mix	2 tomatoes, sliced
1 (4-ounce) can green	1 cup Cheddar cheese,
chilies, chopped, drained	shredded

Heat oven to 400 degrees. Grease pie plate, 10 x 1½-inches. Cook and stir beef and onion until brown; drain. Stir in seasoning mix. Spread in plate; top with chilies. Beat milk, baking mix and eggs until smooth, 15 seconds in blender on high or 1 minute with hand beater. Pour into plate. Bake 25 minutes. Top with tomatoes and cheese. Bake until knife inserted in center comes out clean, 8 to 10 minutes longer. Cool 5 minutes. Serve with sour cream, chopped tomatoes, shredded lettuce and shredded cheese, if desired. Pie makes its own crust. Yield: 6 to 8 servings.

MAMAW'S CHILI CASSEROLE
Mary A. Thurlkill

1 (16-ounce) can tamales	2 (15-ounce) cans chili
1 (16-ounce) can pinto beans	1 cup Cheddar cheese,
1 medium onion, chopped	grated

185

Remove paper from the tamales and lay on the bottom of a greased 8 x 8-inch baking dish. Pour the pinto beans evenly over the tamales. Then put an even layer of chopped onions. Pour the chili evenly over the onions. Top with grated cheese. Bake at 350 degrees for 30 to 40 minutes, or until all is bubbling hot and cheese is melted. Yield: 4 to 6.

MENUDO
Vicky Patton

I make this dish and freeze it in quart containers. It is served in a bowl like chili and makes a nice change and addition to Mexican meals.

8   pounds menudo (beef tripe)   2   (30-ounce) cans hominy
2   pounds ground pork   Menudo spices
2   cloves of garlic   1   tablespoon salt
2   onions

Prepare tripe by washing and trimming away fat. Cut into bite size pieces. Cover with enough water to cover tripe 2 inches. Chop garlic and onions and add to pot. Bring to a boil, after simmering for 1 hour add 10 to 12 tablespoons menudo spice. Stir in hominy and salt and continue to simmer for at least 2 more hours. Yield: 6–8 quarts.

MEXICAN PORK CHOPS
Cynthia Smith

6   pork chops, ¾-inch thick   1   (1¼-ounce) package taco
Salt and pepper to taste   seasoning mix
Oil enough to brown chops   ½   cup Cheddar cheese,
¾   cup uncooked rice, regular   shredded
1½ cups water   1   medium green bell
1   teaspoon salt   pepper, sliced into rings
1   (8-ounce) can tomato sauce

Sprinkle chops with salt and pepper. Brown in small amount of oil on both sides. Drain well on paper towels. Place chops in a 13 x 9 x 2-inch baking dish and sprinkle the raw rice around the chops. Combine water, salt, tomato sauce, taco seasoning and pour over chops and rice. Cover tightly and bake at 350 degrees for 1 hour. Remove cover and sprinkle with cheese and top with the green pepper rings. Cover and bake 15 more minutes or until chops are done and rice is tender. Yield: 6 servings.

186

✿ ✿ ✿ ✿ ✿ ✿ ✿

CARNE ADOVADA

Mary A. Thurlkill

Good served with guacamole, fresh flour tortillas, and ice cold Corona beer. This dish is very spicy.

16 dried, red chile pods	2 teaspoons oregano
3 teaspoons salt	5 pounds pork (any tender
4 cloves garlic	cut)

Preheat oven to 225 degrees. Remove the stems from the chile pods. Place the pods in a pan and bake them for 5 to 10 minutes, stirring occasionally, until the chiles are lightly roasted. Leave the oven door open. Don't breathe the fumes! Place the pods in a medium bowl and cover them with boiling water. Let them sit for 30 minutes. Drain the water from the chile pods. Place the pods in a blender. Add the salt, garlic, and oregano. Barely cover the mixture with water. Blend well for 2 minutes, or until the skins of the pods virtually disappear. Cut the pork in strips that are 2-inches wide and 4-inches long. Place the pork in a plastic container. Add the sauce and thoroughly coat the pork. Cover and refrigerate for 24 hours. Preheat oven to 325 degrees. Place marinated pork and sauce in a baking dish. Cover, and bake for 4 hours, or until the meat is quite tender. Yield: 6 to 8 servings.

CALAVAZA CON PUERCO (Squash with Pork)

Leah Mauck

This is like a stew and a one-dish meal.

1½ pounds pork	2 cups water
2 tablespoons oil	Salt and pepper to taste
1 large onion, chopped	4 medium zucchini squash,
2 cloves garlic, minced	cut in ½-inch slices
1 (8-ounce) can tomato sauce	2 tablespoons picante
1 (17-ounce) can whole	sauce, optional
kernel corn, undrained	

Cut pork in 1-inch cubes; brown in oil, lower heat and add onion and garlic; sauté until clear. Add tomato sauce, corn, water, salt and pepper. Cover and simmer until meat is tender, about 2 hours. Stir occasionally and add water as needed. About 30 minutes before serving, add squash and picante sauce if desired. Serve with tortillas or cornbread sticks. Yield: 6 to 8 servings.

TASTY TACO CHICKEN GRILL   *Moline Lorenz*

This recipe was given to me by my daughter, Patsy Sue Alcorn of Madera, CA.

1 broiler-fryer chicken, cut up	1 tablespoon cooking oil
1 small onion, minced	1 teaspoon salt
1 (8-ounce) can Spanish style	½ teaspoon oregano leaves
tomato sauce	⅛ teaspoon pepper
1 (4-ounce) can taco sauce	½ cup Monterey Jack
¼ cup molasses	cheese, grated, optional
2 tablespoons vinegar	

Place broiler-fryer parts in baking dish and bake in 350 degree oven for 40 minutes. Cool them a bit and pour sauce over chicken. Cover and marinate in refrigerator at least an hour or overnight would be better. When ready to grill, drain excess sauce and reserve. Place chicken on prepared grill, turning a few times for about 20 minutes or until fork can be inserted with ease. Brush generously with reserved sauce during grilling. When chicken is done, place on platter, top with remaining sauce and sprinkle with cheese if desired. Yield: 6 servings.

Sauce: In small saucepan mix onion, tomato sauce, taco sauce, molasses, vinegar, oil, salt, oregano and pepper. Bring to a boil, remove from heat and cool 2 minutes. Yield: 2 cups sauce.

CHICKEN ENCHILADAS   *Ola Matus*

My daughter, Suzanne, won first place at the District 4-H Food Show in Austin with this recipe. She was thirteen years old and received this recipe from her Aunt Sharon Matus in Texas City. Governor Ann Richards was the speaker at the Food Show that day. She was then Commissioner Richards. We were very impressed with her speech; she said, "I am going home this very night and make these enchiladas."

6 chicken breasts	1 onion, chopped
2 cans cream of chicken soup	1 cup chicken broth
1 (16-ounce) container sour	1 pound sharp Cheddar
cream	cheese, grated
2 (4-ounce) cans green chilies	1 package of 12 flour tortillas

Boil chicken in water to cover until fork tender; reserve broth. Cool, chop into small pieces. Combine soup, sour cream, chilies, onion and 1 cup

188

broth. Line 13 x 9 x 2-inch casserole with small amount of soup mixture. Dip tortillas in chicken broth, fill with small amount of chicken and cheese. Roll. Place in casserole. Cover all with rest of soup mixture. Bake 350 degrees for 30 minutes. The last 10 minutes add the grated cheese on top. Yield: 6 servings of 2 enchiladas.

Penny Mengers has the same recipe. She said: I served this to Billy's family and friends when he graduated from the Air Force Academy in 1987 when I was still Penny Liles. It has become a family favorite.

CHICKEN FLAUTAS *Leah Mauck*

I clipped the original recipe from the Austin American-Statesman, *but have changed it some over the years. May be served with Spanish sauce and Guacamole as an appetizer, or with Spanish rice, frijoles and Spanish sauce. May be frozen before baking and then baked as needed.*

2 cups chicken, cooked, finely chopped	32 corn tortillas (6-inch size)
⅔ cups picante sauce	Vegetable oil for frying
¼ cup green onions, chopped	2 cups (8-ounces) Cheddar
¾ teaspoon ground cumin	cheese, shredded

Combine chicken, picante sauce, onion and cumin. Mix well. Heat about ½-inch oil in skillet until hot, but not smoking. Quickly dip each tortilla in oil to soften. About 5 seconds each side. Drain on brown grocery bags, as they are the best for absorbing excess oil. Spoon 1 tablespoonful cheese and chicken mixture down center of each tortilla and roll tightly (about the size of a cigar). Place seam side down on baking sheet. Bake in preheated oven at 400 degrees for 18 to 20 minutes. Serve warm. Yield: 32 flautas.

SPANISH RICE *Ola Matus*

1 cup uncooked rice	½ cup bacon drippings
½ cup onion, chopped	3 cups V-8 Juice
1 clove garlic, minced	Salt and cayenne pepper
½ cup green pepper, chopped	to taste

Sauté rice, onions, garlic and green pepper in bacon drippings until rice is golden. Add V-8 Juice. Cover and simmer for 30 minutes, or after adding juice, pour into greased 1½ quart Pyrex dish, cover and refrigerate. When ready to cook, bake covered at 350 degrees for 45 to 50 minutes. Let sit a few minutes, remove cover, stir with fork, add salt and cayenne pepper to taste. Freezes well after baking. Yield: 6 servings.

FRUIT FILLED KOLACHES

Bernice Milberger

This is a very popular food of my Czech relatives. This is the recipe of my husband's mother, Emma Milberger.

Sweet Dough
2 cups milk, scalded
1 cup sugar
1 teaspoon salt
½ cup butter or ¾ cup shortening
3 eggs, beaten well
2 packages dry yeast
¼ cup warm water
6 cups sifted flour or more

Fruit Filling
12 ounces dried fruit: peach, apple, apricot, prune
½ to ¾ cup water
2 tablespoons butter
1¼ cups sugar or more

Glaze
1 cup powdered sugar
1 to 2 tablespoons milk or water

Pour milk into large crock or glass bowl. Stir in sugar, salt and butter or shortening. Let stand until lukewarm. Blend in eggs. Sprinkle yeast in warm water and stir until yeast is dissolved. Add to milk mixture. Stir in enough flour to make a soft dough. Work this until smooth and not sticky. Cover and set in warm place until doubled in bulk. Make kolaches by pinching off dough in biscuit-size pieces and working with hand into a 3 to 3½-inch circle. Place 2 teaspoonfuls of fruit filling in middle of circle. Pull to the middle two sides and pinch together. Do the same for the other two sides. It will resemble a clover leaf. Brush well with melted shortening and place in a greased baking pan with a little space between each. Let rise again in warm place, about 1 hour. Bake at 400 degrees for 15 to 20 minutes or until light brown. Remove from pan to a rack to cool. When cooled, ice with a thin powdered sugar glaze. If you have dough left, make cinnamon rolls or dinner rolls. Yield: 2 dozen.

Fruit Filling: Cook in saucepan, on low heat, fruit, water and butter. When fruit is tender and can be mashed, stir in sugar. Cool before using.

Glaze: Mix powdered sugar and milk or water until a thin mixture forms. Spoon on top of each kolache.

MARGARET'S KOLACHES

Margaret Mengers

Kolaches are a Czech tradition and this recipe was handed down to me through my mother, Victoria Julia Brandesky Ermis, from her mother, Julia Ann Rocman Brandesky. The Brandesky family were among the original settlers in the Kostoryz community in Corpus Christi. The Ermis family also baked excellent kolaches and their favorite was poppy seed.

190

Dough		Filling	
1	tablespoon sugar	1	(12-ounce) bag prunes
2	packages yeast		without seeds
½	cup warm water	1	teaspoon lemon juice
2	cups milk	1	cup sweetened canned
½	cup plus 2 tablespoons		peaches
	shortening		Sugar to taste
2	teaspoons salt		*Topping*
2	egg yolks, slightly beaten	1	cup brown sugar
½	cup sugar	1	cup flour
6¼	cups flour	½	cup margarine

Sprinkle 1 tablespoon sugar over yeast and dissolve in warm water. Set aside to rise. Heat milk, add shortening to dissolve. Allow to cool to lukewarm; add salt, yolks and sugar. Combine milk/egg mixture and yeast mixture. Add flour gradually and work dough, by hand, wooden spoon or mixer, until glossy. May add a little more flour, if necessary. Cover and let rise until double, about 1 hour. Divide into small egg-shaped portions with spoon and form balls. Place on greased cookie sheet 1-inch apart and butter well. Set oven at 400 degrees. Let rise until light then make indentations in each with four fingers. Fill indented centers with prune filling or make a filling of apples, apricots, pineapple, cottage cheese or poppy seeds. Sprinkle with topping. Let rise 15 minutes. Lower oven temperature to 375 degrees, bake until brown, 15 to 20 minutes. Yield: 5 dozen.

Prune Filling: Cook prunes; cool, mash. Add lemon juice and peaches. Mash. Sweeten to taste. Place 1 teaspoonful or more in indented kolache dough.

Topping: Mix together brown sugar, flour and margarine until crumbly.

POTATO AND APPLE GERMAN SALAD   *Vanessa H. Luce*

My sister, Carol Wiggins, does "Christmas From Different Countries," 1992 was a German Christmas; 1991 was food from The Scandanavian countries and 1990 was from Mexico. The themes were carried out with decorations depicting the Christmas of the Year, with the countries' language greeting you across the front of the house. This year her granddaughter Evelyn commented, "can't we just do a normal Christmas?"

191

½	pound new potatoes	1	tablespoon nuts, chopped
1	cup sliced celery	3	tablespoons salad oil
½	cup Granny Smith		(Safflower)
	apples, diced	2	tablespoons lemon juice
2	dill pickles, diced	1	teaspoon salt (optional)

Dice new potatoes (leave skin on) and boil. When done add next 4 ingredients. Beat oil, lemon juice and salt together until thick. Add to rest of ingredients. Mummm good! Yield: 4 servings.

WIENER SCHNITZEL

Helen Mayfield

My niece Abbie Kroll Green sent me this recipe from Germany.

4	filets of veal (4 to 5 ounces each)	3	eggs
4	tablespoons of flour	5	tablespoons fine bread crumbs
Salt			Cooking oil

Lightly beat (or pound) the filets; flour them and dip in the beaten, salted eggs; then roll them in the bread crumbs and cook quickly on both sides in deep fat until golden brown. Serve immediately. Yield: 4 servings.

LEBKUCHEN

Charlotte Matthews

The mellowing is very important because they are very hard at first.

½	cup honey	1	teaspoon cloves
½	cup molasses	1	teaspoon allspice
¾	cup brown sugar, packed	1	teaspoon nutmeg
1	egg	⅓	cup citron, cut up
1	tablespoon lemon juice	⅓	cup nuts, chopped
1	teaspoon lemon rind, grated		*Glaze*
2¾	cups sifted flour	1	cup sifted powdered sugar
½	teaspoon soda	2	tablespoons water
1	teaspoon cinnamon	½	teaspoon vanilla

Bring to a boil, honey and molasses; cool thoroughly. Stir in sugar, egg, lemon juice and lemon rind. Sift together and stir in flour, soda and spices. Mix in citron and nuts. Chill dough overnight. Roll out small amount at a time, keeping rest chilled. Roll out ¼-inch thick and cut into

192

oblong 1½ x 2½-inches. Place 1-inch apart on greased baking sheet. Bake at 400 degrees for 10 to 12 minutes until when touched lightly no imprint remains. While cookies bake, make glaze. Brush it over cookies the minute they are out of the oven. Then quickly remove from baking sheet. Cool and store to mellow. Mellow about a week in an air tight container. Yield: 6 dozen.

Glaze: Mix sugar, water and vanilla together. Add more water if necessary to make a thin glaze.

SPRITZ COOKIES
Charlotte Matthews

My grandmother brought this recipe with her from Germany. We have been making these at Christmas time for many, many years.

1 cup soft butter	1 teaspoon vanilla
⅔ cup sugar	2½ cups sifted flour
3 egg yolks	

Mix first four ingredients together thoroughly, work the flour in with hands. Force the dough through cookie press onto an ungreased cookie sheet. Bake at 400 degrees for 7 to 10 minutes until set. They taste better if lightly brown on bottom. Yield: About 6 dozen.

GERMAN PRALINES
Patti Knouth

1½ cups sugar	3 tablespoons butter
½ cup brown sugar	6 large marshmallows
3 tablespoons white Karo	1 teaspoon vanilla
½ cup milk	2 cups pecan halves

Cook sugars, Karo and milk until firm ball forms in cold water. Add butter, marshmallows, vanilla and pecans. Beat until it loses its gloss. Take out of pan in a hurry. Drop by teaspoonfuls onto wax paper. Yield: 2½ dozen.

HINTS:

The next time you return a baking ingredient that you borrowed from a neighbor, take along a sample of your baked goodies. She will then be more willing to lend you ingredients in the future.

Marshmallows can easily be cut with scissors dipped in hot water, dried and then cut.

GREEK PASTA SALAD
Theresa Casparis

My husband's favorite salad. It is an exotic exchange from potato salad and goes as well with a New Year's Eve menu as it does with barbecue or a Potluck luncheon.

1 (8-ounce) Vermicelli	1 (2-ounce) jar diced
½ cup extra virgin olive oil	pimientos, drained
2 heaping tablespoons	¼ cup mayonnaise, <u>no</u>
Cavender's Greek Seasoning	substitute
3 tablespoons lemon juice	5 green onions and
1 (4-ounce) can chopped ripe olives	tops, sliced

Cook vermicelli in boiling unsalted water as directed on package. Drain; add olive oil, seasoning and lemon juice. Marinate in refrigerator for 4 hours. Add olives, pimientos, mayonnaise and green onions. Serve immediately or refrigerate awhile to blend flavors. The quality of olive oil used is particularly important in this salad. Extra virgin oil really adds to the flavor. Yield: 6 to 8 servings.

RICE BALLS ITALIANO
Cynthia Smith

When you live most of your life on the Gulf Coast, you learn what to do with all the rice. These are good with spaghetti sauce on top also. Just add a salad.

2 eggs beaten	4 cups cooked white rice
1 teaspoon salt	1½ cups Cheddar cheese,
1 teaspoon dry mustard	grated
¼ teaspoon pepper	½ cup dry Italian bread
1 teaspoon Worcestershire sauce	crumbs
2 tablespoons horseradish sauce	

Combine eggs, salt, mustard and pepper, Worcestershire sauce, and horseradish sauce in a bowl. Add rice and cheese and mix well and then chill. Roll mix in ¾-inch balls, roll in bread crumbs and fry in deep fat at 375 degrees until brown about 4 minutes. Drain. Makes 6 dozen small balls.

JEWISH COFFEE CAKE
Jean Everson

4 eggs	1 teaspoon baking powder
1 cup sugar	1 teaspoon vanilla
1 cup oil	Dash salt
2 cups flour	1 (21-ounce) can lemon pie filling

Beat eggs until thick and add remaining ingredients except pie filling. Pour half of batter into a greased 13 x 9 x 2-inch pan then add lemon filling. Add remaining batter on top and bake at 350 degrees for 40 minutes. Yield: 12 to 15 servings.

POLISH SAUSAGE STEW

Flora Cox

This stew made a hit with all the men and women who sponsored and worked the Phillips Lions Club Fair. I lost the recipe and recently obtained it again from Joel and Leona Lynch from Stinnett, Texas.

1 (16-ounce) package large
  lima beans or 2 cups
  white navy beans
Water
Salt and pepper to taste
2 medium potatoes, diced

3 carrots, diced
1 large onion, diced
3 ribs celery, diced
2 rings of Polish or German
  sausage, sliced thin

Cook beans in water to cover in a Dutch oven until almost tender. Add salt and pepper. Add potatoes, carrots, onion, and celery and cook until tender. About 30 minutes before serving add sausage and simmer. Yield: 12 servings.

POLYNESIAN PORK

Aline Slack

6 pork chops, cut in strips
1 clove garlic, chopped
3 carrots, chopped
½ head cabbage, chopped
½ onion, chopped

3 stalks celery, chopped
2 (3-ounce) packages
  noodles (like Ramen)
4 or 5 shakes of soy sauce
½ to 1 cup water

Brown meat. Add vegetables, cook until limp. Add noodles and water. Cook until tender. Yield: Serves 6.

PUERTO RICAN FRESH HAM

Ruth Blair

10 pepper corns or coarse
   ground black pepper
12 cloves garlic, minced
2 tablespoons dried oregano

3 tablespoons olive oil
3 tablespoons vinegar
Salt to taste
8 to 10-pound fresh ham

Mix first 6 ingredients. Use fresh ham with as much skin left on it as pos-

sible. Cut deep holes in ham and stuff with spice mixture. Rub remaining mixtures on outside of ham. Bake with skin side up at 350 degrees for 35 minutes per pound. Whole piglet may be roasted also. Use 1 teaspoonful of spices for each pound of pork. Yield: About 30 to 40 servings.

SHRIMP OR CHICKEN CURRY
Beverly K. Voron

When Bill and I were in the Peace Corps in Sierra Leone, West Africa, we learned to love curry. There was a sizable number of Pakistanis who lived there and made the dish popular. I remember one wedding reception we attended where this was served. (The African chief had brought the bride a goat for a wedding present.) We love to have this for company. It's a very mild curry, and certainly not very authentic since I've modified it to our taste, leaving out chutney and adding other side dishes we like.

¼	cup plus 2 tablespoons butter	¼	teaspoon ground ginger
½	cup minced onion	2	cups chicken broth
2	tablespoons curry powder	2	cups milk
¼	cup plus 2 tablespoons flour	4	cups cooked, cleaned shrimp or cut-up cooked chicken
½	teaspoon salt	1	teaspoon lemon juice
1½	teaspoons sugar		

Melt butter over low heat in heavy saucepan. Sauté onion and curry powder in melted butter. Blend in flour and seasonings. Cook over low heat until mixture is smooth and bubbly; remove from heat. Stir in chicken broth and milk. Bring to boil, stirring constantly. Boil 1 minute. Add shrimp or chicken and lemon juice. Heat. Serve over rice and have these "chopsies" ready to spoon over the top as each individual desires. Yield: about 8 servings.

onion	green pepper	tomato
cucumber	mandarin oranges	banana
pineapple tidbits	crushed red pepper	grated cheese
chopped peanuts	coconut	toasted coconut
chopped water chestnuts		chow mein noodles

HINT:

If a recipe calls for egg whites use leftover yolks to make mayonnaise, cream sauces, eggnog, or to enrich scrambled eggs or omelets.

196

PUEBLO INDIAN STEW

Peggy Arbon

"Itonaawe" Zuny for "Let's eat!"

2 pounds pork, diced	1 (16-ounce) can whole
1 (4-ounce) can diced green	tomatoes
chilies	1 (17-ounce) whole kernel
½ teaspoon cooking oil	corn
½ onion, chopped	3 cups water
2 diced butternut squash <u>or</u>	Garlic to taste, optional
3 diced large potatoes	Cilantro to taste, optional

Brown pork in cooking oil; add water and bring to boil, lower temperature and cook covered for one hour. Add remaining ingredients and cook 45 minutes longer. Yield: 8 servings.

NOPALITOES

Robyn Henderson

In early spring use tongs to collect new young growth off cactus. Those from 1 inch to 3 inch will be best. Remove thorns by holding the pads with a gloved hand and cut out thorns, or in the case of tough edges, cut off with a sharp knife. When cleaned and washed, put them in a pot and cover with water, salt to taste, boil until tender. (A large clove of garlic or a slice of onion will add flavor, optional.) Drain, rinse with cold water, store in refrigerator until ready to use. It will keep about a week. To cook: dry with towel (paper or dish towel). It can be cooked like okra. Roll in cornmeal mixed with salt, pepper and garlic powder. Fry until slime is gone. Good as a main dish, a vegetable or with salsa.

The kitchen of my mother-in-law, Querida Michael Henderson Lombard, was as different from the one I grew up in as night is from day. Watching that little spunky woman cook was inspiring. Her cooking isn't country, it's good old pioneer. She can cook anything that grows or moves. She eats the flowers off the blooms of the yucca plant. They are full of Vitamin C. She serves them with a dip or chopped for a salad. The unopened flowers have a stronger taste. Wash for bugs and pat dry. Her Indian roots and pioneer spirit shines in much of her cooking. Not only will I pass down her recipes, but I will pass on the gospel songs she sang as she cooked. I call her my "Mother-in-Love."

PUEBLO OVEN BAKED BREAD   *Peggy Arbon*

At the Indian pueblos, the women bake their bread in outdoor beehive-shaped adobe ovens called hornos.

2	packages dry yeast	2	teaspoons salt
2½	cups warm water, divided	9	cups flour
5	tablespoons melted lard <u>or</u> cooking oil		

Place yeast in large bowl, stir in ½ cup of warm water. Stir lard or oil into yeast mixture. Mix salt with flour; add a portion of the flour and 2 cups water alternately and knead final mixture until smooth and elastic. Place ball of dough in large oiled bowl and cover with damp cloth. Let rise for several hours, until double in bulk. Punch down and knead well. Divide into four balls, then place in oiled round 8 or 9-inch cake pans. Let rise again. Bake for 50 to 60 minutes in a 400 degree oven until brown on top of loaf. Yield: 4 round loaves.

INDIAN SOPA BREAD PUDDING   *Peggy Arbon*

With renewed interest and admiration of the American Indians and their wonderful crafts and art, I am delighted to include this Pueblo recipe. "Elahkwa" Thanks in Zuni!

1	loaf of bread, crumbled to ½-inch pieces	½	(15-ounce) package raisins, divided
1	teaspoon cooking oil	2	teaspoons cinnamon, divided
1	pound cheese, grated	½	cup sugar
2	teaspoons vanilla, divided	3	cups water

Brown in oven or toast a loaf of bread. Spread cooking oil on all sides of deep sided baking pan 10 x 8 x 2-inch. Put in crumbled bread, sprinkle ½ the cheese, 1 teaspoon vanilla, ½ raisins, and 1 teaspoon cinnamon. Repeat same ingredients on top layer. Brown the sugar and add water slowly, stirring until all lumps are gone. Pour over ingredients and bake at 350 degrees for 15 minutes. Yield: 8 servings.

HINT:
To make Chinese brown gravy: Use one tablespoon cornstarch, and enough water to thin and add soy sauce to taste. Pour this into the pan of vegetables and stir. Add more water if it is too thick.

CHINESE BARBECUED SPARE RIBS   *Charlotte Matthews*

3   tablespoons soy sauce
5   tablespoons Hoi Sin sauce
2   tablespoons pale dry sherry
¼   teaspoon Chinese Five
     spices powder
½   teaspoon red food coloring, optional

1   tablespoon sugar
2   pieces baby back
     ribs, 2 pounds each
1½ to 2 cups water

Mix first 6 ingredients in a large bowl. Rub the ribs with mixture. Place ribs on a rack in a roasting pan containing water and roast slowly at 350 for 50 minutes or until done. Do not let ribs touch the water. Add more hot water if necessary to keep the bottom of the pan covered while cooking. Baste both sides of ribs halfway through cooking time. When ribs are done, remove water from pan and turn up heat to 450 degrees and brown both sides, about 15 minutes. Cut into strips between the bones. They freeze well after cooking. Food coloring makes them more attractive. We serve the ribs as snacks. Yield: 3 to 4 servings or more for snacks.

LAUREL'S FOO YOUNG FRITTERS   *Donna Hunt*

I got this recipe twenty years ago from a college friend. I not only enjoy the fritters, but also the memories of our friendship every time I make it. It makes a nice meat served with rice.

6   medium eggs, or
      egg-substitute equivalent
1   cup flour
½   teaspoon salt
1½ teaspoons baking powder
1   tablespoon soy sauce
½   teaspoon Worcestershire
      sauce
1   (16-ounce) can bean
      sprouts, drained

1   envelope dry onion soup mix
1   (4-ounce) can sliced
      mushrooms or bamboo
      shoots, drained
1   (5-ounce) can water
      chestnuts, sliced, drained
1   (4½-ounce) can shrimp,
      or (7-ounce) can tuna,
      drained, or ¾ cup
      chopped dried beef

Beat eggs slightly; blend in flour, salt, baking powder, soy sauce and Worcestershire sauce, beat until smooth. Stir in sprouts, soup mix, mushrooms, water chestnuts, and shrimp, tuna, or dried beef. Drop by spoonful into ½ inch hot oil, 375 degrees, in skillet. Fry 2 to 3 minutes on each side until golden. Drain and blot off excess oil on paper towels. Serve with soy sauce and sweet and sour sauce. Mixture can be made and parts frozen or stored in refrigerator, although bean sprouts do loose some crispness. Yield: 6 servings.

Look Who's Cooking?

Macho Meals Men Make,
Including Wild Stuff

CHUCKWAGON, LBJ NATIONAL HISTORIC SITE

Cowboys gathering cattle on the open range required food and drink to keep goin'. For this need, the chuckwagon was born, being of sturdy wood with a box filled with cooking gear and a lid to serve as "Ole Cookie's" workbench. The usual "chuck" was coffee, sour dough biscuits, syrup, bacon, beans and gravy, with occasional fried steak, stew and pie, depending on the cooks' mood. The chuckwagon was the cowboys social center and evenings were spent playin' cards, smokin', singin' and spinnin' yarns.

SHRIMP IN A BLANKET—AGGIE STYLE   *Scott Chambers*

Trial and error by dumb Aggie pursuing ultimate shrimp appetizer, $150 later, perfection was found! If you like recipe . . . send money for kids Texas A&M education!

2 pounds medium to large shrimp, headed and peeled	**Butter**
1 (8-ounce) bottle Vinaigrette or Zesty Italian dressing	**Tony Chachere's Creole seasoning**
1 pound lean bacon	**Lemon juice**

Marinate shrimp with dressing for 2 to 4 hours in large bowl. Cut bacon strips in thirds and wrap around shrimp, secure with toothpick. Place prepared shrimp in pie tins. Add four slices of butter to each tin. Season moderately with Creole seasoning. Add lemon juice, only slightly, to each tin. Place on Bar-B-Que grill on medium heat turning as needed for 15 to 20 minutes or until bacon is crisp. Great for Aggie football games. Yield: 30 to 40.

HOT CHICKEN WINGS   *Ted Hargis*

Very good for a snack while watching football or at a party.

20 chicken wings	**1** tablespoon Worcestershire sauce
¼ pound butter	
½ (6-ounce) bottle Louisiana Hot Sauce	**⅛** teaspoon red pepper
1 tablespoon Tony Chachere's Salt Free Creole seasoning	

Wash wings, split at each joint, discard tips. Deep fry at 400 degrees for 10 to 15 minutes or bake at 400 degrees for 25 minutes until crispy. Drain well. Melt butter and combine with other ingredients, place in deep dish and pour over the wings. Serve hot. Yield: 8 to 10 servings as appetizer or 4 as main dish.

HINT:
Add raw sliced cucumbers, carrot strips or cauliflower flowerets to liquid left in dill pickle jar. Refrigerate for several days to make delicious cocktail snacks.

GLENN'S CHEESE BALL
Glenn Mills

⅛ cup dry chopped onions
1 tablespoon port wine
1 (0.5-ounce) jar Old English cheese spread
2 dashes garlic salt
1 pinch chives, chopped
1 (8-ounce) package cream cheese

2 dashes Worcestershire sauce
1 (3-ounce) jar dried beef, chopped fine or 1 small roll Braunschweiger
½ cup pecans, finely chopped

Soak onion in wine. Mix all the ingredients, except pecans, very well, until very smooth. Place in freezer about 30 minutes, until firm enough to handle. Roll into a ball, then roll in finely chopped pecans. Serve with crackers. Yield: 1 ball.

PEDERNALES PESTO
Rick Reed

Pesto originated in the Mediterranean areas and got its name from the mortar and pestle used to grind the ingredients. Use as a dip with veggies or bread sticks . . . spoon over pastas . . . add to spaghetti sauces, soups. Use as a baste for roast, chicken and turkey.

1½ cups fresh basil (pressed tightly in cup)
2 cloves garlic, chopped

¼ cup olive oil
¼ cup pecans
⅓ cup Parmesan cheese

Put fresh basil, garlic, olive oil, pecans and Parmesan cheese in a blender or food processor and blend until pureed to a thick paste. No Cooking!!! Yield: 2 cups.

ROBERTO'S QUESO
Robert A. Mauck

When the wife is gone for several days, chips and Roberto's Queso will take care of breakfast, lunch and dinner for at least one day. Add about a pound of salad size shrimp and don't share with anyone.

½ cup margarine
1 medium onion, chopped
6 jalapeños, chopped
1 (16-ounce) can tomatoes, chopped

2 pounds Velveeta cheese, cubed

Melt margarine over low heat, add the onion and jalapeños; heat until the

onion is clear. Add tomatoes and cheese; stir until cheese is melted. Remove from heat and allow to cool. If there is any leftovers, divide into small containers and freeze. Yield: About 3 pints.

PORK TENDERLOIN SANDWICHES   *Mike Earney*

2	¾ to 1-inch thick butterfly pork chops **or** 8 thinly sliced, ¼ to ½-inch boneless pork tenderloins	Garlic powder to taste Meat tenderizer, if desired Seasoned salt, to taste Vegetable oil
2	eggs, well beaten	1 (8-pack) hamburger buns
¼ to ½ cup milk		Favorite condiments
½	pound saltine crackers, crushed fine **or** 1 cup cracker meal	

Butterfly pork chops by cutting each chop in half and then slice crosswise making 4 thin pieces from each chop or use boneless tenderloins. Place meat on a large piece of waxed paper on a hard surface. Pound each piece of meat with a tenderizing mallet until very thin, about ⅛-inch. Turn over and pound other side. Sprinkle with meat tenderizer, seasoned salt and garlic powder. Add milk to beaten eggs and mix well. Dip meat in egg mixture and then in cracker crumbs (aluminum pie pans work well for eggs and cracker crumbs). Shake off excess crumbs and deep fry in hot oil (375°) until golden brown and floats to top of oil. Drain on plate covered with paper towels. Serve on buns with whatever condiments you prefer. Yield: 8 sandwiches.

BARBECUE BUNDLES   *Rick Reed*

Originated in Round Mountain, Texas.

Dried herbs, culinary	Dried basil	Dried sage
Dried rosemary	Dried oregano	Dried dill
Dried thyme		

Don't throw out old herb stems and stalks. Tie them with string in bundles of individual herbs or mixed together. Lay them at the edge of the BarBQ Pit so they will get enough heat to smolder but not enough to flame. Let fire cook to coals before laying on herb bundles. Bundles can be soaked in water for a few minutes to prevent flaming. Experiment!! For steak, burgers, or fajitas: try rosemary, oregano or basil; for chicken: sage, thyme or basil; for fish: dill or thyme.

⚑ ⚑ ⚑ ⚑ ⚑ ⚑ ⚑

BILL'S BBQ SAUCE
Bill Lemons

¼ teaspoon dry mustard	2 tablespoons
¼ teaspoon black pepper	Worcestershire sauce
½ teaspoon ground red pepper	4 tablespoons vegetable oil
1 teaspoon sugar	1 teaspoon Liquid Smoke
1 teaspoon salt	(optional)
½ teaspoon garlic powder	1 bay leaf
2 (8-ounce) cans tomato sauce	⅔ cup vinegar

Mix dry ingredients in saucepan. Add liquids and bay leaf. Mix thoroughly. Bring to a boil and simmer 15 minutes. Stores well in glass container in refrigerator. Is good on all kinds of meats. Yield: about 3 cups.

BAR-B-Q RED SAUCE
Denny W. Stevenson

32 ounces ketchup	2 tablespoons onion flakes
6 ounces honey	1 teaspoon salt
2 tablespoons A-1 Sauce	1 tablespoon coarse ground
2 tablespoons Heinz 57 Sauce	pepper
2 tablespoons Worcestershire sauce	¼ teaspoon garlic salt

Mix in large pan (stainless steel) and bring to a boil. Boil slow for 10 minutes. Remove from heat and cool. Refrigerate and serve on Bar-B-Q. Yield: 5¼ cups.

LIONS CLUB BARBECUE SOP
Johnson City Lions Club

These proportions and directions were given to us by Eddie Dyer and Junior Feuge who regularly cook the barbecue for the Lions Club in Johnson City, Texas. The traditional red sauce never touches the meat these fellows cook. It is so good they sell out every time they cook. Delicious.

1 pound margarine	1 (16-ounce) jar corn oil
4 lemons, juiced	1 large onion, chopped, optional

Melt margarine in pot and add the juice of lemons; stir, add corn oil and onion. Cook for ten minutes and then sop on meat with 'sop mop.' Use sop throughout the cooking process. Yield: About 1 quart.

ROBERTO'S PICANTE SAUCE

Robert A. Mauck

When you are out of Roberto's Queso . . . then the Picante and chips will be good for another day or two. Picante and cheese on a chip, and then heated, is good too.

½ cup onion, chopped	24 to 30 Chili Petines
3 cloves garlic, chopped	1 tablespoon vinegar
2 tablespoons vegetable oil	1 teaspoon salt
1 (16-ounce) can tomatoes **or** 2 cups peeled fresh tomatoes	

Sauté onion and garlic in oil. Blend tomatoes and chilies in blender. Add all to saucepan with the vinegar and salt. Simmer for 45 minutes or until thick. Store in refrigerator. Yield: 1½ to 2 cups.

STEVEN'S HOT SAUCE

Steven Koennecke

6 quarts tomatoes, (green and ripe)	2½ cups vinegar
	1 bunch cilantro, chopped
1 (14½-ounce) can stewed tomatoes	4 cups jalapeño peppers, chopped
⅓ cup salt	2 cups serrano peppers, chopped
3 tablespoons garlic, chopped	
4 cups bell peppers (put in blender)	2 cups of favorite hot peppers
6 cups onions (4 cups chopped, 2 cups blended)	

Scald tomatoes, skin and quarter, put into large pot. (Not aluminum.) Add all other ingredients. Cook until onions and peppers are tender. Run sauce through blender but leaving some chunks. Do not blend too much. Cook blended sauce over medium to low heat, stirring often. Do not cover. Cook until desired thickness. Ready to eat when cool. Or while still hot, you can put in clean jars and seal with hot lids. Yield: about 8 quarts.

HINT:
Scoop out fresh vegetables, such as red or green cabbage or fruits like pineapple, cantaloupe, apples, grapefruit or oranges, to use as containers for dips.

GREEN TACO SAUCE

Melvin E. Scherer

Green Taco Sauce is increasingly difficult to find in stores, even here in Texas. This recipe was developed over a three year period, so the family could still enjoy Green Chicken Enchiladas. Tomatillos are planted and cared for in the garden the same as tomatoes or may be purchased fresh in the produce section. This sauce freezes well in plastic pint containers.

3	cups fresh Tomatillos, peel off the papery husk, then quarter	½	teaspoon sugar
		¼	teaspoon cumin
		¼	teaspoon whole coriander seed
1	medium to large onion, chopped		
6	cloves garlic, chopped	4	tablespoons vinegar
2	(4-ounce) cans green chilies	4	tablespoons water
½	teaspoon salt	2	fresh Tabasco peppers (adjust taste if using dried)

Place tomatillos, onion, garlic, green chilies, spices, vinegar, water and peppers in a saucepan and bring to a boil. Simmer for 8 to 10 minutes. Cool, then puree in blender. Yield: 2 pints.

CAJUN SEASONING SALT

Jess Bowden

This seasoning is pure 24 karat "Cajun," but is very, very good on all kinds of meats. Use for cooking gumbos, vegetables, or soups.

26	ounces Morton's salt	1	ounce bottle fine ground garlic powder
1½	ounce box ground black pepper		
2	ounce bottle ground red pepper	1	ounce bottle chili powder
		1	ounce bottle Accent, optional

Mix all ingredients together and shake to mix well. Use as you would salt. This seasoning is used in the Smoked Turkey Gumbo in this cookbook. (p. 222) Yield: about 3 cups.

HINTS:

Freeze soup stock in ice trays and store in plastic bags.

For flavor, rub soup pot with pod of garlic.

FRITO SALAD
George and Eunice Byars

The original recipe appeared on a Frito package in the early "fifties." Tried it and it became a part of the Byars family cookout menu. It was standard fare at Rudolph Lambert Post #7 American Legion in Port Arthur, Texas from 1970-85. Recipe was often requested. It is a different approach to a salad. As one Legionnaire said, "you can make a meal out of this all by itself."

1 cup tomato, diced	½ cup olives, sliced, optional
1 cup bell pepper, diced	½ cup pimientos, chopped,
1 cup white onion or green	optional
onions, chopped	4 to 6 tablespoons
1 cup celery, cut ¼-inch	mayonnaise or salad
slices	dressing
½ head lettuce, torn in	2 to 3 cups regular size
1-inch pieces	Fritos corn chips
1 cup Velveeta or Cheddar	
cheese, grated	

Place tomatoes, peppers, onions, celery and lettuce in large mixing bowl. Add cheese, and olives and pimientos if desired. Mix in mayonnaise; stir until all ingredients are mixed well. Place in refrigerator until needed. When ready to serve, stir in corn chips for a crunchy, tasty salad. Even kids who don't like vegetables, like this salad. This is a good accompaniment to grilled steaks, barbecue, etc. Yield: 6 to 8 servings.

VEGETABLE SALAD
Jerry Sultemeier

This is great to take to barbecues.

½ cup vinegar	1 (17-ounce) can English
½ cup oil	peas, drained
1 cup sugar	1 (16-ounce) can French
1 teaspoon salt	style green beans, drained
1 teaspoon pepper	1 cup bell pepper, chopped
1 (12-ounce) can white	1 cup celery, chopped
shoe-peg corn, drained	1 cup onion, chopped
1 (17-ounce) can whole	
kernel corn, drained	

Combine vinegar, oil, sugar, salt and pepper. Bring to a boil. Let cool. Mix

207

vegetables in a large bowl. Pour vinegar mixture over the vegetables. Refrigerate overnight. Will keep refrigerated for 2 weeks. Yield: about 16 servings.

BARBECUE POT ROAST   *Bob Grimmell*

An old California recipe sponsored by French's Mustard back in the mid 1950s. A very good flavor. Serve with ranch beans and potato salad.

3 **pound beef pot roast** **1½-inch thick**	1 **(16-ounce) jar, French's** **prepared mustard**
1 **pound box Morton's salt**	

Cut all outside fat from roast. Place roast in a BBQ or grill basket (similar to the wire basket used to grill fish or hamburger only this one is deeper), cover the top side of roast with mustard about ¼-inch thick. Sprinkle with enough salt to thicken the mustard so it sticks to meat. Close the basket lid and turn the mustard side of the roast down to cook on a hot BBQ grate 1½-inches from coals or coil. Open the basket and do the same to the other side of the roast. Close basket. Keep turning the roast every 15 minutes until the mustard is black (burned) and cracking. This takes about 25 minutes or more on each side to complete the cooking. When "burned black" remove from heat, let cool for 10 minutes. Open the basket and scrape off all mustard and salt remaining and discard that. The object is that when it is done, the mustard will crack and fall away, leaving the roast tender and flavorful. Roast should be ready to cut into strips and serve. Yield: 6 to 8 servings.

STIR FRY BEEF AND BROCCOLI   *Rex Armstrong*

1 **pound beef tenderloin, cut** **in ½ inch cubes**	½ **cup chicken broth**
2 to 3 **tablespoons vegetable** **oil (more if necessary)**	2 **tablespoons soy sauce** **or lite soy**
½ **cup onion, diced**	1 **teaspoon cornstarch**
1 **pound fresh broccoli, cut in** **flowerettes**	4 **medium fresh tomatoes,** **cut in wedges**

Brown tenderloin cubes in hot oil in wok or skillet on all sides; remove. Drain on paper towel. Cook onion in oil until tender; remove. Add to beef. Set aside. Add broccoli (along with more oil if necessary). Stir fry until broccoli is partially tender. Combine broth, soy sauce and cornstarch in small bowl. Add reserved beef and onion to broccoli; pour broth mix-

ture over all. Stir to mix. Lower heat to simmer; simmer 5 minutes, covered. Add tomato wedges; gently mix with other ingredients. Cook until tomatoes are just heated through. Serve on a bed of rice. Yield: 4 servings.

BEEF STROGON
Duane Lokken

A delightful, tasty and aromatic Swedish main dish. Can be served as an elegant dinner main course.

1	medium onion, chopped	½	teaspoon cloves, divided
2	tablespoons cooking oil	½	teaspoon allspice, divided
8	ounces fresh mushrooms, chopped		Salt and pepper to taste
		½	cup beef bouillon
1½	pounds sirloin, cubed	8	ounces sour cream
½	teaspoon nutmeg, divided		Cooked rice for 4 to 6 servings

Sauté onion in oil; remove from oil, set aside. Sauté mushrooms, remove from oil, set aside. Add beef to cooking oil. Mix nutmeg, cloves and allspice; sprinkle half the mixture over beef; salt and pepper to taste. Brown beef, add bouillon and simmer for 30 minutes or until beef is tender. Add onion and mushrooms to beef. Stir in remaining seasoning mixture and add the sour cream. Heat to serving temperature and serve over rice with a side dish of steamed broccoli. Yield: 4 to 6 servings.

BAKED BEEF STEW
Leonard Talburt

This dish was frequently served by my mother on wash day or any other day she deemed to be a busy day. Regardless how busy her day was, I was always delighted with this taste treat. Served with a pan of cornbread, this meal pleased the most finicky appetites.

2	pounds sirloin, cubed	6	carrots, cut in large pieces
	Flour to coat meat	3	onions, quartered
	Salt to taste	⅛	teaspoon black pepper
3	garlic cloves, minced	¼	teaspoon paprika
1½	cups beef bouillon	2	tablespoons parsley
12	large mushrooms, cut in half	3	potatoes, cut medium pieces
1	cup celery, cut in ½ inch diagonal pieces		

Dust meat with flour and sprinkle with salt. Place meat and garlic in ungreased 3 quart baking dish. Bake at 450 degrees for 18 minutes. Remove from oven. Pour in bouillon and loosen meat from dish. Add mushrooms, celery, carrots, onions and seasonings. Bake in covered dish in moderately hot oven, 375 degrees for 2 hours. Stir once while baking and add potatoes during the last 30 minutes and continue to bake until done. Yield: 6 servings.

PARK RANGER STEW   Harry O'Bryant

This stew was the creation of necessity. In the early 1960s as a National Park Service couple, Helen, my young bride, and I were assigned to a "back country" ranger station high in the mountains of Yosemite National Park, California, twenty-three miles by horse back from civilization. Once a month we replenished our supplies by riding our horses and taking our pack mule, "Billy," to the valley. As a special TREAT we would buy a 7 or 8 pound sirloin roast. Since we had no refrigeration, half would be cut for steaks; the other half to be used in stews.

3	pounds of sirloin roast	1	(8-ounce) can tomato sauce
⅓	cup flour	5	cups boiling water
3	tablespoons fat	8	medium onions
2	teaspoons salt	2	cups canned peas
¼	teaspoon pepper	2	cups canned green beans
1	teaspoon sugar		

Wrap roast in white tea towel and cover with brown wool army blanket and place in cool dry place during day time. At night with meat wrapped in tea towel only, hoist in food safe to high branch of a tall tree near log cabin. Repeat process for five to seven days. Remove meat from towel and clean with white vinegar. Cut meat in 1-inch cubes; dredge with flour. Heat fat in large cast iron pot blackened with age and use. Brown meat on all sides. Add salt, pepper, sugar, tomato sauce and water; simmer covered for 1½ hours on wood cook stove. Add peeled onions and cook for 45 minutes or until meat is done. Add peas and green beans and heat thoroughly. Thicken gravy to taste. Stew is good using fresh meat and modern methods of cooking. Yield: 8 to 10 servings.

RAINBOW STEW   M. D. Terry & Annie Lee West

It is easy to fix; you can get it going and then go about your business. It sure gives you an appetite when you start to smell it cooking. You can hardly wait for it to get ready. Annie Lee West said, "Norma Felps brought this recipe to the Post office."

2 cups dry pinto beans	1 (4-ounce) can chopped
Water to cover beans	green chilies
2 cans cream of mushroom	1 teaspoon cumin
soup, divided	1 teaspoon garlic powder
2 pound roast, cut into parts	½ teaspoon oregano
1 (10-ounce) can Rotel	Rice, optional
tomatoes with green chilies	Flour tortillas, optional

Spray large crock pot with Pam, put 2 cups dry pinto beans in crock pot, cover with water, add 1 can soup, roast, the second can of soup, tomatoes, green chilies, cumin, garlic powder and oregano. Cook on low for 16 to 20 hours. Yield: 8 servings.

OVEN BRISKET
Tim Carter

4 to 5 pound brisket	*Sauce*
1½ teaspoons salt	½ cup sugar
1 teaspoon onion salt	1 cup barbecue
2 teaspoons celery salt	sauce, any kind
1 teaspoon garlic salt	1 cup Russian
2 teaspoons pepper	dressing, not creamy
2 teaspoons Worcestershire sauce	

Trim excess fat from brisket. Mix salts, pepper and Worcestershire sauce and rub into meat on both sides. Bake in covered pan or wrapped in foil in 225 degree oven for 8 hours or overnight. Pour off part of liquid; cool, slice and put back in pan. Mix ingredients for sauce; pour over meat. This is a good time to freeze if desired. Thaw, if frozen. Bake at 300 to 325 degrees for 1 hour or until heated through. Yield: 10 or more servings.

BACHELOR SKILLET DINNER
Buddy Francis

I had to cook for two nephews one time while Evelyn, my wife, and two sons were gone. I prepared this dinner and they had to eat it more than one meal. When my family returned, they said to Evelyn "Please cook us something besides Uncle Buddy's bachelor food!" You can see why we've called this Bachelor Skillet Dinner ever since.

1 pound ground meat	1 tablespoon Worcestershire
½ onion, chopped	sauce
1 (7¼-ounce) box Kraft	Salt and pepper to taste
Macaroni/Cheese dinner	

Brown meat and onion in large skillet or Dutch oven. While browning meat, cook macaroni in water as directed on box. After meat and onion are browned, add macaroni, salt, pepper, Worcestershire sauce and cheese packet. Stir together well and heat thoroughly. Ready to serve. Yield: 4 hungry boy servings.

SMOTHERED BURRITOS

Dick Thomas

<u>Sauce</u>
1   medium onion, chopped
2 to 3 Anaheim peppers,
    chopped
1   tablespoon margarine
1   teaspoon comino seed
½   teaspoon salt
1   (16-ounce) can tomatoes
1   (8-ounce) can tomato sauce

<u>Burritos</u>
1   pound ground meat
1   (1¼-ounce) envelope
    Lawry's Taco Seasoning Mix
¾   cup water
6   flour tortillas, large size
1   (15-ounce) can refried
    beans <u>or</u> 2 cups fresh made
6   ounces cheese, grated

Chop onion and peppers into 1-inch pieces. Sauté onion and peppers in margarine with comino seed. Add remaining ingredients and simmer covered for approximately 1 hour; remove cover and allow sauce to thicken. Brown meat until crumbled, drain. Blend in taco mix and water. Bring to boil; reduce heat and simmer, uncovered, for 15 minutes, stirring occasionally. Prepare burritos by spreading the center of a tortilla with refried beans. Place 2 tablespoons of the meat mixture over the beans, fold over the top and bottom of the tortilla and roll tightly. Repeat. Place burritos in casserole dish and cover with sauce and grated cheese. Bake in 300 degree oven until cheese is melted. Yield: 4 servings.

CHEESEBURGER ONION PIE

Rex Armstrong

1   tablespoon vegetable oil
1   pound mild white onions,
    sliced and quartered to
    make 2 cups
1   pound ground beef
⅓   cup ketchup
2   teaspoons prepared mustard
¼   teaspoon salt
⅛   teaspoon pepper

2   (8-ounce) cans refrigerated
    crescent dinner rolls
1   cup Cheddar cheese,
    shredded
2   eggs, beaten
<u>Glaze</u>
1   egg yolk, beaten
1   tablespoon water

Heat oil in skillet over medium heat. Add onions; cook, covered, for 10

212

minutes, stirring occasionally. Remove onions; set aside. Brown beef; remove from heat and drain off fat. Stir in ketchup, mustard, salt and pepper; set aside. On floured surface, unroll dough from 1 can of rolls. Press together perforations and roll dough to 12-inch square. Place dough in a 9-inch quiche dish, tart pan or pie plate; trim to 1 inch beyond edge of dish. Spoon meat mixture into dish. Sprinkle with cheese; top with onions. Pour two beaten eggs over onion layer. Unroll remaining roll dough; press together perforations and roll out to an 11-inch square. Place on top of onion layer; trim and pinch together with bottom dough layer. Combine glaze ingredients; brush over surface. Bake at 350 for 40 minutes or until browned. Let stand 10 minutes before serving. Serve with chili sauce, if desired. Yield: 8 servings.

ALL-MEAT CHILI
Glynn Teague

Try this over Mexican Red Beans . . . very, very good.

4 pounds ground chuck, venison or turkey	1 tablespoon salt
3 cups water	2 to 3 teaspoons cumin
3 cloves garlic, minced	4 to 6 tablespoons chili powder

Brown meat to remove excess fat, drain. Put all ingredients in a pot; stir thoroughly to mix spices. Cover and cook on high heat for 10 minutes; stir well and simmer for 1 hour. Serve topped with fresh, chopped onions. Yield: 8 or more servings.

TEXAS CHILI
Dr. John Weaver

This is my Mom's recipe. She learned how to make it from a Mexican friend when they lived in the Valley before I was born. I don't want to hear any talk about "real" Texans don't put beans in their chili. I'm a son of a son of a Texan and I've enjoyed beans in my chili all my life. This is originally a beef recipe but I've found that ground venison or turkey, Jerry Lindeman's idea, give excellent results.

3 pounds lean ground beef, venison **or** turkey	1 tablespoon ground cumin
3 medium onions, chopped	4 tablespoons paprika
3 cloves garlic, chopped	1 tablespoon salt
4 tablespoons Gebhardt's chili powder	2 pints boiling water
	⅓ cup cornmeal
	1 pound pinto beans, cooked

213

In a 4-quart pot, cook the meat, onions and garlic until the meat is brown and the onions are clear. Add all the spices, stir well until the meat is coated and cook a little longer. Add the water and cook until the onions all but disappear and the mixture begins to thicken, about 45 minutes. Sprinkle the cornmeal on top and let it begin to sink before stirring it in. Add the cooked beans and simmer a short while, careful not to let it stick to the bottom of the pan. Yield: enough for 8 hungry people with leftovers.

KING RANCH CASSEROLE
Billy Mengers

When I was about four years old, I attended one of the famous Santa Gertrudis sales on the King Ranch at the Big House with my dad, Wilbur Mengers. I tasted this dish there for the first time and it has been one of my favorites ever since. Nowadays, I prepare it for my own family.

3	pounds ground beef	1	(10-ounce) can Rotel
	Salt and pepper to taste		tomatoes with green chilies
	Garlic powder to taste	15	corn tortillas, cut in small
1	medium onion, chopped		pieces
1	can cream of chicken soup		Longhorn or Cheddar cheese,
1	can cream of mushroom soup		grated

Place meat in large skillet. Season with salt, pepper and garlic powder. Add onion and cook until meat is browned. Add soups, tomatoes and tortillas; mix well. Place in a 4-quart casserole; cover with cheese. Bake 1 hour at 350 degrees, uncover last 30 minutes. Yield: 10 to 12 servings.

SKILLET LASAGNA
Rex Armstrong

1½	pounds lean ground beef	6	lasagna noodles, cooked
1	small onion, chopped		and rinsed
1	green pepper, chopped	3	cups (12-ounces)
1	(30-ounce) jar spaghetti		Mozzarella cheese, shredded
	sauce with mushrooms	½	cup Parmesan cheese,
1	teaspoon dried oregano		grated
1	teaspoon dried basil		

In a dutch oven, brown beef, onion and pepper. Drain fat, if necessary. Stir in spaghetti sauce, oregano and basil. Simmer, uncovered, 10 to 15 minutes. In a 10-inch skillet, spread ¼ cup of the meat sauce. Top with 3

noodles, cutting to fit as needed. Spread half the remaining sauce and half the Mozzarella and Parmesan cheeses. Top with remaining noodles, meat sauce and Parmesan. Cover and heat on medium for 3 minutes. Reduce heat to low; cook for 35 minutes. Sprinkle with remaining Mozzarella and let stand 10 minutes with cover ajar. Yield: 6 to 8 servings.

LASAGNA MEAT SAUCE

Glen Hobbs

Make the sauce a day ahead, refrigerate and have lasagna the next day.

3	(16-ounce) cans stewed tomatoes	2	teaspoons seasoned salt
2	garlic cloves, crushed, divided	1	teaspoon basil leaves
		¼	teaspoon oregano
1	teaspoon salt	¼	teaspoon dill seed
¾	teaspoon pepper, divided	1	teaspoon celery salt
1	pound ground round	1	tablespoon honey
½	pound bulk sausage	2	tablespoons parsley flakes
1	tablespoon olive oil	½	cup burgundy wine
1	medium onion, chopped	1	(2½-ounce) jar mushrooms, drained

Combine tomatoes, 1 garlic clove, salt, ¼ teaspoon pepper in saucepan. Simmer over low heat 2½ to 3 hours. Brown meat and sausage in olive oil in a large skillet. Add remaining garlic, ½ teaspoon pepper, onion, seasoned salt, basil and oregano. Cook until onion is tender. Drain off drippings. To meat mixture add tomato mixture, dill seed, celery salt, honey, parsley, Burgundy and mushrooms. Simmer over low heat 8 hours or longer. The sauce will be thick. Yield: about 2 quarts.

LASAGNA

Glen Hobbs

1	(14-ounce) package spinach lasagna noodles		Lasagna Meat Sauce, recipe above
2	(12-ounce) cartons small curd cottage cheese	2	pounds Mozzarella cheese, shredded
1	cup Parmesan cheese, divided	½	pound Muenster cheese, shredded
1	tablespoon parsley flakes	½	pound mild Cheddar cheese, shredded
¾	teaspoon salt		
1	teaspoon oregano leaves		

Cook lasagna noodles according to package directions. Drain. Combine cottage cheese, ½ cup Parmesan cheese, parsley flakes, salt and oregano. Reserve ¾ cup meat sauce. In a 13 x 9 x 2-inch baking dish alternate layers of noodles, meat sauce, Mozzarella cheese, Muenster cheese, Cheddar cheese and cottage cheese mixture. Repeat layers 3 times. Spread reserved meat sauce on top. Sprinkle with ½ cup Parmesan cheese. Bake at 350 degrees for 45 minutes. Yield: 12 to 15 servings.

CHUCK'S MEXICAN CASSEROLE   *Charles Kusy*

I'm a single father so I'm also looking for something good and easy to make. A friend gave me the main ingredients for this and I added a few of my own. My daughter and I really enjoy it. We also like to read and try recipes from the first Potluck on the Pedernales.

1   **pound lean ground beef**
1   **small onion, chopped**
1   **small green bell pepper, chopped**
1   **(4-ounce) can chopped green chiles**
1   **(4½-ounce) can chopped black olives**
1   **envelope Lawry's Enchilada Sauce Mix**
1   **(16-ounce) can Ranch Style beans, undrained**

¼   **teaspoon salt**
¼   **teaspoon pepper**
½   **cup water**
1   **can cream of mushroom soup**
1   **cup Cheddar cheese, grated**
1   **cup Monterey Jack cheese, grated**
2   **cups crushed corn or tortilla chips**

Brown ground meat and add all ingredients except cheese and chips. Simmer for 15 minutes. Layer in a 13 x 9 x 2-inch baking dish starting with 1 cup chips, ½ meat mixture, ½ cheese, then repeat. Bake in 350 degree oven until cheese melts. Yields: 6 to 8 servings.

HINTS:

Sour cream keeps best if stored in the tightly covered container in which it is purchased. If stored upside down in the refrigerator, maximum retention of texture and flavor is assured.

If serving wine with your meal, you might want to wait to serve it until after the salad course if the salad dressing contains vinegar, because vinegar will affect the taste of wine.

DIRTY RICE
Jess Bowden

I fix this at Christmas time and take it to a family of six. It is their Christmas dinner.

2	cups water	⅛	cup parsley, cut up fine
1	pound lean ground beef	2	bay leaves
1	pound lean ground pork	½	teaspoon black pepper
½	pound ground chicken giblets		Salt, to taste (I use Cajun Seasoning Salt — see p 206)
½	cup yellow onion, diced		
½	cup shallots (green onions and tops), diced	1½	tablespoons Worcestershire sauce
¼	cup bell pepper, diced	¼	pound margarine
1	cup celery, diced fine	1	can cream of mushroom soup
¼	cup garlic or 1 teaspoon garlic powder	1	pound long grain rice

Mix water and meats together in heavy pot, on medium-hot burner. Add all vegetables, seasonings, Worcestershire sauce and margarine. Cook on medium heat approximately 4 hours, stirring often. Add cream of mushroom soup. Continue cooking 30 minutes. Cook rice according to package directions. After rice is completely cooked, mix with the meat ingredients thoroughly. Allow to cook on low heat about 30 minutes before serving. Yield: 6 to 8 Cajuns — 12 to 15 regular people.

S.O.S. OR CREAMED CHIPPED BEEF
Duke Rumpf

This is the traditional dish, somewhat glorified, eaten by so many in the armed services. It's great for a breakfast or a Sunday night supper.

2	pounds ground beef	½	cup milk
1	pound bulk pork sausage	½	cup water
2	medium onions, chopped fine		Flour
		1	teaspoon salt
1	medium green pepper, chopped fine	1	tablespoon pepper
2	stalks celery, chopped fine	1	teaspoon garlic powder or 3 buds, crushed

Brown meats until well done, remove from drippings; set aside. Brown onion, bell pepper and celery in drippings until onion is clear and soft; drain. Reserve about 2 to 3 tablespoons grease in skillet; add enough flour

to create a thick brown paste. Add milk and water to thin the paste until it becomes a thick gravy, stirring constantly. Return meat and vegetables to gravy, add salt, pepper and garlic. Simmer for about 15 minutes or until meat is well blended into gravy. Serve over biscuits, toast or crisp hash-brown potatoes. Yield: enough for 6 hearty eaters.

RICE AND PORK CHOP CASSEROLE   *George Byars*

A quick and easy recipe learned as a male single parent in order to keep from starving to death.

2	cups instant rice	1	can French onion soup
4	pork chops, large	1	soup can of water

Into a large casserole place ½ cup of rice as bed and then place on this bed, two large pork chops. Cover chops with another ½ cup of rice and cover this second layer of rice with two more pork chops. Cover with the last one cup of rice. Pour the can of French Onion soup over rice and chops. Add a can of water to the empty soup can and pour into casserole. Place casserole, with lid, in a preheated oven of about 400 degrees for 20 minutes or until done. Chops may be browned, if desired. **Variation:** Substitute creamy onion or cream of mushroom soup. Yield: 4 servings.

POTLUCK BARBEQUED SAUSAGE   *George Byars*

Being a Methodist, a Mason, a Lion, a Volunteer Fireman, an Eagle, and a Legionnaire, I was always going to a 'potluck dinner.' As a male, single parent I had to come up with something I could do that was edible. I came up with a dish that was acceptable.

Ring sausage (any amount you desire)
Hunts Original Recipe Barbecue Sauce
1 to 2 cups onions, chopped

Cut the sausage into two-inch lengths. In a 10-inch Dutch oven, place the quantity of sausage you like. Set the oven at 350 degrees. After about 30 minutes, remove and pour off the grease that has been cooked out of the sausage. Next, pour the bottle of barbecue sauce over the sausage. Add onions and bring back to heat. As soon as the barbecue sauce starts bubbling, the Dutch oven can be removed from heat and begin to cool for travel to the potluck dinner. Yield: Depends on amount sausage used.

FIREMAN'S SPECIALTY GRILLED CHICKEN *Ron Wilson*

I am with the Southlake Fire Department and this is one of the dishes I serve when it is my turn to cook.

4 boneless skinless chicken
    breasts
10 ounces fresh mushrooms,
    sliced

½ cup onion, chopped
1 to 2 tablespoons margarine
4 slices Mozzarella cheese

Grill or bake chicken breasts until done. Sauté mushrooms and onion in margarine until onion is clear. Place chicken breasts in pan that has been sprayed with Pam. Spoon onion and mushrooms over the chicken. Place one piece of cheese on top of each piece of chicken. Bake at 350 degrees until cheese melts coating the chicken and covering the mushrooms. Yield: 4 servings.

CHICKEN FRICASSEE SHORTCUT *Les Sansom*

Any cream soup may be used. Try browning chicken first, we like it that way.

4 large chicken leg quarters
1 can cream of celery soup
1 teaspoon salt

½ teaspoon pepper
1 teaspoon paprika

Wash leg quarters, skin them if you like, and place in deep pan flat on bottom. Mix in a bowl, the soup, salt, pepper and paprika. Spoon the mixture over the chicken, evenly using all of it. Cover the pan with foil tightly and bake in 350 degree oven for 2 hours or until tender. Serve the soup mixture over rice, if desired. Yield: 2 generous servings with some left over.

PICANTE CHICKEN *Bubba Woods*

1 chicken (cut into frying pieces)
Salt, to taste
Black pepper, to taste
2 tablespoons cooking oil

1 (16-ounce) jar of Pace
    Picante Sauce (Mild,
    Medium or Hot, your choice)
Minute Rice

Salt and pepper chicken to taste; to reduce the fat and calories — remove the skin from the chicken before salting and peppering and discard the skin. Heat oil in skillet on medium high heat; add chicken to skillet and brown each side. After browning chicken, drain off oil, return to stove and

219

add 1 jar of picante sauce; bring to a boil, then reduce heat to simmer. Cover skillet and simmer for 30 minutes or until chicken will separate from the bone with ease. While chicken is simmering prepare 4 servings of Minute rice as directed on box. Serve chicken over rice. Yield: 4 servings.

FIREMAN'S SURPRISE
Ron Wilson

Whole chicken **or** chicken pieces
Water to cook chicken
2   stalks celery, sliced
½   onion, quartered and
     chopped
1   (10-ounce) can refrigerated
     biscuits

1   can cream of chicken
     soup
1   can cream of mush-
     room soup
Paprika, salt and pepper
     to taste

Cut up chicken and boil in water to which celery and onion have been added. Cook until tender, about 45 minutes to an hour. Remove chicken, drain saving the liquid. Take chicken off the bone. Cut white meat into small cubes. Roll out biscuit dough very thin. Cut into strips about 3 inch by 2 inches. Place one piece of cubed white meat in this 'dumpling' and roll up. Secure edges by crimping all around. Do this until all the white meat is used. Mix soups and the reserved liquid that the chicken was cooked in, together. Bring the liquid mixture to a boil, stirring to prevent scorching. Add the 'chicken in the dumpling' along with the extra plain dumplings to the liquid. Cook until dumplings are done, about 30 minutes. Add the rest of the chicken and cook a few more minutes. Yield: 8 servings.

CHICKEN STIR FRY WITH RICE
Les Sansom

My wife especially likes this dish. This keeps well in the refrigerator and we eat it as long as it lasts. Various vegetables can be used.

½   pound boned chicken breast
2   cups cabbage, shredded
½   cup celery, sliced thin
1   green bell pepper, cut small
1   medium onion, chopped
1   stalk broccoli, chopped
½   cup carrots, sliced thin
1   cup uncooked rice (prepare
     as directions indicate) to
     make two cups cooked rice

1   teaspoon chicken
     flavored instant bouillon
2   cups water, divided
2   tablespoons corn starch
2   tablespoons soy sauce
2   tablespoons cooking oil
1   teaspoon salt
½   teaspoon ginger

220

Use stir fry pan or large vessel. Cut up chicken in small pieces, set aside. Cut up vegetables in small pieces. Set aside. Mix instant bouillon in one cup of water. Set aside. Mix corn starch in the other cup of water and add soy sauce to mixture. Set aside. Add cooking oil to frying pan. Do not turn on heat yet. Prepare the rice about now so that it will be ready when the stir fry is done. Turn heat on high and when the oil is heated, add the vegetables, sprinkle salt and ginger over them and start stirring. Stir at all times until vegetables are tender crisp. Remove vegetables from pan to container and add chicken to the stir fry pan. Stir chicken until done. Meat will be white and tender. Return vegetables to the pan and add the cup of water to which the bouillon was added and the corn starch/soy sauce mixture with the cup of water. Stir until thickened (very short time). Remove from heat and serve over rice. Yield: 4 servings.

CURRIED RICE AND CHICKEN   *George Byars*

Quick and simple. Can be made all in one pot. This is authentic enough that a lady of Japanese ancestry asked me for the recipe.

1½	cups instant rice	¼	teaspoon powdered garlic
1½	cups water	2	(5-ounce) cans cooked
¼	teaspoon powdered curry		chicken

Cook rice as directed on the box. After rice is cooked, stir in the curry, garlic and chicken. Let set for five to ten minutes. Do not over do curry. Use enough to get the taste but not too much and get the fire. A good curry is S&B Golden Curry Sauce mix. Yield: 2 to 3 servings.

PEDERNALES TURKEY   *Patrick Watson*

This is an original recipe first tried out on a canoe campout trip on the Pedernales river. I have used it on many a hunting trip since. These can be made a day or two ahead and refrigerated until ready to cook. Try chicken or pork chops.

5-inch square foil	1 cup stir fry frozen
No-stick cooking spray	vegetables
4 to 6 ounces turkey breast	1 medium potato, diced
Bon Appetit spice, to taste	1 teaspoon butter or Crisco

Tear off a square of foil large enough to wrap all ingredients and spray with cooking spray. Season turkey with spice and lay on center of foil. Put vegetables over meat and sprinkle with seasoning. Spray light coating of

221

no-stick spray over vegetables. Place butter on top of vegetables. Wrap up foil and seal tightly. Wrap again in extra heavy duty foil if cooking over coals to prevent burning. Cook over hot bed of coals for 15 to 20 minutes per side. Be careful when opening foil. May be cooked in oven at 350 degrees for 1 hour and 15 minutes. Yield: 1 serving.

JERKY

Authur Feuge, Jr.

Delicious hot or cold as hors d'oeuvres or main dish. Makes wonderful sandwiches. This is in great demand at every Lion's Club Christmas party in Johnson City.

    8   ounces Morton's Tender Quick
    15 pounds meat, turkey breast, venison, etc.
    Coarse ground pepper

Rub Tender Quick into meat. Place in plastic bag and refrigerate overnight or 12 hours. Wash in warm water, wipe with paper towels. Pepper well and let set for at least 15 minutes. Place on barbecue grill for 1 hour over light heat turning frequently. Yield: 15 pounds.

SMOKED TURKEY GUMBO

Jess Bowden

This is very good, but mild gumbo.

1   smoked turkey leg <u>or</u> 2 or 3 wings
5   cups water
1   (14½-ounce) can vegetable broth
¾   cup green onions and tops, chopped
½   teaspoon garlic powder
½   cup celery, chopped
2   teaspoons Cajun Seasoning Salt (see page 206)
1   (10-ounce) box frozen cut okra

1   (16-ounce) can tomatoes
1   cup raw rice
2   cups water
2   teaspoons beef bouillon crystals
Salt to taste
½   teaspoon Cajun Seasoning Salt, optional (page 206)
¼ to ½ teaspoon ground red pepper, optional
¼ to ½ teaspoon garlic powder, optional

Put turkey in stock pot and add water. Boil on low 30 to 40 minutes. Remove meat from pot. Remove and discard the skin, tendons and bone.

Cut meat into small pieces. Add meat back to broth. Add vegetable broth, onions, garlic, celery and Cajun Seasoning Salt. Boil on low heat 15 to 20 minutes. Add okra and tomatoes. Bring to low boil and cook until okra is done. Cook rice in pan with water, beef bouillon crystals and salt. Cook until rice is done. Put amount of rice wanted in bowl and dip gumbo over it. For more zest add the last three ingredients. Yield: 6 to 8 servings, not Cajuns.

JUNIOR'S FAMOUS CATFISH *Arthur Feuge, Jr.*

The mustard takes away the "fishy" taste but after cooking leaves no taste of its own. To see if grease is hot enough, drop in one piece. If it starts sizzling, it's right.

Catfish filets	**Cornmeal**
Prepared mustard	**Salt**

In large dish or pan, lightly coat fish with mustard and let sit for 15 minutes. Roll in salted cornmeal and place in hot, deep grease. Cook until golden brown. Allow ½ pound per person.

CAMPFIRE TROUT *Cicero A. Rust III*

While camping in Wyoming and Colorado with Mike and Lisa Moraign, I enjoyed their catching and preparing the fish, their cooking the fish, and our recipe.

Trout	**Lemon, a squeeze of . . .**
Garlic salt, dash	**Butter, enough**
Pepper, sprinkle	**Green onion, thin slices**

In heavy duty foil, place the prepared trout surrounded with the above condiments and butter (I prefer Falfurrias Butter for cooking.) Cook surrounded by coals, for five to ten minutes. Yield: 1 serving.

HINTS:

Keep celery fresh and crisp by wrapping in paper towel; place in a plastic bag in the refrigerator.

Allow 1 cup tossed salad per person.

HELPER AND BOSS CREOLE GUMBO

Jimmy (Boss) &
Lelia (Helper) Sublett

This recipe makes a great casual dinner for about twelve people. Since my husband has made this for years and it takes a lot of preparation, he's the 'boss' and I'm the 'helper.'

8 stalks celery, chopped
3 large onions, chopped
1 green bell pepper, chopped
1 pound fresh <u>or</u> frozen
   okra, sliced
2 cloves garlic, minced
1 cup vegetable oil
1 cup flour
1 (3½ to 4 pound) chicken,
   cooked and boned
2 quarts chicken stock
1 pound center cut ham
   slice, chopped

4 pounds raw shrimp,
   peeled and deveined
2 pounds crab meat
2 quarts water
½ cup Worcestershire sauce
½ cup ketchup
½ (16-ounce) can tomatoes
2 teaspoons salt
2 bay leaves
¼ teaspoon thyme
¼ teaspoon rosemary
Cooked rice
Lemon, optional

Helper: Chops celery, onions and green pepper; slices okra, minces garlic and gives to husband.

Boss: Heats oil in heavy cast iron Dutch oven, slowly adds flour and cooks while stirring until flour becomes medium to dark brown, about the color of a Hershey bar or beer bottle. To the roux add the vegetables, except the okra and cook until soft. In separate pan sauté okra until brown and then add to roux mixture and stir well.

Helper: While husband was creating roux, you bone the cooked chicken which you cooked, reserving 2 quarts of stock. Chop ham, peel and devein shrimp and check crab meat for shells. Reserve seafood for later.

Boss: Adds chicken, ham, stock and water to roux mixture. Stirs well and adds seasonings. Simmers for about 3 hours. Now adds seafood and cooks 30 minutes more.

Serve over cooked rice. Season with lemon if desired. Keeps well in refrigerator and freezes well. Yield: 12 servings.

☆ ☆ ☆ ☆ ☆

HINT:
Leftover vegetables go nicely in a salad.

☆ ☆ ☆ ☆ ☆

OVEN BARBECUED SHRIMP

Allen Law

2	pounds uncooked peeled shrimp	½	lemon, thinly sliced
1	tablespoon minced parsley	1	teaspoon ground red pepper
½	cup unsalted butter	¾	teaspoon Liquid Smoke
3	tablespoons olive oil	½	teaspoon dried oregano
1	teaspoon paprika	¼	teaspoon Tabasco sauce
1	tablespoon Worcestershire sauce	½	teaspoon salt
1	tablespoon fresh lemon juice	½	teaspoon black pepper

Wash and peel shrimp. Combine remaining ingredients in a saucepan; simmer for 10 minutes. Cool. Pour over shrimp and mix thoroughly. Cover and refrigerate at least 2 to 3 hours, stirring occasionally. Preheat oven to 300 degrees. Place shrimp and sauce in a shallow pan or black iron skillet. Bake shrimp, turning frequently until they just turn pink, about 15 to 20 minutes. DO NOT OVER BAKE. Shrimp should be tender. Yield: 4 to 6 servings.

BOILED SEAFOOD CAJUN STYLE

Russell LeBlanc

Suggest you cover your table with thick newspapers, then pour the Boiled Seafood in the center of the table, give everyone several napkins or paper towels and dig-in! When eating boiled crawfish, sucking heads is permitted. I've been in Texas for fifteen years, originally from Louisiana, and still have one foot stuck in the mud.

5	pounds shrimp, crab, and/or crawfish	3	lemons cut in half
6	medium red onions (Creole onions)	1	bag Zatarain's Crab Boil Seasoning
6 to 8	small to medium whole potatoes		Salt to taste
6 to 8	corn on the cob		Cayenne pepper to taste
			Water

Pot used for cooking depends on the amount of seafood boiled. I've used a 4-quart pan on the stove to a #3 washtub on an outside burner. Rinse seafood and set aside. Wash onions, potatoes and corn. Combine vegetables in cooking pot along with lemons, the Zatarain's crab boil seasoning, salt and pepper. Add water to fill about ¾ full. Bring to a rapid boil, add seafood and bring to a second boil. Continue boiling 15 minutes; then

turn off heat and let it stand for 20 minutes to allow seafood to absorb seasonings. After soaking, drain off water and throw the crab boil seasoning bag away. Yield: 4 servings.

ROAST VENISON
Bob Grimmell

This recipe comes from Bielefeld, Germany, and dates from my grandfather's time. Serve with "Spatzle" or Egg Noodles and a fresh garden vegetable.

2¼ to 3¼ pounds backstrap		½	cup sour cream **or**
Salt			sour milk
1½	ounces butter **or** margarine	2	teaspoons corn starch
3	ounces fat bacon	1	tablespoon water
1	cup water		

Skin the meat, rub with salt and brush with butter. Rinse out roasting pan with water and put in the meat and cover it with bacon strips. Place pan in middle of oven. Add a little water to pan from time to time to prevent the drippings from becoming too brown. Roast at 375 degrees for 45 to 60 minutes. About ten minutes before the meat is cooked, pour the cream or milk over it. When meat is done turn off heat. Remove roast from pan and keep it warm while making gravy. Place pan with the drippings on top of stove on a burner. Stir the residue away from the bottom and add enough water to dissolve the juices. Scrape the pan well. Strain through sieve (if necessary). Thicken with corn starch mixed with 1 tablespoon water. Yield: 8 servings.

GRILLED VENISON STEAKS
Roger Lawson

Venison is better for us than beef. Let it age in a cooler at least a week, if not two, before processing to help tenderize the meat.

4 venison steaks	Worcestershire sauce, to taste
Salt, pepper, seasoning salt,	¼ to ½ cup margarine,
garlic powder to taste	melted

Tenderize steaks by beating with meat mallet. Sprinkle both sides of meat with spices and Worcestershire sauce. Let sit at least 20 minutes, longer if desired. Before grilling, drizzle butter over meat. The meat can then be grilled outdoors or baked in the oven at 350 degrees until meat suits your taste. Thickness of steak will also determine cooking time. The steaks are tender fixed medium to medium well. Yield: 4 servings.

🦃 🦃 🦃 🦃 🦃 🦃 🦃

BILL'S VENISON STEAKS

Bill Lemons

Even people who "don't like" venison – love this!

8 to 10 venison steaks	1 teaspoon paprika
Teriyaki sauce	1 teaspoon garlic salt
¾ cup Bisquick	Cooking oil
2 teaspoons seasoned salt <u>or</u> No-Salt	

Marinate steaks in Teriyaki sauce at least two hours. Mix Bisquick, salt, paprika and garlic salt; dredge steaks in Bisquick mixture. Fry in ½-inch hot oil. Drain on paper towels. Do not over cook or it will be tough. Make cream gravy, if desired. Freeze leftover coating mixture for use at another time. Yield: 8 to 10 small steaks.

Variation: *Violet Waters* also prepares venison this way. Sometimes rather than using Teriyaki sauce, she soaks the steaks in milk for 30 minutes <u>or</u> in water that 1 teaspoon of baking soda or vinegar, to a cup of water, has been added. Hot biscuits are a must.

BRAISED VENISON TIPS

Allen Law

2 pounds venison <u>or</u> beef cut into 1 inch cubes	½ teaspoon garlic powder
	¼ teaspoon onion powder
1 (10½-ounce) can beef consomme	2 tablespoons cornstarch
	¼ cup water
⅓ cup red burgundy wine	Hot cooked rice <u>or</u>
2 tablespoons soy sauce	egg noodles

Brown meat on all sides in a large heavy skillet. Add consomme, wine, soy sauce, garlic powder and onion powder. Heat to boiling. Reduce heat, cover and simmer 1 hour. Blend cornstarch and water and stir gradually into meat mixture. Cook, stirring constantly, until gravy thickens and boils. Cook 1 minute more. Serve over rice or noodles. Yield: 6 servings.

VENISON CHILI

Bob Grimmell

Texans don't put beans in chili, I know, but beans lower cholesterol. Chili always tastes better when cooled and reheated. Round steak or pot roast may be substituted for venison.

227

☆ ☆ ☆ ☆ ☆ ☆ ☆

2 pound shoulder of deer	3 cups canned tomatoes with juice
¼ cup flour	1 (12-ounce) can beer
Salt and pepper to taste	Water <u>or</u> tomato sauce, if
1 large onion, chopped	necessary
2 cloves garlic, minced	Crushed red pepper <u>or</u>
2 tablespoons oil	Tabasco sauce, to taste
2 teaspoons cumin	1 (23-ounce) can ranch
2 tablespoons chili powder	style beans

Cube meat into ½-inch pieces. Place meat in bag with flour, salt and pepper and shake. Brown onion and garlic in oil and add meat. Brown meat and onion until onion is limp. Add cumin and chili powder, stir. Add tomatoes and beer. Lower heat and simmer uncovered until meat is tender and sauce has thickened. Add water or tomato sauce as necessary. Stir in crushed red pepper or Tabasco after chili is cooked. Add beans just before serving. Yield: 6 servings without beans, 8 servings with beans.

BEER STEW
Pat Smith

This is a good way to use up the deer meat while on the hunting trip, so the wife and kids don't have to eat it. There is usually some beer at the deer camp, so pop a top and have some beer stew. This could all be done in a crock pot, freeing up the camp cook to do some more hunting. Beer taste disappears.

1 cup boiling water	2 tablespoons flour
¼ pound diced lean bacon	2 teaspoons salt
1 tablespoon margarine	¼ teaspoon pepper
20 peeled, small white boiling	1 (12-ounce) can <u>or</u> bottle
onions	of beer
1 large garlic clove, minced	1 tablespoon lemon juice
2 pounds boneless venison <u>or</u>	
chuck cut in 1½-inch cubes	

Pour boiling water over diced raw bacon and let it stand for 1 minute. Drain. Put bacon and margarine into a large skillet or Dutch oven. Cook until the bacon is limp and transparent. Add the onions and garlic. Cook stirring frequently until the onions are golden. Add the meat, venison or beef to the fat in the Dutch oven . . . a few pieces at a time. Brown over high heat. Transfer the meat to a plate after browning, stir in the flour, salt and pepper and the beer. Put all back into the skillet. Just cover the meat with the beer. Add more beer as it cooks if more liquid is needed. You may drink or discard the rest of the beer if any is left. Bring to a boil,

reduce heat and simmer covered for 1½ hours or until meat is tender. Remove from heat and add 1 tablespoon lemon juice, stir. Serve with noodles or rice and top with chopped parsley. Can be done in crock pot just as well, dump all ingredients together and cook on low heat for 6 to 8 hours. Yield: 8 servings.

WOK VENISON
Roger Lawson

I cook like Justin Wilson, never measuring anything. This may be made as is or add to it. Beef or chicken may be substituted for the venison.

Worcestershire sauce
(approximately 2 tablespoons)
2 steaks of venison, cut in bite
size pieces
1 onion, thin sliced and halved

1 bell pepper, thin sliced
Garlic powder, to taste
Seasoning salt, to taste
Pepper, to taste

Heat wok to medium heat. Put Worcestershire sauce in wok and add meat and brown. Move meat to side and add vegetables and spices. Sauté until tender. Mix meat and vegetables. Sauté 10 to 15 minutes. Serve over rice. Yield: 4 servings.

DEER SAUSAGE
Clemens R. Lorenz

This was passed down from my grandpa. The better the meat, the better the sausage.

20 pounds deer meat or beef
20 pounds pork
1 cup salt

½ cup fine ground black
pepper
1 pinch red pepper

Grind all meat and mix with all ingredients. Makes good ring sausage and pan sausage. Yield: 40 pounds.

HOMEMADE VENISON SAUSAGE
Felix Sultemeier

I have made sausage for years and this is our families favorite recipe. The success of good sausage is processing the deer as soon as possible, using sharp knives and removing all fat and muscles.

☆ ☆ ☆ ☆ ☆ ☆ ☆

2 cloves garlic, slice thin	½ level tablespoon fresh
1 cup boiling water	ground black pepper
Set of casings	for 2 pounds of meat
60 pounds venison	(25 tablespoons)
40 pounds fresh pork shoulder	Sage <u>or</u> red pepper to
1 level tablespoon pickling	taste, optional
salt for 2 pounds of meat	
(50 tablespoons)	

Place garlic in boiling water and set aside to cool; strain. Wash casing in warm water and cut in 12 to 14-inch strips. Weigh all meat, season with salt, and half as much pepper as salt, garlic water and sage or red pepper, then grind meat as fine as possible. Stuff meat into casings and tie securely at both ends. Hang in smokehouse. Smoke immediately with live oak wood chips (damp chips make a good smoke), do not let the chips flame. Smoke for 3 days. Time depends on weather and the moon sign. Dark of the moon causes sausage to shrink quicker. For dry sausage hang longer. Freeze. (50 tablespoons equals 3⅛ cups and 25 tablespoons equals 1½ cups plus 1 tablespoon.) Yield: 100 pounds.

MENGERS FAMILY SAUSAGE   *William L. Mengers*

This sausage seasoning has been in the Mengers family for generations, and is apparently a German standard, as it is very similar to recipes used here in the Hill Country. The Mengers originally settled further south in Tynan, near Corpus Christi, Texas.

20 pounds venison	4 tablespoons red pepper
30 pounds pork	1 teaspoon saltpeter
16 ounces salt	2½ tablespoons sage
6 tablespoons black pepper	1¼ tablespoons garlic

Grind altogether. Place in casings or use as pan sausage. Recipe may be doubled. Yield: 50 pounds.

PATTY SAUSAGE   *Gary Hobbs*

John Stevenson taught me how to mix sausage when I was fourteen years old.

6 pounds venison	1 tablespoon red pepper
6 pounds lean pork	1 tablespoon chili powder
4 tablespoons salt	¼ teaspoon garlic powder
4 tablespoons black pepper	

Cut up meat to fit the grinder. Mix the seasonings in a bowl and sprinkle over the meat. Grind in grinder with fine wheel. Yield: 12 pounds.

SAUSAGE
J. E. Sublett, Jr.

My in-laws, Mr. and Mrs. Walter Duecker, taught me to make this sausage.

20 pounds of meat (pork, beef, venison) <u>or</u> a mix of any of these	1 cup salt
	½ cup black pepper
	4 teaspoons red pepper

Grind and mix together, shape into patties and freeze with a paper between each patty, or shape into loaves, or put in casings. Yield: 20 pounds.

TURKEY SAUSAGE
Arthur Feuge, Jr.

I make this from wild turkey and wild hogs that I shoot, as well as the deer.

2 pounds venison	½ cup salt
8 pounds dark meat turkey	¾ cup medium ground pepper
10 pounds pork	½ tablespoon saltpeter

Mix thoroughly and let set 30 minutes. Grind using regular grinder blade. Use as pan sausage or stuff into casings and smoke for 30 minutes or according to taste. Yield: 20 pounds.

BRAD'S ROAST MOUFLON SHEEP
Bradley Smith

If you, like me, don't consider yourself a sheep lover, I think you will find this recipe a surprise. This recipe is best done with a young ewe, but it's tasty with even the old trophy ram. I was taught not to shoot anything I wouldn't eat. Mom cooked, and I have at least tasted, birds, pigeons, squirrel, possum and wild turkey. It was an experience for both of us. Obviously I am still harvesting, and now cooking for myself, some exotic meat. Now I insist that Mom tastes a bite.

4 or 5 pound Mouflon sheep ham <u>or</u> butt	Water
	3 tablespoons vinegar

If frozen, thaw in water and vinegar. Remove and pat dry. Preheat oven to 425 degrees. Place meat in roaster and bake uncovered until seared, about 35 minutes. Reduce heat to 350 degrees and cook, uncovered, for 3½ hours, basting often with sauce. Yield: 20 servings.

Basting Sauce

½ cup butter	2 tablespoons Dijon mustard
1 (5-ounce) bottle Worcestershire sauce	1 medium purple onion, grated
½ cup water	2 tablespoons brown sugar
Juice of two limes	2 tablespoons Tex Joy Steak Seasoning or Fiesta Fajita
½ lime rind, grated	Seasoning
2 tablespoons wine vinegar	

Place all ingredients in pan and heat. Baste meat with sauce often. Yield: about 2 cups sauce.

PINTO BEAN SQUARES   *E. B. Seals*

Pinto beans were always a favorite during our growing up years on the farm. In the later years, our Aunt Eula found that she could make them even better. This recipe was served at a lot of church 'dinner on the grounds' gatherings and at funeral meals.

2 cups cooked pinto beans	½ teaspoon dry mustard
1 egg, beaten	¼ cup green onion, minced
1 cup milk	1 cup cooked rice
1 teaspoon Worcestershire sauce	1½ cups Cheddar cheese, grated, divided

Combine all ingredients reserving ½ cup grated cheese for topping. Pour into well greased or Pam sprayed 8-inch square baking pan. Bake at 325 degrees for 45 to 50 minutes until set. Sprinkle with reserved cheese and bake another 5 to 10 minutes. Allow to set for 10 minutes before cutting into squares and serving. Yield: 6 servings.

HOMINY CASSEROLE   *Dennis R. Bushnell*

When I was in college at Texas Tech, a lovely lady, Charlotte Goeth, who was the aunt of a friend, Debbie Jones, would have us out to eat. I had not liked hominy before, but most anyone will like it fixed this way.

1 (30-ounce) can hominy	1 cup Monterey Jack cheese, grated
1 cup sour cream	
1 (4-ounce) can chopped green chilies	

Drain hominy and put into a one-quart casserole. Stir in sour cream and

green chilies. Sprinkle the cheese on top and place in 325 degree oven until casserole is hot and bubbly, or until cheese is melted, about 30 minutes. Yield: 4 to 6 servings.

ONION RINGS LA MACCHIA
Mike LaMacchia

This makes enough onion rings to feed a football team; you will have to make adjustments. Mixture should not be too thick, not as thick as a pancake mixture. Mike LaMacchia is the owner of Mike's Grill, a sport's bar in San Antonio, where the motto is: "Great food, fun and sports." These are good onion rings!

Jumbo yellow onions (Texas
   1015 if in season)
½ gallon buttermilk
2 or 3 large eggs, beaten
Salt, pepper, garlic powder to taste

Flour
Vegetable oil (Canola Oil,
   preferably)

Cut onions ½ inch thick, leave in solid piece, but soak all the onion pieces in sugar water overnight. This causes them to sweeten as well as come apart, into 'rings' easier. Drain onions. Mix eggs into buttermilk. First, dip onion rings into flour that has been seasoned with pepper, salt and garlic powder; this is an important step. Then dredge into buttermilk and egg mixture, then back into flour. Do not double dip except into the flour. Deep fry in oil at 300 degrees to 310 degrees. Do not get it too hot. Important to know the temperature.

EARL'S POTATOES
Earl Rosson

4 potatoes
3 tablespoons butter
1½ teaspoons salt
Dash pepper

½ cup Cheddar cheese, grated
2 tablespoons parsley,
   chopped
½ cup heavy cream

Cut potatoes in chunks like a slice of lemon. Cut a 48-inch length of foil and fold in half. Put potatoes in center of foil, add butter, salt, pepper, cheese, and parsley. Pull edges of foil up by four corners, pour in cream. Fold over foil and seal seams tight. Bake at 450 degrees for 1 hour. Yield: 4 servings.

HOT POTATO SALAD

Rex Armstrong

6 medium size potatoes
2 cups shredded Cheddar
   cheese
6 tablespoons margarine,
   divided

1½ cups commercial sour
   cream
3 green onions, chopped
1 teaspoon salt
¼ teaspoon pepper

Cook potatoes in skins; cool and dice. Combine cheese and 4 tablespoons margarine in saucepan; heat and stir until cheese is almost melted. Remove from heat; blend in sour cream, onions, salt and pepper. Fold in potatoes, and spoon into a greased 2-quart casserole. Dot with 2 tablespoons margarine. Cover, and bake at 300 about 25 minutes. Yield: 6 servings.

SQUASH CASSEROLE

D. R. Bushnell

We visited the Country Dinner Playhouse in Austin and they served a squash dish on this order. I couldn't find a recipe that was anything like theirs, so I made my own.

2 pounds yellow squash, sliced
1 large onion, sliced
1 cup water
Salt and pepper to taste

1 can cream of celery soup
½ cup American cheese, grated
1½ cups crumbled cornbread

Put squash, onions, water, salt, and pepper in saucepan with lid and cook until tender. Stir in soup; add cornbread, then stir in cheese. Adjust cornbread to soak up just the right amount of liquid, you do not want it dry or too soupy. Pour into a 1½-quart casserole dish and bake at 325 degrees until casserole bubbles, about 30 minutes. Yield: 8 servings.

TOMATOES IN A MARINADE

Terry A. Carter

This recipe came about because a way was needed to serve the tomatoes my wife produces in the garden.

4 large tomatoes, sliced
⅓ cup salad oil
¼ cup red wine vinegar
1 teaspoon chopped onion
2 teaspoons parsley flakes
1 teaspoon Italian seasoning

½ teaspoon sugar
¼ teaspoon garlic salt
1 teaspoon salt
¼ teaspoon coarsely ground
   pepper

Put tomato slices in a shallow, oblong, one quart dish. Combine all the remaining ingredients, mix well, pour over tomatoes. Cover with plastic wrap or lid and marinate several hours in refrigerator. The tomatoes are also good in salads and the marinade makes a good salad dressing. Yield: 8 servings.

CHEESY ZUCCHINI BAKE
Rex Armstrong

2   medium tomatoes, peeled
    and cut into wedges
2   small zucchini, sliced
2   small yellow summer
    squash, sliced
⅛   teaspoon dried thyme
½   teaspoon dried basil
Dash garlic powder

½   cup shredded Cheddar
    cheese
½   cup grated Parmesan
    cheese
⅓   cup dry bread crumbs
1   cup (4-ounces) shredded
    Mozzarella cheese

Combine tomatoes, squash, seasonings and Cheddar cheese. Place in a 1½ quart casserole. Top with the Parmesan cheese and bread crumbs. Bake at 350 degrees for about 45 minutes or until vegetables are tender. Sprinkle with Mozzarella cheese and let stand for 5 minutes before serving. Add some Italian sausage for zest! Yield: 6-8 servings.

CAT HEAD BISCUITS
Clifford Connell

This recipe was submitted by Bobbie Connell, Clifford's wife. She said "It is an old cowboy recipe. I am married to one of the oldest cowboys in Blanco County. Called cat head because you pinch the biscuits off like you would a cat's head."

1   sack flour
1   cup clabber or sour milk

1   teaspoon salt
2   teaspoons soda

Open top of flour sack; make hole in flour. Put milk into the hole with salt and soda. (About a teaspoon, he cupped his hand to show how much). Mix by hand, working flour into milk mixture until the dough is just right. Pinch off a wad and work into a smooth ball. Put into a well greased Dutch oven. Keep pinching off dough and adding to oven until all used up. Put lid on oven and set on a bed of coals, put coals on lid. After about 15 minutes take lid off and eat. These may not be the lightest biscuits you ever ate, but remember it was 'trail drive fare.' Next day take the same flour sack, make another hole, and make more biscuits. Yield: about 6.

GOEBEL'S GUNNERS FISH FRY BISCUITS   *Will Dahmann*

All hunters will love these biscuits.

3   dozen prebaked biscuits

Place 3 dozen prebaked biscuits into basket of fish fryer. Stand biscuits on sides. Install basket into fish fryer pan. Must have 3 empty beer cans (any brand) upright in bottom of pan to keep biscuits from burning on bottom. Cover the top with a lid or foil. Bake for 15 minutes on medium fire. Yield: 3 dozen.

FLAKY BISCUITS   *Rex Armstrong*

2 cups sifted unbleached flour	½ teaspoon cream of tartar
4 teaspoons baking powder	½ cup butter, chilled (no
3 tablespoons sugar	substitutes)
½ teaspoon salt	¾ cup milk, room temperature

Sift together into large mixing bowl: flour, baking powder, sugar, salt and cream of tartar. Cut in butter until bits of butter are the size of medium peas. Mix in milk, only until ingredients are blended. **Do not over-mix.** Form into a ball; pat out on floured board to ¾ inch thickness. Cut into biscuits using a 2½ inch biscuit cutter. Place on ungreased cookie sheet or in 13 x 9 x 2 inch pan. Bake at 475 for 10 minutes or until golden brown. Yield: 10 biscuits.

SOURDOUGH BISCUITS   *Bill Wiemers*

Get a starter from a friend who has some or purchase a starter packet and follow the directions for making a starter.

I keep my starter (2½ cups) in a 40-ounce glass peanut butter jar with straight sides. The starter is most active around 85 degrees. When the temperature is lowered it becomes less active. If you use the starter only 2 or 3 times a month, 38 degrees is a good temperature. It can be frozen. To thaw, let it come to room temperature gradually. **Do not apply heat.** TEMPERATURE ABOVE 95 DEGREES WILL KILL THE STARTER.

The starter needs to be prepared the day before you plan to serve the biscuits. I leave about ½ cup of the starter* in the container and put the rest of the starter, approximately 1½ cups, into a 4 to 5 quart container (not metal).

To starter in large container add:

236

½	cup powdered milk	2	cups flour
4	teaspoons sugar		

Stir well, using wooden or plastic spoon; add enough warm water to make a mush (not soupy) mixture. Cover with a lid or plastic wrap and place in warmest area of kitchen.

*To the starter (½ cup), in the glass/plastic starter container, add about a cup of flour and enough warm water to make a sticky consistency; mix well. Put on the lid and let it sit with the above mixture for 8-12 hours. Stir each container once or twice during this time.

When ready to prepare biscuits — stir contents of both containers. Put the starter in the jar back into the refrigerator, with the lid on tight. To the larger container add:

1	teaspoon salt	1	teaspoon baking soda
1	teaspoon baking powder	¾	cup cooking oil

Stir until well mixed. Add enough flour to bring the dough to a stiff consistency which can be rolled out with a rolling pin. Work the dough with your hands several times. Flour the surface where the dough will be rolled. Flour the rolling pin and gently roll the dough until it is ⅓ inch thick. Using a 2-inch round cutter, gently cut out the biscuits.

Put 2-4 tablespoons of cooking oil into a 11 x 17 inch pan. I use the first biscuit to spread the oil around the bottom and sides of the pan. Carefully coat both sides of each biscuit with the oil and place them close together in the pan: about 35 biscuits fit in this size pan. If I have extra biscuits, I put them in a smaller pan to bake. I cover the pan(s) with plastic wrap and refrigerate for several hours or overnight.

TWO HOURS before baking remove the biscuits from the refrigerator and let them rise in a warm place. Bake at 350 degrees for 30 minutes, until golden brown.

HUNGARIAN COFFEECAKE   *Glen Hobbs*

1	cup lukewarm water	½	cup margarine, melted
1	package yeast	¾	cup sugar
3½	cups flour	1	tablespoon cinnamon
¼	cup sugar	1 to 2	cups pecans, chopped
1	tablespoon salt	1	cup raisins, chopped

Mix water and yeast. In large bowl mix flour, sugar, and salt; add yeast mixture. Cover with cloth and let rise until double. Punch down and let

rise again. Make dough into walnut size balls and dip into margarine, then into sugar mixed with cinnamon. Put dough balls in well greased 10-inch tube pan or Bundt pan. Press nuts and raisins between the dough and around edge of pan. I roll balls in the pecans before putting in pan and sprinkle raisins around each layer. Let rise until double. Bake at 350 degrees for 35 minutes. Yield: 1 large loaf.

RAISIN NUT ZUCCHINI BREAD   *Harry Carpenter*

All of my life I have enjoyed this bread. It is great toasted with your favorite jelly or jam. Keeps well in the refrigerator and makes a nice gift.

4	eggs	1½	teaspoons cinnamon
2	cups sugar	2	cups zucchini, grated
1	cup oil	1½	teaspoons vanilla
3½	cups flour	1	cup pecans, chopped
¾	teaspoon baking powder	1	cup raisins
1½	teaspoons baking soda		

Beat the eggs, add sugar and oil. Combine the dry ingredients, and add to the above. Stir in the zucchini, add vanilla, nuts and raisins. Put into two greased 9 x 5 x 3 loaf pans. Bake at 350 degrees for 45 to 60 minutes. Yield: 2 loaves.

OATMEAL PANCAKES   *Ray Zesch*

I brought this 'stick to your ribs' pancake recipe from my family in Mason. Good cooking is a family tradition. I have joined my dad, Gary, in the restaurant business in San Angelo.

1	cup oatmeal	1½	cups flour
1½	cups buttermilk	2	tablespoons brown sugar
¾	cup milk	1	teaspoon baking powder
2	eggs, beaten	1	teaspoon soda
¼	cup margarine, melted	½	teaspoon salt

Combine oatmeal, and milks together. Set aside for 5 minutes. Add eggs and margarine to oat mixture, mixing well. Combine dry ingredients; add to oat mixture, stirring until blended. Pour ¼ cup batter onto a hot griddle, grease if necessary. Cook until edges are dry and turn to cook the other side. Yield: 4-6 servings.

238

❧ ❧ ❧ ❧ ❧ ❧ ❧

CRUNCHY FRENCH TOAST

Tim Carter

My mother taught me to cook. Week-end meals are my specialty, especially breakfast.

1	egg	1½	tablespoons baking powder
½	cup milk	4	slices white bread
½	cup flour	1½	cups vegetable oil
⅛	teaspoon salt		

Beat egg slightly; add milk and blend. Add flour, salt and baking powder (1½ tablespoons is right) and beat with a whisk. Cut bread diagonally to form triangles. Dip bread in batter. Fry halves in hot oil until golden brown. Serve with syrup, jam or powdered sugar. Yield: 4 servings.

DEER CAMP EGGS

Joel Honeycutt

It is a good idea to be down wind when cooking this; the smell will always draw a crowd!

1	(15-ounce) can hominy	6 to 8 eggs, beaten
½	pound pan sausage	Salt and pepper to taste
½	cup onion, chopped	

Mash ½ of the hominy with a fork, leave other ½ whole. In skillet brown the sausage, add onion and cook until sausage is almost done. Stir in mashed and whole hominy; fold in eggs and cook until done. Yield: 6 to 8 servings.

DIRTY 'GREEN' EGGS

Pat Smith

The 'green' in the title of this recipe has nothing to do with the color of the eggs, but everything to do with the inventor John W. Green of Timpson, Texas. On every hunting trip I made with this friend, these were served. John Green was the breakfast cook and the reason was obvious to all who ever had the great pleasure of his company. This man knew how to 'do breakfast.' He usually cooked nice thick pork chops, sometimes sausage or bacon. He would pour off some of the grease to use for his famous cream gravy (which is another recipe) and then stir into this pan all the beaten eggs it would hold. The eggs were dirty from the drippings, with bits of bacon or pork chops, and so good. Breakfast was definitely something to look forward to.

239

Bacon, ham, sausage or pork   6   eggs
   chops   ⅛   cup evaporated milk

Fry meat as usual, drain off the grease and save. Do not touch the bottom of the pan with a scraper. Beat eggs and add milk; stir like crazy. Pour into the hot skillet with the meat drippings and a little grease to keep them from sticking. Let the eggs 'set' a minute or two and stir, getting up the meat particles and mix with the eggs. Cook until just right; eggs will be dirty, but good. Yield: 4 servings.

STUFFED EGGS   *Pat Smith*

Wife's comment: Many years ago, my husband offered to help get the eggs ready for a picnic, I was at work and he was off. He called asking me how to 'skin' an egg. He had boiled them until all the water was nearly gone and the membrane (skin) was stuck to the egg. You should have seen the eggs when he got through 'skinning.' They looked like the surface of the moon looks through a telescope. They were not the best looking eggs, but tasted pretty good.

6   hard-boiled eggs (boil hard till they crack)
Mayonnaise and mustard until it looks pale yellow
Salt and pepper to taste

Boil the eggs until they crack, that way you know they are done. Be sure you use clean eggs to start with. Then beat the eggs on the counter to crack them more, take off the shell, then 'skin' them (get off the membrane). Cut them in half the long way. Take out the yellow stuff and put in a bowl. Be careful not to dig too deep and get white with the yellow. Mix mayonnaise and mustard with the yellow of the egg, add the salt and pepper and stir. Stuff all this into the white shell that will fit. Run finger around the bowl and lick all that is left over. Don't make too runny. Yield: 12 halves if you are lucky and don't ruin any.

HILLTOP BREAKFAST TACOS   *D. J. Whittington, Jr.*

I developed this recipe while a member of the local Soil Conservation Service District committee. We serve breakfast annually to the Blanco County pastors and interested landowners working to improve their soil and water. I also used this recipe for the first annual Cowboy Breakfast held in conjunction with Lights Spectacular, Hill Country Style.

40 flour tortillas
1 pound fresh pan sausage (as hot as you like)
2 dozen (24) eggs

Remove tortillas from plastic bag. Wrap in foil, and place in oven at 250 degrees for approximately 1 hour. Using extra large skillet, put pan sausage into skillet on medium heat. Stir meat as it is cooking and browning. When meat is well done, add the 24 eggs which are well-beaten as for scrambling. Continue to stir until the eggs are cooked. Remove from heat, or turn heat on very low temperature. Serve approximately 3 tablespoons mixture on each tortilla. Yield: Feeds approximately 20 people.

CINNAMON ANGEL FOOD CAKE   *Sterling Bingham*

A dietician at the Heart Institute put Angel Food Cake on my diet plan. I came up with this version.

1 Duncan Hines Angel Food   Candy sprinkles
**   Cake Mix   Chopped pecans (optional)**
Cinnamon

Follow mixing directions on box of cake mix. Cover bottom of ungreased angel food cake pan with dough, then sprinkle large amount of cinnamon, candy sprinkles, and chopped pecans (optional) over batter. Repeat process. Be sure to add plenty of cinnamon. When all is layered, take spatula and insert vertically and swirl through to remove 'bubbles' and swirl ingredients. Bake 37 minutes in a 375 degree oven. Yield: 1 large cake.

Alternate cake: Leave out cinnamon, bake and serve fresh strawberries on a slice. Most delicious — few calories.

BALENA BREAD (German Fruit Cake)   *Homer Blackwood*

This recipe comes from Lela Sublett. "An old German janitor in a school where my dad taught, shared this recipe with him. For the next forty-five years dad baked this fruit bread and shared it with friends and family. My job, as a child, was to shake the very hot pieces in powdered sugar as fast as he cut it up. I'd scorch my fingers, but it was worth it to be a part of this holiday tradition. I hope some new families will enjoy this experience together also."

2   pints water
2   pounds brown sugar
1   pound nuts, chopped
½   pound raisins

½   pound dates, chopped
2   teaspoons soda
4½   cups flour
Powdered sugar

Bring water to boil and set off burner. Add sugar, nuts, raisins and dates, stir. Mix in soda and flour. Place dough in a greased 15 x 11 x 2-inch pan ¾ inches thick. Bake at 325 degrees for one hour. Cut into 1½ to 2-inch squares as soon as it is taken out of oven. Shake in bag with powdered sugar to coat. When cool, put in a tight can to store. Yield: 40 to 70 squares.

FLUFFY BANANA CAKE
Bennie Ray Fuelberg

A family favorite!

2   cups flour
½   teaspoon baking powder
¾   teaspoon soda
½   teaspoon salt
½   cup shortening
1½   cups sugar
2   eggs
1   teaspoon vanilla

¼   cup buttermilk
1   cup mashed bananas
Icing
½   banana, mashed
1½   cups powdered sugar
2   tablespoons butter,
     softened
Evaporated milk

Sift dry ingredients. Cream shortening and sugar, eggs and vanilla; add buttermilk. Add flour mixture and bananas alternately. Mix well. Pour into 2 8-inch greased and floured cake pans. Bake at 350 degrees for 30 to 35 minutes.

Icing: Mix banana, powdered sugar, butter and enough evaporated milk to desired consistency. Don't make too thin. Ice while cake is still warm. Yield: 1 2-layer cake.

CHOCOLATE CHIP CAKE
Chuck Matus

This cake is quick and easy and is great when served while still warm, covered with vanilla ice cream.

1   package yellow cake mix
2   (3.9-ounce) packages of
     instant chocolate pudding
4   eggs
½   cup vegetable oil

1½   cups water
1   teaspoon vanilla
1   (12-ounce) package
     chocolate chips <u>or</u> 2 cups
¾   cup nuts, chopped

Mix dry ingredients together; add eggs, oil, water and vanilla. Mix well. Stir in chips and nuts. Pour into a greased and floured Bundt pan. Bake 1 hour at 350 degrees. Yield: 10-inch cake.

DEVIL'S FOOD CAKE   *Raymond Casparis*

This recipe has been a favorite of the Howard Casparis family for years. It was a yearly tradition to serve this at Christmas. This was handed down to Regina Casparis, my mother, by her mother, Mrs. Flora Smith of Llano, Texas. It was known in our home as "Lee's Favorite"!

1 cup molasses	1 teaspoon allspice
½ teaspoon baking soda	1 teaspoon nutmeg
1 cup sweet whipping cream	1 teaspoon cloves
1 teaspoon cream of tartar	1 teaspoon cinnamon
½ cup cocoa	About 4 cups flour
1 cup boiling water	*Mocha Icing*
2 cups pecans, chopped	12 tablespoons cocoa
¼ cup citron, diced	12 tablespoons hot coffee
2 cups raisins	12 tablespoons butter <u>or</u>
4 eggs	margarine, melted
1 cup butter <u>or</u> margarine,	2 teaspoons vanilla extract
melted	6 cups powdered sugar
2 cups sugar	

Preheat oven to 350 degrees. Mix molasses with baking soda. Mix whipping cream with cream of tartar. Mix cocoa with boiling water. Mix pecans, citron, and raisins with a small amount of the flour to lightly coat these ingredients. Combine all ingredients in a large mixing bowl, adding flour last, being sure not to get batter too stiff. Pour batter into 4 greased 9-inch cake pans and bake in 350 degrees oven for 45 minutes. Use caution during baking time so as not to cause cake layers to fall.

Mocha Icing: Combine cocoa and coffee. Add butter or margarine and vanilla extract. Then add powdered sugar gradually until thoroughly mixed and of spreading consistency. Place first cake layer on cake plate and spread icing evenly. Repeat layers spreading each with icing. Spread icing over top and sides of cake.

HINT:
Swallow your pride occasionally; it's not fattening.

243

LEMON PUDDING CAKE
Leonard Talburt

This recipe was an old standby with my mother. I always found it wise to try to get the first serving, just in case it ran out before my turn.

2 eggs, separated	1 cup sugar
1 teaspoon grated lemon peel	¼ cup all purpose flour
¼ cup lemon juice	¼ teaspoon salt
⅔ cup milk	Whipped cream, optional

Heat oven to 350 degrees. Beat egg whites until stiff peaks form; set aside. Beat egg yolks; blend in lemon peel, juice and milk. Add sugar, flour and salt; beat until smooth. Fold in egg whites. Pour into ungreased 1-quart casserole. Place casserole in pan of very hot water about 1-inch deep. Bake 45 to 50 minutes. Serve warm or cool, and if desired, with whipped cream. Yield: 6 servings.

MINIATURE CHEESECAKES
Chuck Matus

This recipe was given to me many years ago by Suzanne O'Brien, a co-worker at Ford Aerospace in Houston.

No-stick Spray	¾ cup sugar
Graham cracker crumbs	*Topping* 
3 eggs, separated	¾ cup sour cream
2 (8-ounce) packages cream	2 tablespoons sugar
cheese, softened	1 teaspoon vanilla

Spray 4 miniature muffin tins with no-stick spray and dust with graham cracker crumbs. Beat egg whites until stiff, set aside. Combine cream cheese, egg yolks and sugar; beat until thick and creamy. Fold in egg whites. Spoon into muffin tins and bake at 350 degrees for 15 minutes.

Topping: Combine sour cream, sugar and vanilla and mix thoroughly. Put 1 teaspoon of topping on each cake and return to oven for 5 minutes. Cool completely before attempting to remove from pans. Yield: 48 miniature cakes.

★ ★ ★ ★ ★

HINT:

Refrigerate cheese in its original wrapper until opened. After opening, rewrap in plastic wrap, plastic bags, or foil, or place in airtight containers and refrigerate.

BANANA BLUEBERRY PIE

Harry Carpenter

As a boy this was one of my favorites. Sets up well in the refrigerator and goes great with milk or hot coffee.

2 8-inch pie shells <u>or</u> graham cracker crusts	1 (8-ounce) cream cheese
3 bananas, sliced	1 cup sugar
1 (21-ounce) can blueberry pie filling	1 (12-ounce) carton whipped topping
	1 teaspoon milk

If using dough crust, prebake. Place a layer of bananas on bottom of each shell, divide blueberries on top of bananas. Mix cream cheese, sugar and whipped topping; add milk to smooth. Spread on top of blueberries. Keep refrigerated until ready to serve. Yield: 2 8-inch pies.

MAMA'S TEA CAKES

Truman Fawcett

1 cup butter, softened	¼ teaspoon salt
½ cup powdered sugar	¾ cup nuts, finely chopped
1 teaspoon vanilla	Colored sugar or powdered
2¼ cups flour	sugar

Heat oven to 400 degrees. Mix thoroughly butter, sugar and vanilla. Work in flour, salt and nuts until dough holds together. Shape dough into 1-inch balls. Place on ungreased baking sheet. Bake 10-12 minutes until set but not brown. While warm roll in powdered sugar or colored sugar before baking. Yield: about 4 dozen.

SOUR CREAM FUDGE

Robert Hemphill

2 cups sugar	2 tablespoons butter
⅔ cup sour cream	1 teaspoon vanilla
¼ cup milk	½ cup pecans <u>or</u>
2 tablespoons light corn syrup	walnuts, chopped

In a 1½ or 2 quart deep saucepan put sugar, sour cream and corn syrup. Over medium heat melt these ingredients while stirring occasionally. Bring to a boil and then cover for two minutes. Uncover and stir constantly until mixture reaches 232 degree on candy thermometer. Remove from heat and cool for ten minutes. Beat in butter and vanilla for a few minutes, then add nuts. Pour into greased 8 x 8 x 2-inch or 9 x 9 x 2-inch pan. Cut

into squares and cool at room temperature until hardened. (While stirring the mixture, do not scrape sides of the pan. If you do, the sugar will crystallize out and the fudge will not be creamy). Yield: 25 to 36 squares.

TURRON
Cicero A. Rust III

While traveling in Mexico with students of Lyndon B. Johnson High School, we find the "dulces" of either Mexico City or Copper Canyon to be inviting.

1	pound slivered almonds	2	tablespoons honey
1¼	cups sugar	3	tablespoons almonds,
½	cup honey		ground
2	tablespoons milk		Butter

Toast the slivered almonds on a cookie sheet in a preheated 350 degree oven for eight minutes. Place toasted almonds, sugar and honey in a saucepan and stir the mixture over low heat until golden. Add the remaining two tablespoons honey, milk and ground almonds. Remove from heat; beat for ten minutes until mixture becomes firm. Butter a cookie sheet and spread in a ½ inch thick layer. Cut into squares and cool completely. Yield: 1 batch — about 24.

ROBERT'S ORANGE SHERBET
Robert A. Mauck

Great after you have eaten Roberto's Picante and Queso for two or three days.

4	(12-ounce) cans Orange Crush	1	(14-ounce) can sweetened condensed milk
1	(12-ounce) can Seven-Up	1	(6-ounce) jar maraschino cherries, chopped
1	(15-ounce) can crushed pineapple		

Combine above ingredients in 1 gallon ice cream freezer, electric or hand cranked. Yield: 1 gallon.

WILMA'S SUGAR PECANS
Truman Fawcett

Family recipe passed down from mother-in-law, Mrs. R. L. Green.

¼	cup butter	1	tablespoon cinnamon
3	cups pecan halves	1½	teaspoons ginger
½	cup sugar	1½	teaspoons nutmeg

246

Melt butter in a skillet. Stir in pecans and sugar. Cook over medium heat, stirring until sugar melts and nuts brown, 8-12 minutes. Combine remaining ingredients in a large bowl. Stir in pecans and coat well. Spread on waxed paper and cool completely. Yield: 3 cups.

GREEN TOMATO RELISH
Duke Rumpf

10 to 12 very green tomatoes
2 medium <u>or</u> 1 large onion
4 stalks celery
½ cup 90 grain vinegar <u>or</u> ⅔ cup of 50 grain vinegar
½ cup granulated sugar
1 teaspoon dill <u>or</u> dill weed crushed

1 teaspoon mustard seed
1 teaspoon coarse black pepper
1 tablespoon salt
½ teaspoon celery seed
Pinch of allspice
Pinch of nutmeg

In food processor or food grinder, chop vegetables to coarse texture (make sure to save all juices). Blend vinegar, sugar and spices; pour over vegetables in saucepan. Cook on low to medium heat until onions are clear, stirring occasionally. When onions are clear, taste, adding vinegar or sugar to suit your taste. Can in very hot, freshly scalded Mason jars, sealing immediately. When all lids 'ping' and are solid to touch, they may be stored to enjoy later. These are basic proportions and may be multiplied to account for availability of more green tomatoes. It's tart! Yield: 4-6 pints.

HINTS:

To speed up salad making, wash, trim and dry all ingredients for the salad as soon as you buy them; tie ingredients together in a plastic bag, store in the refrigerator.

If your beef jerky gets a little mold on it, don't throw it away. Dampen a cloth with vinegar, wipe the mold away, let dry and it is ready to eat.

To cut biscuits quickly, roll dough out in rectangles and cut out with an old metal ice tray divider. Place on baking sheet and bake. Biscuits will separate easily at dividing lines.

In recipes using yeast and potatoes, boil potatoes saving liquid for the yeast to rise in.

The Good Old Days
Tried and True Recipes Fifty Years Old or More

Genera Eubanks '93

JOHN BRUCKNER BARN

This large stone barn was built by German immigrant John BRUCKNER, Sr. in 1884 on land purchased from James Polk Johnson. Typical German architecture is reflected in its dog-trot style. Stone for the barn was quarried in the hills to the south and hauled to the site by ox cart. Used primarily for storing wheat and corn, it also sheltered buggies and farm implements. Now part of the LBJ National Historic Site, the barn is restored and stands as an historical landmark.

248

BOILED CUSTARD   *Patty Casparis*

My mother made this when I was a little girl in Kentucky, and before the days of electric refrigerators. In the winter-time, Mother would set this on a table outside our kitchen window until it reached an icy consistency. The original recipe called for bourbon to taste. Mother would not allow liquor in the house, so she would add a teaspoon of vanilla flavoring to each of our glasses. (This is a drink.)

6 tablespoons flour	10 eggs, separated
2 cups sugar	2 tablespoons vanilla, or to
Salt to taste	taste, (bourbon to taste)
½ gallon milk	

Mix flour, sugar and salt. Beat egg yolks, then add to flour mixture. Heat milk and gradually add to custard. Cook until desired thickness, stirring constantly. It should coat spoon and be thin enough to drink. Cool. Beat egg whites and fold into custard. Can be chilled. Yields: 10 cups.

GRANDMA SALLIE'S PUNCH   *Louise Gravenor*

This is a sweet drink. It will keep a long time refrigerated.

5 cups sugar	½ dozen lemons, juiced
3 cups water	Water to make 2 gallons
1 (46-ounce) can orange juice	1 teaspoon almond extract
1 (46-ounce) can pineapple	1 teaspoon vanilla extract
juice	

Bring sugar and 3 cups water to boil to melt sugar. Let cool. Add other ingredients, stirring well. Yield: 2 gallons.

GRANDPA'S HOMEMADE EGG NOG   *Vicky Patton*

This eggnog is so thick you may want a spoon!

12 eggs	2 quarts milk
2 cups sugar	Nutmeg (optional)
½ teaspoon salt	Whiskey (optional)
1 quart whipping cream	

Beat eggs, sugar and salt together until foamy and sugar is dissolved — set aside. Beat whipping cream until peaks hold firm — set aside. Gradually add milk to egg mixture, then gently fold in whipped cream. Serve plain

or with whiskey and nutmeg to taste. Keep chilled or serve in a punch bowl set in ice. Yield: 20 cups.

MOTHER'S MILK SOUP
Louise Gravenor

This was my request when I was home sick as a child.

½ cup dry rice	**Noodles**
1 quart milk	1 egg
Pinch of salt	Pinch salt
¼ cup margarine	½ teaspoon baking powder
	Flour to make stiff dough

Cook rice in water as directed on package. Heat milk, salt and margarine in a large pan. Do not boil! While heating, prepare noodles. In a small bowl, beat egg with a fork. Add salt, baking powder, and enough flour to make a stiff dough. Roll out thin on a floured surface. Cut into ¼ inch wide strips. When milk almost boils, add rice and noodles. Lower heat and simmer for 15 minutes. Most of the time I like to add sugar and cinnamon to mine. Yield: 4-6 servings.

OYSTER STEW
Dardanella Gipson

My mother served this Christmas Eve for dinner, before our church group went Christmas caroling. If we had snow, we went in a sleigh drawn by two horses – no snow, we used a wagon. In northern Virginia, we always had snow at Christmas, but sometimes the streets would be cleared.

½ gallon sweet milk	1 pint oysters
1 (12-ounce) can evaporated milk	Juice from oysters
½ cup butter **or** margarine	Salt to taste (about ½ teaspoon)

Heat milk and evaporated milk in large container. Just before boiling stage, add butter or margarine, salt, oysters and juice. Cook over low heat for 15 to 20 minutes. DO NOT let come to a boil. Serve with crackers. Yield: 10 cups.

HINT:
Freeze soup stock in ice trays and store in plastic bags.

PICKLED BEETS AND EGGS

Leah Mauck

This is an Easter tradition in Bob's family, as well as in ours. I must say, the first time I had Easter dinner at his Mother's, I really had my doubts as to how I would be able to be gracious and eat this, as I am not an "egg person." It was delicious and we now have it on other occasions, as well as at Eastertime.

1 (16-ounce) can sliced beets, drained, reserve juice	½ teaspoon salt
1 cup beet juice	1 cinnamon stick, broken
1 cup vinegar	½ teaspoon whole cloves
2 tablespoons brown sugar	8 hard boiled eggs, shelled

Add water to reserved juice to make 1 cup. Combine juice, vinegar, sugar and spices. Bring to a boil, boiling 1 minute, or until sugar is dissolved. Place beets and eggs in a container with a tight lid. Pour boiling juice mixture over beets and eggs. Refrigerate for 2 to 3 days, stirring every day to turn eggs, in order for the white of the eggs to pick up the color and flavor of the beets. Yield: 8 servings.

PICKLED EGGS AND BEETS

Ruth Matthews

Grandmother Virginia (Jenny) Shuff lived on small farms in Mingo County, West Virginia and Pike County, Kentucky, most of her life. She cooked the produce most often available or grown on their farm and then passed the recipes down to family members for more than sixty years.

5 hard boiled eggs	½ cup cider vinegar
1 (16-ounce) can small whole beets	1 scant teaspoon salt
	1 scant teaspoon sugar

Peel eggs, set aside. Place beets and juice in a fairly large saucepan over a low fire. Add vinegar, salt and sugar, stirring to dissolve. Place eggs in pan with beets, stirring gently to submerge all eggs. May add more vinegar and a bit of water, but taste for tartness. When boiling point is reached, remove from fire and place in a glass or ceramic deep bowl. Refrigerate for 2 to 3 days. Stir gently, occasionally, to insure that all eggs color evenly and that eggs and beets are immersed for the pickling process. To serve: slice eggs and beets to make a lovely garnish or serve whole if desired. Yield: 5 servings or more.

⌘ ⌘ ⌘ ⌘ ⌘ ⌘ ⌘

APPLE SALAD

Helen Mayfield

2 apples, peeled and grated
Lemon juice
2 bananas, sliced
Sugar <u>or</u> honey to taste

Lettuce leaves
Whipped cream
Pecans, chopped
Maraschino cherries

Grate fresh apples (allow 1 apple for two people). Sprinkle with lemon juice to prevent darkening of apples. Place apples in colander to drain off juice. When ready to serve, slice bananas and mix with apples. Sweeten to taste. Put enough for 1 serving on lettuce leaf on individual salad plate. Put whipped cream, nuts and maraschino cherry on top and serve. Yield: 4 servings.

PEA SALAD

Ima Hobbs

2 (10½-ounce) cans English peas, drained
1 cup Colby <u>or</u> Cheddar cheese, finely cubed
½ cup Miracle Whip salad dressing

Salt and pepper to taste
¼ cup bell pepper, chopped (optional)
¼ cup onion, finely chopped (optional)

Pour peas and cheese in bowl. Add bell pepper and onion if desired. Add Miracle Whip, salt, and pepper. Toss until Miracle Whip is thoroughly mixed, tossing gently, or the peas will be mashed. Keep refrigerated until ready to serve. Yield: 8 servings.

MACARONI AND LETTUCE SALAD

Ima Hobbs

I always fix this for church potluck dinners and family gatherings. It's an old recipe my Mother received from Etta Beauchamp. One time I did not take this salad and all the boys at the family gathering asked if I was mad at them! I told them "no, why"? They thought I was because I hadn't brought this salad.

2 cups water
1 teaspoon salt
1 cup macaroni, uncooked
Salt and pepper to taste
½ cup Miracle Whip salad dressing
2 eggs, boiled, chopped

⅔ cup onion, chopped
1 small head lettuce, chopped (about 3 cups)
¼ cup Miracle Whip salad dressing (more or less, to moisten)

252

Bring water to boil, add salt and macaroni and cook until tender. (Do not overcook.) Drain, then cool in ice water. Drain well. Place in bowl and add salt, pepper and salad dressing. Mix well. Place in refrigerator overnight to allow flavors to be absorbed. When ready to serve, mix eggs, onion and lettuce with the macaroni mixture. Mix well. Add additional salad dressing to moisten, if needed. Yield: 10 to 12 servings.

WILTED WATERCRESS SALAD   *Adelia Felps*

This recipe was passed down from my grandmother. In the early springtime the Hill Country has many springs and creeks with watercress in them. Ask around, and if you hear or know of someone with watercress, they usually are happy to share with you.

3 slices bacon, save drippings
1 tablespoon sugar
2 or 3 tablespoons vinegar
2 large handfuls or bunches watercress, washed, stemmed and
   patted dry with paper towel

Salt and pepper to taste
2 hard-boiled eggs,
   sieved or sliced
   (optional)

In 10 x 3 inch iron skillet, fry bacon until crisp. Remove bacon, crumble and set aside. Remove skillet from heat and add all remaining ingredients, including crumbled bacon and bacon drippings. Return to heat if needed, stirring and mixing until watercress is just wilted. Turn out into bowl and add sieved eggs if desired. Eat while still warm. Very good with warm sourdough bread or cornbread. Olive oil and bacon bits may be substituted for the bacon and drippings. Yield: 2 servings.

MACARONI AND CHEESE SALAD   *Helen Mayfield*

1 (7¼-ounce) box macaroni
   and cheese
¼ cup mayonnaise
½ cup sour cream

½ cup ham, chopped
¼ cup green onion, diced
¼ cup bell pepper, diced
¼ cup celery, diced

Prepare macaroni in 6 cups boiling water, cook until tender, drain and add cheese packet. Do not use milk or margarine. Stir in mayonnaise and sour cream; add ham and vegetables. Mix well. Refrigerate overnight. Other vegetables may be added. Yield: 4 to 6 servings.

HOMEMADE MAYONNAISE

Jewell Sultemeier

I have made this mayonnaise since 1935 before we could buy it in jars.

1	egg		Dash of pepper
1	teaspoon sugar	2	cups vegetable oil, divided
¾	teaspoon salt	1½	tablespoons lemon juice
1	teaspoon dry mustard	1	tablespoon boiling water
½	teaspoon paprika		

Beat egg in deep bowl at high speed of an electric mixer until thick and lemon colored. Add sugar and next 4 ingredients, mixing well. Add 1 cup oil in a very thin stream, beating at high speed until it begins to thicken. Add lemon juice and mix well. Add the remaining oil in a very thin stream, beating until thickened. Add water and mix well. Spoon mayonnaise into glass container. Chill. Yields: 2 cups.

SMOTHERED BEEFSTEAK

Kittie Clyde Leonard

This recipe was taken from my mother's cookbook, which was published in 1906.

1	large thin round steak	Chopped onion, as desired
1	cup bread crumbs	Enough milk to soften
½	teaspoon salt	Few slices bacon
Pepper to taste		½ pint water
1	tablespoon butter	Flour to thicken gravy
¼	teaspoon sage	

Take one large thin round steak. Prepare a dressing by mixing the next seven ingredients. Spread over meat, roll it up carefully and tie the ends with string. Fry bacon and place the roll of beef in the fat. Brown on all sides then add water and stew until tender. When cooked sufficiently, remove the meat, thicken the gravy and pour over the meat. Carve crosswise. Yield: 6 servings.

HINT:

When out of bacon or salt pork use left over bacon grease to flavor brown beans.

TEXAS SPAGHETTI

Margaret Withers

This is a favorite in the Withers family and has been for many years. It was handed down from my mother-in-law.

1½	pounds ground beef		Spaghetti, approximately
1	cup onion, chopped		8 ounces
2	tablespoons chili powder	3	quarts water
1	teaspoon garlic salt,	1	teaspoon salt
	optional	1	tablespoon margarine
2	teaspoons salt	1	cup Cheddar cheese,
1	(16-ounce) can tomatoes		grated

In large skillet, lightly brown meat and onions; add chili powder, garlic salt, salt and tomatoes. (I use stewed Mexican tomatoes now.) Simmer with enough water to prevent scorching. Cook spaghetti, adding salt and margarine. Drain well. Combine with meat mixture and add cheese. Serve as a casserole with crisp green salad and hot rolls. Yield: 6 to 8 servings.

GRANNIE SLAYTON'S DUPER DOGS

Delores Fenton

Long before we had our present day Dairy Queens, there were Dairy Kings. My mother, Gladys Slayton, better known as Grannie Slayton, worked for the Dairy King chain for several years. She became a master at making these. She has made them for at least three generations of our family.

1	cup flour	Milk, enough to make a thick
½	teaspoon salt	batter
1	teaspoon baking powder	Weiners, 8 to 10
½	cup sugar	Sticks
1	egg	Oil, enough to make dogs float

Mix all dry ingredients together. Add egg and milk, mixing well. Push sticks into weiners leaving enough out to hold onto. Dip the weiners into the thick batter, then drop into a deep fryer, with oil hot. Fry until golden brown, 8 to 10 minutes. These are similar to corn dogs, but without the corn meal. This batter also makes great onion rings. Yield: 8 to 10 duper dogs.

HINTS:
Freeze bread for easier cutting for fancy sandwiches.

OLD FASHIONED PRESSED CHICKEN   *Kittie Clyde Leonard*

This recipe came from the San Antonio Express *on December 14, 1932.*

1 stewing chicken	2 tablespoons Picante Sauce,
Water, boiling	optional
Salt and pepper	

Cut up a stewing chicken. Add just enough boiling water to cover. Simmer until tender. When done, remove bird from broth and shred with fork or put through food chopper. Add salt and pepper to taste. Put in mold. Simmer broth until it is reduced to about one-third of it's original quantity. Add Picante Sauce, then pour over chicken. Cover with lid that leaves an inch around edge. Put light weight on lid and chill. Slice and serve. Yield: 6 to 8 servings.

SPANISH CHICKEN   *Leah Mauck*

This was always my choice when we could choose whatever we wanted for our "birthday dinner." It is still one of my favorites. It is from my mother and she can't remember exactly when she got the recipe, but probably sometime in the late 1930s. It came from a Betty Crocker Radio Show.

1 (2½-pound) chicken	1 (17-ounce) can sweet peas,
Salt and pepper	drain and reserve juice
Flour	1 (4-ounce) can sliced mush-
Oil	rooms, drain and reserve
1 large onion, chopped	juice
1 large green pepper, chopped	Flour to thicken
Garlic, to taste	1 (3-ounce) jar stuffed green
1 (8-ounce) can tomato sauce	olives, drain and slice

Cut chicken for frying. Salt, pepper and flour, then brown in deep fat. Remove chicken, leaving a small amount of fat in pan. Add onion, green pepper and garlic. Sauté slowly until tender. Add tomato sauce, juice from peas and mushrooms. Add chicken and enough water to cover. Simmer slowly until chicken is tender. Remove chicken and cool enough to handle. Bone and cut into small pieces. Thicken stock with flour. Add chicken peas, mushrooms, olives, salt and pepper to taste. Serve over steamed rice. Yield: 6 to 8 servings.

FRIED EGGPLANT OR 'ROUND FISH'

Cynthia Smith

My grandmother must have grown eggplant because she had a zillion recipes for it. However, the only way I ever served eggplant was fried. My children wouldn't have eaten anything called eggplant, so I called it 'Round Fish.' The mistake I made is in never telling them when they were old enough to know the truth, that it really was only eggplant. They were served it in someone else's home, and commented on how good the 'round fish' was! Much laughter ensued, as well as embarrassment, on the part of my teenagers. Mothers will do much to get children to eat vegetables!

Eggplant	Bread crumbs
1 egg, beaten	Fat to fry in

Wash and peel eggplant, cut in slices about $1/8$ inch thick. Arrange slices in layers, press to remove water. Dip each slice into beaten egg then bread crumbs, and fry in deep hot fat. Drain on paper toweling. Yield: 6 servings.

FRIED ONIONS AND APPLES

Helen Mayfield

This came from an old cookbook, dated 1931.

3 tablespoons margarine	1 medium onion, sliced thin
1 quart tart apples, sliced	1 teaspoon salt
¼ inch thick	1 tablespoon sugar

Melt margarine in heavy skillet. Add apples, onions, salt, and sugar. Cover and cook slowly, stirring frequently to prevent scorching. Remove cover and continue cooking until done. Serve while hot. This is very good with meat dishes. Yield: 6 to 8 servings.

FRIED GREEN TOMATOES

Ruth Matthews

Grandma Jenny's family recipe.

6 green tomatoes	1 teaspoon salt
¾ cup cornmeal	2 tablespoons cooking oil
1 tablespoon flour	

Choose medium to large green tomatoes that are beginning to ripen; will have pale pinkish stripes. Cut the stem end from the tomatoes. Cut tomatoes crosswise in thick slices. Sift together meal, flour and salt. Place oil in skillet over medium to low heat. Dredge tomato slices in cornmeal mix-

ture and sauté in oil, turning to brown on each side, until golden brown. May dampen the slices with water if they seem too dry to hold cornmeal mixture. Yield: 5 to 6 servings.

SCALLOPED POTATOES
Janey Wiemers

This is a recipe from the PRACTICAL COOKERY COOKBOOK, which my mother made throughout the years I was growing up. It has always been a favorite. She graduated from Kansas State in the early 1900's with a degree in Home Economics and the PRACTICAL COOKERY book published by the University was her favorite for basic 'how to's,' planning, recipes and serving.

4 large potatoes, peeled and sliced	¼ cup flour
½ large onion, chopped	1 (12-ounce) can condensed milk (evaporated)
Salt and pepper to taste	Margarine

Peel potatoes and slice, then arrange potatoes in an oiled baking 11 x 7 x 2-inch pan or in a 13 x 9 x 2-inch pan if you double this recipe. Sprinkle each layer with salt, pepper, chopped onion and flour. Dot with pieces of margarine. Continue to layer the above ingredients until the dish is no more than ¾ full, then add the milk to cover the contents of the dish. Bake in a 350 degree to 400 degree oven until the potatoes are tender. Cover during the first part of the cooking. Yield: 4 to 6 servings.

MAMAW'S DIRTY RICE
Jerry Nixon

My grandmother, "Mamaw," we called her as they do in Cajun/French, always sprinkled bread crumbs over the top. She toasted her own bread, or used day old dry bread and crumbled it herself. This was being served long before 'bread crumbs in a can' was available. She cooked this special dish at holiday times.

2 medium eggplants, peeled and chopped	1 cup chicken giblets <u>or</u> chicken livers <u>or</u> a mixture of these, cooked, drained and chopped
1 pound ground beef <u>or</u> pan sausage	
1 medium onion, chopped	Cayenne (red) pepper to taste
2 cups cooked, white rice	Salt and pepper to taste
1 egg, beaten	Bread crumbs, optional

Soak eggplant in salted water for 10 minutes, drain, and add water to

cover and cook until fork tender. Drain again and mash eggplant. Cook the meat, but do not brown, then drain well. Mix the meat and eggplant and all the other ingredients. Pour into a 10-inch baking dish and bake at 350 degrees until the top browns. I use a 10-inch cast iron skillet so I can cook the meat and then bake in the same utensil! Saves washing another pot. The livers or giblets are what gives this the 'dirty' look, and a distinct taste. Yield: 6 to 8 servings.

GRANDMA'S CRACKER DRESSING   *Jean Everson*

This recipe was my favorite dish that Grandma Payman served with her baked chicken. She had sixteen children and as she said "this serves four or six of them, so just multiply the recipe as many times as kids were home, plus the grandkids they brought with them!"

1 pound crackers, crumbled	2 teaspoons parsley
4 hard boiled eggs, chopped	Chicken broth
1 medium onion, minced	Flour
1 cup celery, chopped	

Mix the first five ingredients with enough chicken gravy to make it moist. Make gravy by thickening chicken broth with flour. Bake in 13 x 9 x 2-inch pan for 25 minutes or until light brown at 300 degrees. Yield: 6 or more servings.

HARD BOILED EGGS   *Jane Mills*

I found this in a small tablet that belonged to my mother-in-law. The tablet was dated 1929. She and Dad had married in March of 1929. I found other recipes along with this one, so I am assuming she had a few friends write down some of their favorite recipes. This egg recipe was signed by two ladies and I know they must have had a great time writing it down!! My mother-in-law was a good cook, but as a new bride, who knows!!

10 gallons of water	12 dozen eggs

Start with a wood stove. Build up a good hot fire. Place a very large kettle with 10 gallons of water on the hot stove. Let the fire go out. Build it up again. Scorch water to a medium brown. Drop 12 dozen eggs into the water. The water may run over, but don't mind that. Let the eggs boil from 10 to 12 hours. Take them off and put on ice. Crack them on a man's head. Serve on lettuce leaf with a pinch of paris green.

☆ ☆ ☆ ☆ ☆ ☆ ☆

PANCAKES/SOUR-SWEET GRAVY

Elnora Kneese

My grandmother, Matilde Neumann, used this recipe for gravy in the early 1900s, serving it with pancakes.

Gravy
⅔ cup sugar
⅓ cup flour

¼ teaspoon salt
2 cups water
½ tablespoon vinegar

Mix sugar, flour and salt. Bring water to a boil. Add sugar/flour mixture, stirring until blended and becomes thickened. Stir in vinegar. Makes about 2 cups.

Pancakes

2 cups flour
4 teaspoons baking powder
1 teaspoon salt
2 tablespoons sugar

1 egg
1½ to 1¾ cups milk
2 tablespoons butter, melted

Mix flour, baking powder, salt and sugar. Add the egg and milk, mixing until it's a smooth and creamy batter. Heat skillet with 1 tablespoon shortening. Using ½ cup batter per pancake, pour batter into hot skillet. Brown on first side until brown around edges. Flip over and brown on second side. Fresh garden lettuce, mixed with a little salt, vinegar, sugar and a little bacon grease may be served with the pancakes. Yield: 3 to 4 servings.

APPLE STRUDEL

Julie Mengers Zesch

The apple strudel was traditional in all branches of the family. I decided to use it as a 4-H entry when I was in LBJ High School, in Johnson City. Grandma Vicki Ermis wrote down the recipe and I practiced on the family, then entered the 4-H competition, going all the way to the state contest. Now my family count on me to bring the strudel to all the family gatherings!

¾ cup margarine
1 cup warm milk
2 egg yolks
3 cups flour, sifted
½ cup margarine, melted
9 apples, pared and sliced
1 cup sugar

3 tablespoons cinnamon
1 cup raisins
1 cup pecans, chopped
1 cup coconut
1 cup vanilla wafers, crushed
Margarine

Melt ¾ cup margarine in milk. Stir in egg yolks and flour. Mix well. Chill

dough in refrigerator for 2 hours or overnight. Divide dough into three parts. Roll each part very thin on lightly floured board. Melt ½ cup margarine, then brush on dough. Place 3 apples on top of margarine. Sprinkle each strudel with ⅓ cup sugar, 1 tablespoon cinnamon, ⅓ cup raisins, ⅓ cup pecans, ⅓ cup coconut, and ⅓ cup vanilla wafers. Dot each with margarine. Roll and place on cookie sheet. Brush with melted margarine. Bake at 350 degrees about 45 minutes. Serves a big crowd! Yield: 3 large strudels.

APRICOT STREUSEL COFFEE CAKE   *Janey Wiemers*

This was often baked by my mother, Zella Smith, to serve at WCSC meetings at the church. It became a goodie I took to WSCS meetings, after Bill was ordained and we started serving churches in Southwest Texas.

1	(12-ounce) package dried apricots	3	teaspoons baking powder
¼	cup sugar	½	teaspoon salt
	Water to cover ¾ inch over apricots	¼	cup margarine
		1	egg
1½	cups flour, sifted	½	cup milk
¾	cup sugar	1	teaspoon vanilla

Bring apricots to a boil, then reducing heat to simmer until tender. Remove from heat and mash. Set aside. Sift together flour, sugar, baking powder and salt. Cut in the margarine. Stir in the egg, milk and vanilla. Grease and flour a 9-inch square baking pan. Spread ½ of the mixture over bottom of pan, then spread with apricots. Cover with remaining batter. Sprinkle with streusel mix.

Streusel Mix

¼	cup brown sugar	1	tablespoon margarine, melted
1	tablespoon flour		
1	teaspoon cinnamon	¼	cup nuts, chopped

Bake 25 to 30 minutes at 375 degrees. Yield: 10 to 12 servings.

HINT:
To prevent a soggy crust in pudding and custard pies, or quiche, brush slightly beaten egg white on the uncooked pie shell; bake at 425 degrees for 5 to 10 minutes. Add filling and finish according to recipe directions.

261

GRANDMA'S COFFEE CAKE   *Leah Mauck*

This is exactly as it was given to me – after much trial and error, I found it must be mixed in a very large bowl. I use a bread crock that belonged to my grandmother. This really makes a large amount of dough.

1	cake yeast	2	tablespoons butter
1	cup lukewarm water	1	tablespoon salt
2	cups flour	2	cups sugar
2	eggs, well beaten	10	cups flour
1	quart lukewarm milk		

Put 1 yeast cake in 1 cup lukewarm water to dissolve. Put 2 cups flour in mixing bowl; make small hole in center and pour in dissolved yeast. Sprinkle small amount of flour over top and let stand 1 hour. Add 2 well beaten eggs. To 1 quart of lukewarm milk, add 2 tablespoon butter, 1 tablespoon salt, 2 cups sugar and add to sponge. Add enough flour (approximately 10 cups) to make a thick dough. Beat smooth and let rise 2 hours. Pour in well greased shallow pans, 8 x 8 x 2-inches, about ½ full, and let rise until double. Dot with butter and sprinkle sugar and coconut (optional). Bake at 350 degrees for 20 minutes. Yield: 6 to 8 cakes.

RADIO COFFEE CAKE   *Madeline Casparis*

I was born in 1915. When I was sixteen years old, I heard this recipe given on our Philco radio. Hence the title, RADIO COFFEE CAKE. Our family has enjoyed it throughout the years.

1⅓	cups sugar	⅔ cup pecans, chopped
⅓	cup shortening	1 to 2 tablespoons
1	egg, well beaten	butter, melted
1	cup milk	Sugar
½	teaspoon salt	Nutmeg
4	teaspoons baking powder	Cinnamon
2½	cups flour, reserve ¼ cup	
⅔	cup raisins or maraschino cherries, chopped	

Mix sugar and shortening. Add egg and milk. Add salt and baking powder to 2¼ cups flour, sifting together two times, then add to sugar mixture. Mix ¼ cup flour with raisins/cherries and pecans and add to batter. Pour into a greased 9 x 13-inch baking dish. Spread melted butter over top,

then lightly sprinkle with sugar, nutmeg, and cinnamon. Bake in 350 degree oven for 30 to 40 minutes. Cherry juice may be used, but reduce milk proportionately. Yield: 15 servings.

DATE LOAF CAKE   *Elnora Kneese*

½ cup butter or shortening	½ teaspoon salt
1 cup sugar	¾ teaspoon soda
1 egg	1 cup dates, chopped
⅔ cup sour milk <u>or</u> buttermilk	1 cup pecans, chopped
2 cups flour	Grated rind of 1 orange

Cream butter and sugar, add egg and milk. Mix well. Add rest of ingredients. Mix well. Pour into a greased 13 x 9 x 2-inch pan. Bake at 350 degrees for 30 minutes.

Sauce

Juice of 2 lemons (6 tablespoons)	**Juice of 2 oranges (⅔ cup)**
	1 cup sugar

Mix well and pour over cake while cake is still warm. Yield: 18 to 24 servings.

GOLD MINE DEVIL'S FOOD CAKE   *Leah Mauck*

This was my "gold mine" during high school. There were several ladies that wanted this cake every Saturday. Mother and Dad furnished all the ingredients, as well as the car and gas to deliver them – I kept all the profit!!!

2 squares bitter chocolate, melted	2 eggs, well beaten
1 teaspoon vanilla	2 cups flour
½ cup shortening	½ teaspoon salt
1¼ cups sugar	1 teaspoon soda
	1 cup buttermilk

Mix chocolate and vanilla together and set aside. Cream shortening thoroughly, gradually add sugar and cream until well mixed. Sift flour, salt and soda together. Add alternately with milk to creamed mixture. Blend in cooled chocolate mixture. Bake in 2 greased and floured 9-inch round pans, at 350 degrees for 30 minutes or in a 13 x 9 x 2-inch pan for 35 minutes. Cool on wire rack 10 to 15 minutes, then mix frosting and frost. Yield: 12 to 15 servings.

Frosting

1 **(3-ounce) package cream cheese, softened**	2 **cups powdered sugar**
1 **tablespoon butter, softened**	1 **teaspoon vanilla**
2 **squares bitter chocolate, melted**	**Milk, to obtain desired consistency to spread**

Mix cream cheese and butter, creaming well. Add chocolate and pow-dered sugar, mixing well, then add vanilla. Add milk, a few drops at a time, mixing well, until of the desired consistency to spread.

PINEAPPLE-BANANA NUT CAKE   *Flora Cox*

My mother-in-law baked this cake for the children, when they were very small. My sister-in-law, Meribell, now bakes this cake for special occasions.

1½ **cups sugar**	1 **teaspoon vanilla**
3 **bananas, mashed**	1½ **cups flour**
½ **cup butter**	1 **heaping teaspoon**
2 **eggs**	**baking soda**
4 **tablespoons buttermilk**	1½ **cups pecans, chopped**

Cream sugar, bananas and butter. Add eggs, buttermilk and vanilla, mix-ing well. Sift flour and baking soda together, then add to creamed mix-ture, mixing well. Add nuts. Bake in 3 8-inch round greased and floured cake pans, 20-25 minutes at 350 degrees. Cool on wire rack 10 to 15 min-utes. Frost with Pineapple Filling. Yield: 12 to 15 servings.

Pineapple Filling

1 **(20-ounce) can crushed pineapple**	2 **tablespoons butter <u>or</u> margarine**
1 **cup sugar**	¾ **cup pecans, chopped**
2 **tablespoons flour**	

Strain or drain pineapple juice in cooking pan. Add sugar, flour and but-ter/margarine and cook until thick, stirring constantly. Add pineapple pulp, stirring well. Spread ⅓ filling between each layer of cake, topping with ¼ of pecans. Spread top with remaining filling and pecans.

★ ★ ★ ★ ★

HINTS:
Fresh pineapple does not ripen further after it is picked. Choose one slightly soft to the touch and fresh looking, and use within 3 to 5 days.

SNOWBALL CAKE

Evelyn Fuelberg

My mother, Emma Reue, made this cake which my family always enjoyed.

2 packages unflavored gelatin
2 tablespoons cold water
1 cup boiling water
1 cup sugar
2 tablespoons lemon juice
1 (20-ounce) can crushed pineapple with juice
1 (10-ounce) bottle maraschino cherries, halved

1 cup coconut
1 cup pecans, chopped
3 packages Dream Whip, divided
1 angel food cake, torn in small pieces
Additional coconut

Dissolve gelatin in 2 tablespoons cold water. Add boiling water and mix. Add sugar, lemon juice, pineapple with juice, cherries, coconut and pecans. Mix well and place in refrigerator until partially jelled. Prepare 2 packages of Dream Whip and add to mixture. Line large mixing bowl or angel food cake pan with wax paper. Alternate pieces of cake and mixture in bowl or pan. Chill. When cold turn over on plate, remove wax paper. Ice with the other package of prepared Dream Whip and sprinkle with additional coconut. Keep refrigerated until ready to serve. Yield: 12 to 15 servings.

COON OIL COOKIES

Janey Wiemers

¾ cup coon oil (may substitute pure lard)
2 eggs
2 cups sugar
1 teaspoon soda

2 teaspoons cream of tartar
¼ teaspoon salt
3 cups flour
1 teaspoon vanilla

Baking instructions not given. This was handed out by Eliese Deike, from Kerrville, at the Institute of Texan Cultures Folklife Festival, about ten years ago. Good luck!! Yield: about 5 to 6 dozen.

CORN FLAKE COOKIES

Emma Reue

4 egg whites, beaten stiff
1½ cups sugar
1 cup coconut

1 cup pecans, chopped
1 teaspoon vanilla
3½ cups corn flakes

Mix all ingredients together. Drop by tablespoonfuls one-inch apart on well-greased cookie sheet. Bake 325 to 350 degrees for 25 to 30 minutes. Yield: 4 dozen.

ROCK CAKES
Vicky Patton

When my mother came from England to live here in Johnson City, she brought this recipe with her. We children grew up expecting ROCK CAKES at Christmas. These are not a real sweet cookie. Usually we have them with hot tea or coffee. I like them best made with the white sugar.

1	cup butter <u>or</u> margarine	½	teaspoon nutmeg
2	cups brown <u>or</u> white sugar	1	teaspoon baking soda
2	eggs	1½	teaspoons cinnamon
½	cup cold coffee	1	teaspoon vanilla
4½	cups flour	2	cups currants <u>or</u> raisins
1	teaspoon baking powder	1½	cups nuts, broken
½	teaspoon salt		

Mix first 4 ingredients until smooth. Fold in flour, baking powder, salt, nutmeg, soda, cinnamon and vanilla. Add currants and nuts and mix well. Mixture will be stiff. Drop by tablespoonfuls onto a greased cookie sheet and bake at 400 degrees until golden brown, about 8 minutes. Yield: 6 dozen.

GRANNY BOOTS CAKES
Robyn Henderson

This came from Louisiana over fifty years ago by my husband's "Granny Boots." She could not walk, but she pulled herself up to the kitchen cabinets and baked some great things. Granny Boots and Grandad lived in one of the oldest stagecoach depots in Texas. There was a lot of history in the Michael house. My mother-in-law says that Granny Boots used lard in this recipe, but most people use shortening, such as Crisco.

1¾	cups shortening	3	cups flour
3	cups sugar	2	tablespoons baking powder
6	eggs	¼	teaspoon salt
2	teaspoons vanilla		

In large bowl cream shortening and sugar, then add eggs and vanilla, beating well. Sift dry ingredients together and add to creamed mixture. Roll out on counter dusted lightly with flour. Cut with favorite cookie cutters. Add chips, fruit or whatever you desire. Bake in 400 degree oven for 10 to 12 minutes. Batter may be colored with food coloring if desired. For making drop cookies, add 1 more cup of flour. The amount of cookies made will depend on size of cookie cutters, or whether drop cookies are made. Cookies are soft and not hard to mess up! Yield: about 5 to 6 dozen.

GRANNIE SLAYTON'S TEA CAKES   *Delores Slayton Fenton*

My mother has almost one hundred grandchildren, great-grandchildren, and great-great-grandchildren. They all have learned from an early age that Grannie's cookie jar always held some of these tasty treats.

1	cup butter	1	teaspoon vanilla
2	cups sugar	2	teaspoons baking powder
2	eggs	⅛ to ¼ teaspoon soda
2	tablespoons buttermilk	3	cups flour

Cream butter and sugar together well. Add eggs, buttermilk and vanilla, creaming well. Add dry ingredients and mix thoroughly. These can be dropped by teaspoon onto an ungreased cookie sheet and pressed flat with a fork. They can also be rolled out and cut with cookie cutters. Bake in 400 degree oven for about 8 minutes, or until lightly brown. Yield: 5 dozen.

ROSE'S SUGAR COOKIES   *Rita Reiner*

My mother, Rose Krueger, has made these cookies for years. They make such good cut-outs for Valentine Day, Christmas and other holidays.

3	cups flour	1	cup shortening
1	teaspoon baking powder	3	eggs
Pinch of salt		1	teaspoon vanilla
1¼	cups sugar		

Sift dry ingredients together. Add shortening, mixing with a fork. Add eggs and vanilla, mixing well. Roll out very thin on floured board. Cut with cookie cutter. Place on lightly greased cookie sheet. Bake in 375 degree oven for about 8 minutes or until <u>very</u> lightly browned. Yield: 5½ dozen.

HINTS:

Spice your apple pies with cardamom instead of cinnamon. It's a nice change.

Put a layer of marshmallows in the bottom of a pumpkin pie, then add the filling. You will have a nice topping as the marshmallows will come to the top.

MOMMA'S SUGAR COOKIES

Bettye Prehn

My mother, Sue Krueger Johnson, used to make these. They make a bunch.

1 cup margarine	4½ cups flour
1 cup sugar	Dash of salt
1 cup confectioners sugar	1 teaspoon soda
2 eggs	1 teaspoon cream of tartar
1 cup vegetable oil	1 cup pecans, chopped
1 teaspoon vanilla	

Cream margarine, then add sugars, mixing well. Beat in eggs. Add oil and vanilla. Sift dry ingredients together once. Add to batter, mixing well. Add pecans. After mixing well, place in refrigerator to chill ½ to 1 hour. When ready to bake, preheat oven to 350 degrees. Shape dough into small balls and press flat on an ungreased cookie sheet. Bake for 10 minutes or until lightly brown. Yield: 7 dozen.

FIG DAINTIES

Leah Mauck

My mother sort of 'manufactured' this recipe in order to get us children to eat figs – it worked! The preserves make it nice and moist.

1 cup flour	½ teaspoon vanilla
1½ teaspoons baking powder	1 cup pecans, broken
⅛ teaspoon salt	8 ounces fig preserves,
3 eggs	drained and chopped
¾ cup sugar	

Sift flour once, measure and add baking powder and salt. Sift together 3 times. Set aside. Beat eggs until thick and lemon colored. Add sugar, a little at a time and continue beating as vanilla is added. Mix nuts and figs and add to egg mixture, mixing well. Carefully fold in dry ingredients, mixing thoroughly. Bake in greased and floured 8 x 8-inch pan at 350 degrees, for 30 to 35 minutes, or until toothpick comes out clean. When cold, cut into squares and sprinkle with powdered sugar, Yields: 9 to 12 squares.

HINT:
Line a pastry shell with wax paper and fill with dried peas to prevent air bubbles on a baked pie crust. Bake about 5 minutes or until shell is set; then remove paper and peas.

HONEY CAKES

Dorothy C. Lackey

My grandmother made these each Christmas. My mother then started making them and now I make them. The tradition continues, as it wouldn't be Christmas without them.

¼ pound German Sweet Chocolate
½ cup butter
¾ cup sugar
3 egg yolks
1 cup honey
¼ teaspoon baking powder

2½ to 3 cups flour
1 teaspoon cinnamon
¼ teaspoon ground cloves
½ teaspoon nutmeg
½ to ¾ cup milk
¼ pound pecans, chopped

Grate chocolate and set aside. Cream butter and sugar. Add egg yolks and mix well. Add honey. Sift all dry ingredients together. Add to creamed mixture, alternately with milk. The batter will be stiff. Add nuts and press into a greased and floured sheet cake pan. Wet hands to do this. Bake at 350 degrees for 25 to 30 minutes. Cut while warm. Can be iced and decorated for Christmas, if desired. Yield: about 30 cookies.

POORMAN'S COOKIES

Janey Wiemers

This recipe was given me by my Aunt Nellie. It is the only recipe I have from my Grandmother, Mrs. B. B. Kouns.

1 cup raisins
2 cups water
½ cup sugar
½ cup shortening
1 egg
2 cups flour (may need a scant more)

1 teaspoon cinnamon
1 teaspoon allspice
1 teaspoon cloves
1 teaspoon baking soda
¼ teaspoon salt

Cook raisins in water until 1 cup of juice is left. If not enough juice remains to make 1 cup, add coffee, milk or fruit juice to make the cupful. While juice is warm, add sugar and shortening, stirring until melted. Add egg, flour, cinnamon, allspice, cloves, soda and salt. Bake in a greased jelly roll pan (flat pan ½-inch thick) in moderate oven, 350 degrees for 30 minutes. Ice with powdered sugar icing, using strong coffee for liquid. Yield: 35 squares.

CREAM AND SUGAR PIE OR "FINGER PIE"   *Leah Mauck*

Forget the calories and cholesterol!! This is an 'Old Southern Recipe' from my Aunt Gladys Thompson Rawlinson who was always a 'perfect Southern lady.'

1 9-inch deep unbaked pie shell	½ teaspoon cinnamon
1 pint coffee cream	½ teaspoon nutmeg
1 cup sugar	¼ teaspoon salt
3 tablespoons flour	½ cup light brown sugar

Pour cream into unbaked pie shell. Mix granulated sugar, flour, cinnamon, nutmeg and salt. Sprinkle mixture on top of cream — then stir very gently with fingers, making figure eights just until sugar mixture goes under. Be sure to stop stirring when sugar sinks. Sprinkle brown sugar over top and (optional) dot with butter. Bake immediately in preheated oven 400 degrees for 20 minutes. Lower temperature to 300 degrees and bake approximately 40 minutes. This pie is always served warm and may be served with whipped cream. Yield: 8 to 12 servings.

FIVE IN ONE PIE   *Shirley Rosson*

This is Grandmother Gum's recipe. It is at least seventy-five years old. My mother owned a restaurant and it was always my job to stir the custard every morning before going to school.

Custard	3 egg yolks, beaten
1 cup sugar	2 tablespoons margarine
4 generous tablespoons flour	1 teaspoon vanilla
1¾ cups milk	

Mix sugar and flour in a quart size saucepan. Add egg yolks, milk and margarine. Cook on medium, stirring constantly, until thick. After it cools add vanilla. Yield: 8 to 12 servings. Add one of the following to make a pie:

Coconut: Add one cup coconut to custard and stir. Pour into a 9-inch baked pie shell. May make meringue out of egg whites or serve with whipped topping.

Pineapple: Add 1 (8-ounce) can of crushed pineapple, drained

Chocolate: Add ¼ cup cocoa.

Cherry Cream: Pour custard into crust and add 1 (16-ounce) can cherry pie filling.

Banana Pudding: Line a quart-size bowl with vanilla wafers, slice 1 to 2 bananas over wafers then pour half of custard and repeat.

JOHN'S PECAN CREAM PIE   *Wretha Allen*

This recipe is from my niece, Johnnie Mae Briggs, from West Texas, who got it from her husband's great-grandmother. It's the best Pecan Pie you will ever eat.

1 9-inch pie shell	1 cup pecans, chopped
1½ cups milk, scalded	2 tablespoons butter
½ cup sugar	1 teaspoon vanilla
½ teaspoon salt	3 egg whites
5 tablespoons flour	1 tablespoon sugar
¼ cup cold milk	
3 egg yolks, beaten (reserve whites)	

Bake pie shell as to instructions. In 1½-quart double boiler, scald 1½ cups milk, then set aside. Mix sugar, salt, and flour with ¼ cup cold milk. Add to scalded milk. Cook until it begins to thicken. Add beaten egg yolks, cooking again until mixed well. Add pecans and cook until desired thickness. Cool slightly. Add butter and vanilla. Pour into baked pie shell. When cool, top with meringue.

Meringue: Beat egg whites until very stiff. Add 1 tablespoon sugar, beating until dissolved. Place over pie. Put under broiler, just until meringue starts to turn brown. Remove promptly. (Only takes a short time! Watch carefully.) Yield: 9-inch pie.

GRANDMA WAGENER'S BREAD PUDDING   *Geneva Eubanks*

My Grandmother, Ida Wagener, was widowed at a young age and was left to raise six children on a farm. She lived to be ninety-seven years old and cooked until she was ninety. This is one of my favorite desserts. She fixed it often. She always called the sauce "Schmeer."

10 to 12 slices day old <u>or</u> stale white bread	Dash of salt
Milk	3 eggs, beaten
¾ to 1 cup sugar	1 cup raisins
	1½ teaspoons vanilla extract

Break bread into small pieces and soak in enough milk to make it very juicy. Add all ingredients. Bake in buttered dish or pan at 350 degrees about an hour or until a knife inserted into center comes out clean.

Lemon Sauce

1 cup sugar

2 level tablespoons flour

1½ cups water

Juice of 1 lemon

Dash of salt

In saucepan mix sugar and flour, then add water and juice. Heat slowly until it boils, stirring to keep smooth. Cook about 2 minutes. Add a dash of salt. Pour over hot pudding and serve while warm. Yield: about 6 to 8 servings.

FRANCIS' PUDDING

Rosie Hunter

This was my great-grandmother's recipe.

1 cup sugar

4 eggs, separated

1 pint milk

2 tablespoons Knox gelatin

½ cup cold water

1 small glass cherry juice, (¼ cup)

½ cup maraschino cherries, drained, chopped

2 cups small marshmallows

1 cup pecans, chopped

Whipped cream

Cream sugar and egg yolks together; add milk. Dissolve gelatin in water; add to sugar mixture. Cook in double boiler until thick. Beat the egg whites until very stiff. Add egg whites, cherry juice, cherries, marshmallows and pecans. Pour into a 13 x 9 x 2-inch Pyrex dish. Chill. Cut into squares and serve with a tablespoon of whipped cream on top. Yield: 12 to 15 servings.

LEMON CHEESE

Cynthia Smith

Sounds awful, lemon cheese, but it is delicious spread on a shortbread or Ritz cracker. A friend, whose mother was English, gave me this recipe and they sometimes called it Lemon Curd. Makes a nice gift at Christmas, in a pretty jar.

½ pound margarine

2 cups sugar

4 eggs, well beaten

Juice of 3 or 4 lemons

Place all the ingredients in the top of a double-boiler and cook slowly until very thick. Stir frequently to prevent scorching. This is very much like filling for a lemon pie, except richer. Yield: 3 cups.

HINTS:

Fold leftover vegetables into a cream sauce to serve over a plain omelet; add to fritter batter or marinate in French dressing for salad.

✧ ✧ ✧ ✧ ✧ ✧ ✧

LEMON DELIGHTFUL

Cynthia Smith

⅓	cup fresh lemon juice		Dash of salt
2	eggs, separated	1	(12-ounce) can evaporated
1	tablespoon lemon rind, grated		milk, chilled in freezer 45 minutes
1½	cups sugar, divided in 3 parts	6	ounces vanilla wafers, crushed

In a pan combine the lemon juice, egg yolks, lemon rind, ½ cup sugar and salt. Cook until just thickened. Remove from heat and cool. In a bowl whip milk and ½ cup sugar. In a separate bowl, beat egg whites and remaining ½ cup sugar until stiff. Into the beaten egg whites, fold the whipped milk and the cooked mixture. Butter lightly, a 13 x 9 x 2-inch pan. Sprinkle ½ of the crushed wafers in the pan, then pour the lemon mixture over the wafers evenly. Sprinkle with remaining crumbs and freeze. This can be cut into squares to serve or spooned into pretty sherbet or other dishes. Can be kept in freezer, covered, for several weeks. This is light in texture, but rich. Yield: 12 servings.

FRIED PEACHES

Grace Hobbs

There has never been a recipe for this. My Grandma Page always fixed this when peaches were in season. I think she learned it from her mother, Great-Grandma Cox. It is made more or less to your own taste.

- 2 heaping cups sliced fresh peaches, unpeeled
- ½ cup sugar
- 3 slices bacon, fried crisp, crumbled
- 3 tablespoons bacon drippings
- 1 teaspoon vanilla

Cover peaches with water and add sugar. Boil 10 to 15 minutes. Add crumbled bacon, drippings and vanilla. Thicken with your favorite thickening. This makes a small amount. Yield: about 4 servings.

CHOCOLATE FUDGE

Dardanella Gipson

I have used this recipe since I was a child. It came from my Grandmother Hamlett, who lived in Lynchburg, Virginia. She was a good cook – she had to be with fourteen children.

2 cups sugar	2 tablespoons margarine
⅔ cup milk	1 teaspoon vanilla
2 tablespoons white corn syrup	1 cup pecans or black walnuts, chopped
3 tablespoons cocoa	

Cook sugar, milk, corn syrup and cocoa until it forms a soft ball (either in cold water or on a candy thermometer). Usually takes 7 to 9 minutes. Take margarine and lightly butter a dish. When candy reaches right stage, remove from heat. Add remaining margarine and vanilla. Beat until it passes a glossy stage. Add nuts and pour into dish. When cooled, cut into squares. Yields: about 24 pieces.

AUNTIE MARGARET'S FAILURE FUDGE   *Margaret Dannecker*

This recipe is so old it originally called for "top milk" and "molasses." I began trying to update it twenty years ago, but found it wildly unpredictable. Sometimes it was too dry, sometimes grainy and always "setting up" or hardening too fast. But the richness and flavor was so good, that even the failures never went begging. The family just named it "Auntie Margaret's Failure Fudge" and insisted on getting some every Christmas whatever the flaws. After years of experimentation and trauma, I finally discovered the missing ingredient... "PATIENCE" on the part of Auntie Margaret. Patience to let the syrup come 'slowly to a full boil,' as the recipe called for and patience to let the fudge cool down equally slowly (without cheating and putting the pan into a sink of cold water to hurry it along). One warning: if you serve this to a true chocoholic, you, too, will be condemned to making it every Christmas for the rest of your life!!

3 tablespoons butter	¾ cup half 'n half milk
3 cups sugar	3 squares unsweetened chocolate
½ teaspoon vinegar	¼ teaspoon cream of tartar
Dash of salt	1 teaspoon vanilla
3 tablespoons dark corn syrup	1 cup pecans, chopped

Melt butter in heavy saucepan and brown slightly. Add sugar, vinegar, salt, syrup and milk. Stir until well blended. Cover and bring slowly to a full boil. Add chocolate (broken into small chunks) and boil rapidly until candy forms a soft ball when a drop or two is tried in cold water (236-238 degrees on a candy thermometer). Keep covered during cooking. Just before removing from fire, sprinkle ¼ teaspoon cream of tartar into mix-

In large 3 to 4 quart saucepan, add sugar, vinegar, and spices. Bring this to a boil. Add squash mixture. Cook at least 3 minutes, stirring well. Put into clean sterilized jars and seal. Very good with meat or beans. Yield: 6 pints.

COLD PACK SUN PICKLES   *Wretha Allen*

I have made these pickles for years. My mother-in-law taught me to can. This was one of her favorites.

10 cups water	**Green jalapeño peppers**
2 cups salt (not iodized)	**Grape leaves**
Cider vinegar	**Fresh dill**
Garlic pods	**Fresh whole cucumbers**

In large 5-quart saucepan simmer water and salt for 10 minutes. Cool. Mix equal parts vinegar and salt brine. In sterilized quart jars place 1 garlic pod, 1 jalapeño pepper, 3 grape leaves and a sprig of fresh dill. Stand in cucumbers – DO NOT CUT. Pour in vinegar mixture to fill jar. Seal. Place in full sun for 10 days. Chill when ready to serve. Yield: 10 quarts.

PEAR PRESERVES   *Ola Matus*

This is Aunt Pauline Gipson's recipe. She could make the best pear preserves I have ever eaten. Sometimes she would add pineapple to this recipe.

10 pounds pears, pared and sliced	1 lemon, sliced thin
5 cups water	2 (15-ounce) cans crushed
10 cups sugar	pineapple, optional

Soak pears while peeling in one tablespoon salt to one quart water. Rinse well. Boil sugar and water five minutes. Add pears and lemon. Cook until pears are clear and syrup is thick. Pack into clean hot jars and seal at once. Yields: 10 pints.

HINTS:
Small amounts of jelly left in jars may be combined, melted and used to glaze ham.

When canning vegetables the salt may be left out of recipe. It's purpose is to add flavor. Pickles are an exception, they need salt to prevent spoilage.

Jarring Ideas
Puttin' Up, Advice, Hints, Proverbs and
a Few Lies

JOHNSON CITY STATE BANK

The Johnson City State Bank, constructed of native, white, hewn stone, was chartered and opened for business in 1906. In 1937 the bank was liquidated, thereafter various businesses occupied the building, changing the face and interior over the years. In 1986 William Trapani, Jr. purchased the building and restored it to its original beauty.

278

⇨ ⇨ ⇨ ⇨ ⇨ ⇨ ⇨

BEST EVER BREAD & BUTTER PICKLES   *Geneva Eubanks*

These pickles are our family's favorite. Our grandchildren love them and always ask if these are "Neva's" pickles. Easy to fix and crisp.

34 (4-inch) or 52 (3½-inch) cucumbers	½ teaspoon ground cloves
8 small onions	2 teaspoons celery seed
½ cup ice cream salt	1½ teaspoons turmeric
Cracked ice	2 teaspoons mustard seed
5 cups sugar	5 cups white vinegar

Wash cucumbers and slice thin, unpeeled. Slice onions. Place in large container, add salt and mix with hands. Cover with ice and let stand 3 hours, stirring occasionally. Drain. Combine sugar, spices and vinegar. Put cucumbers and onions in large pot, pour sugar/vinegar mixture over cucumbers. Bring to a boil on high heat, turn off heat, do not cook. Pack into hot sterilized jars and seal. Let set few days to a week before serving. Yield: about 5 quarts. Note: Use enamel or stainless pots.

BREAD AND BUTTER PICKLES   *Mary Gipson*

6 pints sliced cucumbers, 18 to 20 medium size	2 cloves garlic
6 medium onions, sliced	5 cups sugar
2 green peppers, sliced	3 cups cider vinegar
2 red sweet peppers, sliced	1½ teaspoons turmeric
⅓ cup pickling salt	1½ teaspoons celery seed
5 pounds crushed ice <u>or</u> 4 cube trays	3 tablespoons mustard seed

Place sliced cucumbers, onions and peppers in a large enamel roaster pan. Pour salt over them and mix well. Put cracked ice on top; cover and let stand at least 3 hours. Meanwhile prepare jars and lids for canning. Mix other ingredients in large canning pot and bring to boil. Remove garlic cloves after it starts to boil. Drain water and ice from cucumber mixture and drop into boiling liquid. Stir and bring to boil (cucumbers will change to an olive color). Turn off heat and fill jars with pickles and adjust lids. Put in boiling water bath and cover. Let boil 10 minutes. Remove and cool on cloth. After cooling check for seal on jar. Store about a month before serving. Chill for nice crisp pickles. Yield: 8 to 10 pints.

GROWING CUCUMBERS by *Mary Gipson.* I would like to share mine and G. R.'s method of growing cucumbers. This past spring, 1992, was a very wet one here in Central Texas. It made it very difficult to plow the

garden, so I gathered up three old tubs with holes in the bottom. I prepared peat moss, potting soil and dirt from under oak trees out in the pasture, filled the tubs and planted cucumbers in each tub, about 4 plants to each tub. G. R. made cages about three feet high around each tub. We fertilized about once a week with about 2 tablespoons of 18-10-5 fertilizer and watered every other day. I never saw cucumbers grow like that before. They grew to the top of the cages and back down to the ground. I made about 100 jars of pickles from those three tubs, not to mention what I gave away. From now on, this is the way I will grow my cucumbers. The above is my favorite recipe for bread and butter pickles.

SWEET PICKLES FROM DILLS   *Dolores Fasel Bozeman*

A simple but easy way to make sweet pickles. They are great!

1	pint hamburger dill chips	½	teaspoon mustard seed
1	cup sugar		

Wash and drain chips. Mix with sugar and mustard seed. Place back in jar. Let set overnight in refrigerator. Yield: 1 pint.

CHOW CHOW   *Annie Lee West*

This recipe can easily be used for larger quantities. Just keep the proportions the same: for example, if you have 1 gallon of green tomatoes, chopped, then you need approximately 1 gallon of the remainder of vegetables, chopped.

2½	quarts green tomatoes, coarsely chopped	1 to 2	fresh hot peppers, chopped, if desired
½	cup salt	4½	cups white vinegar, 5% acidity
1	quart cabbage, coarsely chopped	3	cups sugar
3	carrots, peeled and chopped	1½	teaspoons celery seeds
2	large onions, coarsely chopped	½	teaspoon cayenne pepper
1½	large bell peppers, chopped	1½	teaspoons dry mustard
1	large red sweet pepper, chopped	1½	teaspoons cinnamon
		1½	teaspoons whole cloves
		½	teaspoon ground ginger
		1	teaspoon black pepper

Chop green tomatoes and put into a bowl. Cover with the salt and let set while chopping remaining vegetables. When all the chopping is complete, lightly drain juice from tomatoes. Mix all the vegetables together in a large saucepan. Add vinegar, sugar and spices. Cook over moderate heat with vegetables at full boil until all are tender, especially the carrots, approximately 1½ hours. Pour into sterile, hot jars and seal. Yield: 8 pints.

STRAWBERRY FIG PRESERVES
Jewell Sultemeier

When our children were growing up we had several fig trees. We would get tired of fig preserves, so I used this recipe for a change for we did not waste anything.

3 cups figs, mashed	2 (3-ounce) packages
3 cups sugar	strawberry gelatin

Cook 20 minutes. Place in sterilized pint jars and seal. Yield: 1½ to 2 pints.

HOMESTEAD HONEY
Janey Wiemers

It is used and tastes like honey. These ingredients were all readily available in Alaska and substituted for native honey. Some Alaskan recipes were pretty far-fetched, but this one could be made and enjoyed. It was given to me by a close friend, Edie Diver.

10 cups sugar	30 white clover blossoms
1 teaspoon powdered alum	18 red clover blossoms
3 cups boiling water	18 fireweed blossoms

Boil sugar, alum, and boiling water together for 10 minutes. Remove from the burner and drop in blossoms. Let set for 10 minutes. Strain out the blossoms. Pour into jars and seal. Yield: 2 pints.

HERB—SALT SUBSTITUTE
Shirley Spurlock Rosson

½ teaspoon garlic powder	½ teaspoon paprika
½ teaspoon onion powder	¼ teaspoon powdered thyme
½ teaspoon dry mustard	¼ teaspoon ground celery
½ teaspoon white pepper	seed

Mix and store in shaker bottle. Yield: 1 tablespoon.

PAN COATER
Chuck Matus

My wife, Leslie, got this from one of her cake decorating classes.

1 cup Crisco shortening
1 cup flour

1 cup Crisco oil

Mix ingredients into a paste and store in refrigerator. Keeps indefinitely. Use to coat pans instead of greasing and flouring. Yield: 3 cups.

This & That

PERFUMED SACHETS FOR LINENS
Peggy Hudspith

This is from "Family Receipt Book" published in 1819.

1 quart rose petals, dried
1 ounce each of cloves, mace, lavender and allspice ground in mortar

Pine shavings can be added if desired but increase rose petals

Mix and put in small linen bags.

WHIPPED BUTTER
Thelma Elm

You don't have to give up butter for economy sake. Let one pound of butter reach room temperature, then beat it well, add two cups of evaporated milk to the butter and beat until milk is absorbed. Chill butter and you will have two pounds of butter instead of one.

ALL-PURPOSE INSECT SPRAY
Holly Lawson

Garlic, onion and hot peppers have repellent qualities. The soap makes it cling to plant leaves.

1 garlic bulb
1 small onion
1 tablespoon cayenne pepper

1 quart water
1 tablespoon liquid soap detergent

Chop or grind garlic and onion, add cayenne, and mix with water. Let steep 1 hour, then add liquid soap detergent. Store in a tightly-covered jar in the refrigerator up to 1 week.

FORMULA FOR ROACH EXTERMINATING   *Holly Lawson*

This is Heloise's Boric Acid Formula. Keep out of reach of children.

¼ cup shortening or bacon drippings	½ cup flour
⅛ cup sugar	½ small onion, chopped, optional
8 ounces powdered boric acid	Water to form soft dough

Cream shortening and sugar, mix boric acid, flour and onion. Add to sugar and shortening. Blend well, then add water to form soft dough. Shape into small balls. Place balls throughout the house in places normally inhabited by roaches. (If balls are placed in open sandwich bags they'll stay soft longer.) When dough becomes brick hard, replace with a fresh batch.

Household Hints

To remove skunk spray from animals, shampoo with Grease Relief laundry detergent; on clothing apply liberally, then wash with regular laundry detergent. — Bill Lemons

To clean stuffed toys use dry cornstarch. Rub it in, wait about 5 minutes and brush off.

To clean varnished floors or woodwork, rub with cold tea.

Try shaving cream and wash with club soda to remove spots.

For healthier house plants, try a little tender loving care and castor oil.

If you shrink your best wool sweater, soak it in tepid water with shampoo, then reshape.

When one glass is stuck inside another, do not force them apart but fill top glass with cold water, then dip lower glass in hot water. They will come apart without breaking.

To remove candle wax from napkins: rub with an ice cube until wax hardens, then scrape off with a dull knife. Place napkin between layers of paper towels and press with a warm iron until all wax has been absorbed.

To open a stubborn jar pour a handful of salt into a bowl. Turn the jar upside down into the salt to immmerse the lid, allowing the grains to slip between the lid and the threads of the jar. Turn right side up, twist and the jar opens.

To remove grease stains, dampen spot with cold water and cover with powdered starch. Let dry. Brush off and the stain will be gone.

Garlic: If you have never cooked with fresh garlic you should start. When purchasing garlic, find full heads and store on the shelf. Do not store in the refrigerator. To prepare: with the palm of your hand crush the entire head so that the cloves fall apart. Select a clove, and bang it with the bottom of a drinking glass or crack it with the flat side of a large knife. Place knife flat over the clove and hit the knife gently with your hand. The cracked clove will render itself skinless. Now dice. Eating fresh garlic is great for hair and skin and keeping mosquitoes from biting. — Robyn Henderson

Directions for trussing poultry: Cut 20 inches of soft white string. Place chicken on flat surface, with feet toward you. Push the legs back close to the body of the chicken. Put the center of the string across the end of the legs and bring it around and up between the legs, forming a figure 8. Then put the string between the legs and breast. Turn the chicken over and put the string through the wings. After making sure the neck skin is pulled over the vent, tie the string in a bow between the wings. — Debbie Wiemers Hemphill

Old Hints

Ear of corn that has lots of shuck means a cold winter is coming.

If a mesquite tree grows beans it means you'll have a cold winter.

If it thunders in February, it will frost in April on the same date as it thundered in February.

It is a sure bet there will be no other frosts after the mesquite trees have put out leaves.

If the sun goes down behind a cloud on Sunday, it will rain by Wednesday or if the sun goes down behind a cloud on Wednesday it will rain by Sunday.

Whatever the first twelve days of January are ie; sunny, rainy, cloudy, windy, cold or mild, that is how the rest of the months will be that year on each particular day.

If it rains on the full of the moon it will rain again within the next two weeks, but not every day.

Make homemade soap in the dark of the moon.

Make plum jelly in the dark of the moon.

Butcher in the dark of the moon, so the meat won't drip.

Rules for testing fat for frying: Drop a piece of soft bread into hot fat, if the bread browns in 40 seconds, the temperature is right.

To 'try out fat': Any odd pieces of fat may be tried out more easily in a double saucepan, than by putting into the oven; it will then take less watching.

Old Home Remedies

Dr. Christian Althaus was a pioneer doctor in the Fredericksburg area. He was born in Prussia in 1821 and died in Gillespie County, Texas in 1915. He practiced medicine using mainly medicines made from herbs, seeds, roots and bark. Honey and juices of fruits were used to make the liquids and tonics. His treatments were so successful that he was asked by the United States Government to travel to Bandera during their diphtheria epidemic in 1862. Using the serum he developed from the bark of the Blackjack tree, he cured thirty-four out of the thirty-five patients. — Pat Althaus

DR. ALTHAUS' SALVE

Sweet oil	Resin
Beeswax	Terpentine (turpentine)
Deer taller (tallow)	

Equal parts of above, then melt first four ingredients and add terpentine last.

DR. ALTHAUS' THROAT WASH

1	pint vinegar	3 tablespoons of honey
1	pint strong sage tea	Alum, size of bird egg
1	handful of Blackjack bark	

Take the old rough bark off use the incide (inside) — cook it to a strong tea, strain, have about half pint of the tea then mix all together and let come to a boil. Use as a throat wash. In case of diphtheria use spirits of musterd (mustard) put it on the glans (glands) let stay five minutes and take it off. I mean on the out sid (side) of the throat. (Mustard Plaster).

Dr. Althaus used:

Horehound for cough medicine

The Elderberry for different ailments

Camellia tea for cramps and pain reliever

Combination of bitters (herbs) for liver medication

For Sore Throat: Make a poultice of kerosene, turpentine and pure lard and place this on your neck. In five minutes you will be able to taste the kerosene in your throat, and the cure will have begun. Then take two or three drops of kerosene oil in a spoon with a pinch of sugar and swallow this to complete the treatment.

Take a sock you have worn inside a boot and worked in for about a week so that it has a bad odor. Tie it around your neck. — Sadie Sharp

Hold a nutmeg in the mouth, be careful, don't get strangled. After a few minutes spit out the nutmeg.

Take a couple of peppermint drops and slowly let them dissolve in the mouth. This coats the throat and helps the hurt.

For Hair: Vaseline or petroleum jelly, with a little sulphur mixed in it and rubbed well into the scalp, makes hair grow thicker; and the sulphur, too, is said to prevent the hair from turning gray, as it feeds the roots with new coloring material. Leave on all night. Should you try this I advise using a old pillow to sleep on; it is likely to ruin or damage nice bed pillows. — Sadie Sharp

For Hiccoughs: Drink pineapple juice. — Sadie Sharp

For Snake Bite: This came out of my Grandmother's remedy box which she had back in the 1800s. Mix equal parts of gun powder, hog lard and a little salt to make a paste. Apply a poultice of the mixture, directly to bite as soon as possible. In thirty minutes remove poultice and the poison drawn from the wound will have tinged the poultice a green color. Apply another poultice until all pain and swelling are gone. This is safe, and the ingredients are at hand in most farmers or ranchers home. — Helen Mayfield

Poultice for Thorns: Take a knife and scrape soap, any kind of soap, enough to make a paste. Add a little sugar and turpentine to make a paste and then place it on the thorn and cover with a bandage. Leave it on over night, it will draw the thorn out.

Bee Sting: If you get stung by a bee, put a copper penny on the sting for 10 to 15 minutes. Old pennies work best because they have more copper in them. It takes away the poison, reducing the sting and the itch. — Holly Lawson

Chewing tobacco juice applied to sting.

Use household ammonia on insect sting.

Apply a paste of soda and table vinegar.

For Growing Pains: Keep a bowl of salted water in sleeping room, ready for emergency. When pain starts wring a towel from salted water, wrap limb in it from the ankle to knee, without taking the child from his bed, and then swathe with dry flannels, thick and warm, tucking the blankets about him a little closer, and relief is sure.

For Diphtheria: A gargle of sulphur and water has been used with much

success in cases of diphtheria. Let the patient swallow a little of the mixture.

For Regularity: Boil package of prunes in water. Cook down slowly until a nice thick syrup is left. Pour up the syrup and store in refrigerator. Each night, pour out a tablespoon of the thick prune syrup and add several ounces cold water, stir and drink.

For Headache: Rub a little Vick's VapoRub on the place where the head aches.

For mild headache wet a towel in cold water and hold on forehead or use ice pack.

Wet a piece of brown paper bag with vinegar; coat with baking soda and tie on head with something tight.

Bind wilted beet leaves on the forehead.

Sure-Cure Remedy. Pick-me-up for the elderly.

1 egg, divided	**Dash of salt**
1 tablespoon powdered sugar	**1 tablespoon brandy**

Separate eggs; beat yolk until thick and lemon colored, add sugar, salt and brandy and beat again. Blend the white of egg whipped to a stiff froth, add to mixture. This will be so thick you can eat it with a spoon, or you may add 1 cup milk with a little more sugar—gives added strength. —Janey Wiemers

HINTS — EGGS:

Raw eggs separate more easily when cold but egg whites for meringue should reach room temperature before beating. For egg whites to come to room temperature it takes about 1 hour.

When boiling eggs, add 1 teaspoon salt to the water. This prevents a cracked egg from draining into the water.

Eggs should be stored large end up in their container. This allows the yolk to stay centered, which is important when deviling eggs or using sliced hard-cooked eggs as a garnish.

Eggs should never be boiled. To hard-cook, put eggs in a pot with enough water to cover 1 inch above eggs. Bring to a rapid boil. Turn heat off and cover. Let eggs stand 15 minutes. Cool completely under cold running water.

To cut down on cholesterol, substitute two egg whites stiffly beaten for each whole egg called for in a cake recipe.

HINTS:

Dried fruits such as raisins, dates, prunes, peaches and apricots are good sources of iron. In addition to being healthful, they are great for snacking — sweet and delicious.

If you have leftover coffee and like ice coffee try this. Pour the coffee in ice trays and freeze. This uses up the coffee plus the cubes do not dilute the ice coffee.

To make cold drinks look special, serve in water goblets, pilsners, mugs, brandy snifters, tankards, wine or champagne glasses as well as in tumblers.

Ladle punch and party beverages from punch bowls, glass salad bowls or mixing bowls, or pour from attractive pitchers.

Leftover warm punch is good cold, too.

When tea is steeped or cooled too long, it sometimes becomes cloudy when added to ice. Just add a small amount of boiling water to make it clear again.

The key to the best tasting coffee is buying fresh coffee beans and grinding them just before brewing.

Use leftover liquid from canned or cooked fruits in frozen desserts, gelatins, soups or punch drinks.

Yogurt, sour cream or cream cheese is good to use in place of milk in mashed potatoes.

Bake potatoes in half the usual time; let them stand in boiling water for 15 minutes before baking in a very hot oven. Even faster, use a microwave oven.

To peel small white onions easily, pour boiling water over onions in a bowl and let stand 1 minute; drain and cover with cold water. Peel when cool.

If you have an abundance of squash, try steaming, mashing and freezing any extra squash. Use it all year in recipes that call for pumpkin, like breads, cakes and pies.

To reheat cooked pasta or rice, place it in a strainer over a pan of boiling water. Cover and steam 10 to 15 minutes.

Should you grease more muffin tins than can be filled; fill the empty ones with water to keep the grease from baking on the pans.

Place wax paper directly on surface of hot cooked puddings to prevent a skin from forming.

Where's It At . . . Index